JUDGING LEMASS
The measure of the man

THIRTY CENTS

JULY 12, 19

TIME

THE WEEKLY NEWSMAGAZINE

IRELAND
New Spirit in the Ould Sod

PRIME MINISTER
SEAN LEMASS

TIME cover, 12 July 1963.

Judging

LEMASS

THE MEASURE OF THE MAN

Tom Garvin

RIA
ROYAL IRISH ACADEMY

Judging Lemass: The measure of the man

First published 2009

by Royal Irish Academy
19 Dawson Street
Dublin 2
www.ria.ie

The author and publisher are grateful to the following for permission to reproduce the documents, photographs and illustrations in this book: Seán O'Connor (private collection); Eileen and Seán Lemass (private collection); Henry Sheridan (private collection); Irish Press Plc; National Library of Ireland (NLI); UCD Archives, School of History and Archives (UCDA); the UCD–OFM Partnership (UCD–OFM); National Archives of Ireland (NAI); Dublin Diocesan Archives (DDA); Getty Images; Ken Bloomfield (private collection); the *Irish Times*; The National Archives, London (TNA); *TIME*; United Press International; Advertising Archives; British Pathé Film; ILO Historical Photographic Archives; Bord na Móna; Vincent Browne; and Lensmen Photographic Archive.

During the production process some documents, photographs and illustrations have been retouched or tinted for aesthetic purposes. Every effort has been made to trace the copyright holders of these items and to ensure the accuracy of their captions. See Photo Credits pp. 299–300.

ISBN 978-1-904890-57-7

British Library Cataloguing in Publication Data. A CIP catalogue record for this book is available from the British Library.

Printed in Ireland by Turner Print Group.

10 9 8 7 6 5 4 3 2 1

CONTENTS ✺

O'Connell's Schools' junior and middle grade exhibitioners, 1915. Seán Lemass is first from the left in the first row standing. (Courtesy of Seán O'Connor)

'Home Rule: vote for the colleens', postcard, c. 1912. In 1912 a bill proposing the introduction of votes for women was defeated by (the previously supportive) Irish nationalists. Their obstruction sought to allow a clear path for the introduction of a bill supporting Home Rule. (NLI, Ephemera Collection, POL/1910-20/14)

PUBLISHER'S NOTE ✳

The Royal Irish Academy is very grateful to the family of Seán Lemass for allowing access to family photographs and documents for use in this book. Thanks are particularly due to his grandsons, Seán O'Connor, Seán Haughey and Seán Lemass in this regard. Eamon de Valera, too, was very generous with his time and with access to the *Irish Press* collection of photographs (allowing those photographs of Lemass to be digitally archived by UCD Archives, School of History and Archives).

The Academy would also like to thank the directors of the National Archives of Ireland and the National Library of Ireland, and the various archives whose staff gave of their time, expertise and enthusiasm to enable the production of *Judging Lemass*. Particular thanks are due to Seamus Helferty at UCD Archives, School of History and Archives; Aideen Ireland at the National Archives; Mary Broderick, Ephemera Librarian, at the National Library of Ireland; Noelle Dowling at the Dublin Diocesan Archives; Anne Dolan at the Department of History, Trinity College Dublin; and Tony Kenna at Bord na Móna.

Thanks to Dermot Ryan who gave his time to discuss the interviews he conducted with Lemass in the late 1960s.

The Academy is also grateful to Ken Bloomfield and T.K. Whitaker for their guidance and good counsel.

Finally, thanks to Ciara Meehan, who worked as a researcher on the book and John Paul Owens, who has since left the Academy, who copy-edited it.

The original idea for the book was conceived and commissioned by Pauric Dempsey.

Terence O'Neill, prime minister of Northern Ireland; Cecil Bateman, Cabinet secretary; and Lemass pose for a photograph at Stormont House, 14 January 1965. (© Irish Press Plc)

FOREWORD

The appearance of yet another biography of Seán Lemass, who died 38 years ago, reflects an abiding interest in an exceptionally able and dedicated politician. This is not to be wondered at. Lemass was, indeed, a dynamic patriot of great force and ability. I was in the Department of Finance for most of his ministerial career—in the war-time Department of Supplies, in Industry and Commerce, and finally as Taoiseach. I greatly admired his good sense and his decisiveness. Deferring a decision was, for him, the worst decision of all. His intelligence was a shield against error, making of his life an active learning process. Imbued originally, like many of his contemporaries, with the Sinn Féin aspirations of Arthur Griffith, he came, through his war-time responsibilities and experience, to realise the deficiencies of such a policy. His commitment to national progress moved full circle from reliance on lavish protectionism to partnership in a wide free-trading group of nations.

Just as the arch-patriot, de Gaulle, could most acceptably abandon French sovereignty over Algeria, so the chief promoter of Irish industrial development, Seán Lemass, could most acceptably abandon protectionism in favour of free trade. Unfortunately, he did not live to see us enthusiastically enter the European Economic Community in 1973.

In perceptive summary towards the end of this fine biography Tom Garvin writes: 'The promotion of a politics of the practical and a rhetoric of reality may have been the most lasting and most important of his many legacies to the people of Ireland'.

T.K. Whitaker

T.K. Whitaker

Aer Lingus timetable (back cover shot), 1950/1. (NLI, Ephemera Collection, TVL/1950-60/6)

INTRODUCTION ✺

Seán Lemass is commonly seen as the architect of modern Ireland. An almost mythical narrative has grown up around him and his short career as Taoiseach of the Republic of Ireland from 1959 to 1966. People tend to forget that he was the chief manager of the country's economy during most of the period between 1932 and 1959, and that he was behind the creation of Aer Lingus, Bord na Móna, Irish Shipping Ltd and many other semi-state bodies designed to further the modernisation of Ireland. These institutions were also designed to industrialise the country and to escape from what he regarded as the strait jacket of dependence on an agrarian sector of questionable efficiency. He was also the principal architect of the semi-corporate industrial-relations system that evolved in Ireland after the setting up of the Labour Court in 1946. He was not infallible; he opposed from the outset the founding, by Daniel Morrissey of Fine Gael in 1950, of the Industrial Development Authority (IDA), an agency that was modelled on Czech and Puerto Rican originals and is itself widely imitated around the world by developing countries. Later he showed his flexibility and wisdom by publicly changing his mind and putting his considerable political heft behind an expanded version of the IDA. Nor was he a monopolist of economic inventiveness; it was a Fine Gael minister for finance (Gerard Sweetman) who instituted export tax relief in 1956. However, Lemass took up the scheme and expanded it. Again, he was to ratify and back politically a rather statist version of the economic policies put forward by T.K. Whitaker and his colleagues in 1957–8.

Lemass was responsible for not one but two economic revolutions in Ireland during his time in office. Between 1932 and 1957 he was the prime mover behind the protectionist 'Import Substitution Industrialisation' (ISI) of the country, a policy that is still controversial; behind high tariff barriers, the Irish tried to build up industries catering for the tiny home market; it made sense of a sort in a world preparing for war. By 1939 the Irish were indeed self-sufficient in basic clothing supplies and foodstuffs, but at a high price in loss of comparative advantage. Few realise, however, that Lemass was quite sceptical of ISI and was, even as a very young man, a convinced free trader. Ever the pragmatist, he saw that the post-1918 world that he lived in was one of many belligerent nation states all playing the same protectionist game; he believed Ireland would also have to play this game. His real ideal, as far back as 1929, was a prophetic one. He dreamed of a European free-trade area with a huge market that would rival that of the US, at that time a large economic world sufficient unto itself. To even contemplate a united Europe at that time marked him out from most inhabitants of the British Isles, for whom the great reality was still the British Empire, the superpower of the era, resting in splendid isolation from continental Europe behind the guns of the invincible Royal Navy.

The second economic revolution he led was the dismantling of protectionism from 1957 on and a complete reversal of the old policy of discouraging foreign investment in the country. The IDA and other semi-governmental organisations, with his blessing, set about attracting foreign companies, with their money, international connections and know-how. The results were, to the people of that time, magical. The Irish economy doubled in size between 1957 and 1977, mainly due to this historical change of policy, combined, of course, with the general falling away of trade barriers in the British Isles and, later, western Europe as Lemass's dream finally came true.

Lemass was a confirmed Irish nationalist. Like so many of his time, he saw British rule in Ireland not so much as tyrannical as simply negligent, and he felt that unless the Irish rid themselves of the dead hand of London they would never get anywhere. This did not stop him displaying his characteristic inventiveness and flexibility with regard to Northern Ireland. His dramatic and unheralded visit to the prime minister of Northern Ireland, Terence O'Neill, at Stormont in January 1965 ended a sterile cold war between the two Irish states.

The economic policy turnabout occurred while Lemass was minister for industry and commerce and Eamon de Valera (Dev) was still Taoiseach. However, during his seven years as Taoiseach, Lemass initiated not only a new era in North–South relations but also an educational revolution, through his policy of promoting young and aggressive ministers of education in place of the aging ex-revolutionaries of de Valera's government and the almost equally veteran leaders of the governments led by Fine Gael. A succession of ministers transformed the semi-moribund and still-Victorian educational system, approaching rapidly a modern system of universal education that lasts far into young adulthood. Although he did not live to see it develop, Lemass had much to do with founding the great revolution in educational standards and content that has fuelled the growth of the country over the last half-century.

Lemass was himself an ex-revolutionary. It has been persistently alleged that he was one of Michael Collins's hit squad that killed British agents and spies on Bloody Sunday, 20 November 1920. This book assesses the ambivalent evidence on Lemass's military career. Later on he certainly became passionately convinced of the futility of armed struggle in pursuit of political reform or gain, and this conviction was held by one who had witnessed the horrors of political violence up close. His brother, Noel Lemass, was tortured, mutilated and murdered by Irish government agents from Oriel House, the army special branch formed mainly from Collins's squad, in late 1923. Lemass believed he knew the identity of the murderer, but never spoke about it publicly, and he worked for reconciliation in an embittered little country for the rest of his life.

Lemass was a student all through his adult years, reading voraciously on economics, political economy, political science and history. He seems to have had little interest in general literature, and was somewhat uninterested in general ideas for their own sake. He was, however, fascinated by the application of ideas that might solve some problem. On the other hand, his favourite subjects were history and mathematics, and he often said that, had he not been swept up into politics, he would have happily spent his life solving mathematical problems. Perhaps he wished he had lived at a time when he might have been permitted to be interested in ideas for their own sake.

This book looks in particular at the cultural and family background of this unusual figure in Irish political life. His background was one of milliners and tailors; measurement was the basic and honourable skill of his family, and the sub-title was suggested by this trait of Lemass. All his life he assessed opinions, or measured them, and quickly accepted or rejected them according to a rather ruthless private calculus of his own. This tradition of skill, accuracy and work ethic was unusual for an Irish revolutionary and political leader. He was of remote French extraction and of Huguenot artisan tradition. Physically, he reflected this in his 'un-Irish' dark skin, his brown eyes and, possibly, his unorthodox ability to change his mind in quite radical ways; he evidently thought consistency the hobgoblin of small minds, but then he always denied that his basic outlook on things ever changed. His immediate family were hatters from central Dublin, and there was a strong tradition of hard work, skilled creativity and family loyalty. His political ancestry was staunchly Parnellite, and in some ways his personality seems to have echoed unconsciously the enigmatic and solitary character of that legendary fallen hero, a Protestant leader of a Catholic people. He was quite handsome as a young man, in a striking film noir style, and he was a sharp dresser, favouring stylish suits and snap-brim hats. His fastidiousness he explained by saying it was good for morale. Coming from a work-obsessed subculture, he was an extraordinarily energetic and single-minded worker in a somewhat laid-back and leisurely agrarian country. His period as Taoiseach marked the beginning of a long process that has transformed Ireland from an agrarian province of the British Isles to a successful developed country that has been seen as a model for many aspirant underdeveloped countries.

I owe much to many people; the conclusions in this book are my own, but they have been heavily informed by the writings of, and conversations with, previous biographers of Lemass over the years, in particular my old friend and colleague Brian Farrell. Lemass's most complete and authoritative recent biography is the work of John Horgan, with whom I have spent many hours discussing our common fascinations. John has shown extraordinary generosity in giving me unfettered access to his unique and irreplaceable archive of interviews and other research materials, a data source that lies behind his own study of ten years ago. This book is also heavily indebted to John's pioneering work. Michael Mills, Henry Sheridan, Evelyn Sheridan, Eileen Lemass, Seán O'Connor, Maurice Manning, Myles Tierney, Cormac Ó Gráda and T.K. Whitaker were generous with their time and gave me lively insights into the character and purposes of Lemass as a key political actor for so many years in Irish life. The sub-title is derived from a suggestion by Bryan Fanning, who has also listened patiently to my occasionally obsessional out-loud meditations. Michael Laffan listened also, and put me right from time to time. Andreas Hess read an early draft and gave me the perspective of a German-trained sociologist-cum-political-scientist. John Coakley of the School of Politics and International Relations (SPIRE) in University College Dublin (UCD) gave this veteran generous intellectual and physical houseroom. Paul Gill of SPIRE proofread an early version. I have benefited from conversations with my colleagues in the Institute for British–Irish Studies at SPIRE, in particular Michael Anderson, Christopher Farrington and Susan McDermott. A conversation long ago with Breffni Tomlin gave an insight into the relationship between Lemass and de Valera. Pauric Dempsey and Ruth Hegarty of the Royal Irish Academy have been towers of strength, and Pauric suggested this foray into the history of the Irish polity in the first place. Ciara Meehan has been a quietly efficient and good-humoured research assistant. Jonathan Golden of Belfast has been an informed and sympathetic listener and fellow researcher. The Royal Irish Academy has been the instigator and generous patron of this project. As usual, I am indebted to the National Archives of Ireland and Catriona Crowe, to the National Library of Ireland and to that excellent institution that used to be referred to as the Archives Department of UCD. My sojourn as Burns Professor at Boston College (BC) in 2006–7 permitted me respite from my duties at UCD and sowed seeds that led to several things, including this study. In particular, conversations with Bob Savage at BC gave me new insights into the career of this historically crucial Irish political leader.

Tom Garvin

'Now, let's hear what you boys have been doing?', *Dublin Opinion* (July 1948), 161. (Courtesy of the National Library of Ireland)

Right: 'Ireland Week in London', *c*. September 1960. Illustrated poster, designed by Pieter Sluis. (NLI, Ephemera Collection, TVL/1960-70/3)

" Now, let's hear what you boys have been doing? Don't tell me Costello's Government is in still!"

SEPTEMBER 26-30 IN LONDON
SPONSORED BY:—IRISH EXPORT BOARD·
AER LINGUS-IRISH·IRISH TOURIST BOARD

IRELAND
WEEK

ONE

States of Ireland

Lemass photo by Colman Doyle, late 1950s. (© Irish Press Plc)

On 14 January 1965 the young son of
the secretary of the Department of
Finance informed his father that there
was a big policeman at the gate of their
house on the Stillorgan Road, near
Donnybrook in the south suburbs of
Dublin. Perhaps he wondered what
Daddy had done. T.K. Whitaker was
among the few people who knew what
the Garda was there for, and went out to
meet Seán Lemass, Taoiseach and leader
of the Fianna Fáil party, in his Garda-
driven prime-ministerial Mercedes-Benz.
Whitaker got into the car, and the
Taoiseach greeted his senior civil service
official and informal advisor on
Northern Ireland. Lemass growled at the
driver, 'Henry: Belfast!' Lemass did not
even tell Kathleen, his wife of 40 years,
where he was going that morning; that
way, things could be kept quiet for a bit
longer. However, Henry Sheridan, the
Taoiseach's Garda driver since 1961,
remarked to his wife, Evelyn, the night
before that he had been told to prepare
for a long day's drive, and it occurred to
both of them that it involved a visit either
to an agrarian outbreak in the midlands
or possibly to Northern Ireland. Henry
fuelled the car up in anticipation. Evelyn
intuited the North; it must have been in
the air, somehow. On the way to
Northern Ireland, Lemass, not a great
man for small talk and rather given to
long silences unless there was evidently
something necessary and germane to be

said, treated Whitaker to an impromptu seminar on the virtues of the American Constitution of 1789, emphasising the unique system of separation of powers, federalism and judicial review that characterises that classic document of political architecture.[1] Presumably, federalism was on his mind yet again; over the years he had taken an interest in federal devices as they worked elsewhere in the democratic world. The car paused on the Republic's side of the border for some minutes so as not to arrive too early; Lemass was a stickler for punctuality: be neither early nor late. To his mind, to be early could cause embarrassment, to be late was insulting.[2] The party duly crossed the frontier, and Jim Malley, ex-Spitfire pilot and private secretary to Terence O'Neill, prime minister of Northern Ireland, met them at the British customs post outside Newry, as arranged. On the second leg of the journey to Stormont, this one with a Royal Ulster Constabulary (RUC) motorcycle escort, the small talk was about poker, a passion of Lemass's.[3] Malley was fascinated by Lemass, apparently almost as though he were some exotic creature. He described him as 'a most extraordinary man'.[4]

Someone in Cabinet in Dublin had leaked the information about the projected visit to the *Irish Times*, and the paper had despatched a cameraman to the border to snap the historic occasion.[5] This may be how Mrs Sheridan correctly guessed the destination of the journey, even though an official blanket of secrecy had covered the operation. Perhaps there was no connection, but there was a well-established tradition even then of leaks from Charles Haughey, an up-and-coming young TD and minister, who was also Lemass's son-in-law, to John Healy, political correspondent of the *Irish Times*.

On arrival at Stormont, O'Neill welcomed Lemass with the carefully phrased greeting 'Welcome to the North', thereby avoiding the possibly taboo words 'Northern Ireland' and 'Ulster'. Lemass did not reply, increasing O'Neill's unease. He suggested that the Taoiseach might wish to wash his hands after what was such a long journey by the Irish standards of that time, and a far longer one politically than geographically. There seems to have been a prolonged and somewhat uneasy silence as the two men walked to the toilets. O'Neill reminisced:

> Eventually, in the rather spacious loo at Stormont House he suddenly said, 'I shall get into terrible trouble for this.' 'No, Mr. Lemass,' I replied, 'it is I who will get into trouble for this.' I then took him into the drawing room and introduced him to my wife and Cecil Bateman and Ken Bloomfield of the Cabinet Office staff. From then on he thawed out and became a very pleasant and amusing guest.[6]

The conversation was quite free, even somewhat politically incorrect. At one early stage one of the northerners, to break the ice, remarked that he personally regretted that the partition of 1920 had not included the west-Ulster county of Donegal; it would have rounded off Northern Ireland nicely, he felt. Perhaps he also thought a shorter border might have been a good thing: easier to patrol. Lemass riposted humorously that they were welcome to Donegal, as long as they took Neil Blaney, a rather rambunctious and very anti-partitionist Fianna Fáil politician in that county, with it.[7] Even Lemass seems to have had trouble with Blaney, who was quite a firebrand. Some years later, under Taoiseach Jack Lynch, a quiet Corkman who lacked Lemass's authoritativeness, Blaney, as a senior minister in the Irish government, was to publicly call O'Neill a 'bigot', which he quite transparently was not.[8] Blaney was to get away with it, and would not have done so under Lemass; Lynch lacked Lemass's revolutionary pedigree. However, back in January 1965 the northerners seem to have been somewhat surprised by Lemass, possibly expecting some wild-eyed revolutionary. One of them thought that the southerner, always a sharp dresser, had a 'gangster's suit';[9] but then, in southern eyes, northerners dressed square. Ken Bloomfield, a senior officer in the Northern Ireland civil service and therefore Whitaker's opposite number, thought Lemass at first sight had a rough charm:

> The taoiseach was burly, leonine and gruff, like some veteran French politician of the left. He spoke with a delicious growl. When O'Neill asked him if he knew well the then leader of the [British Conservative] Opposition, Alec Douglas-Hume, he confessed he had always 'had some reservations about the innate capacity of the Fourteenth Earl'.[10]

North–South rapprochement had been in the air for some time, and the end of the IRA 'Operation Harvest' campaign in 1962 offered a window of opportunity. The possibility of North–South co-operation in a number of important areas, in particular transport and electric power (including nuclear energy), was mooted at a meeting between Lemass and Harold Wilson on 16 March 1964. Wilson was leader of the opposition at the time but was expected to become prime minister of the UK shortly. Long before the Belfast meeting, O'Neill acknowledged Whitaker's role in taking the initiative. He remarked to Tony Grey of the *Irish Times* that he had once told Whitaker that if he ever replaced Lord Brookeborough as prime minister, he wanted a meeting with Lemass to be arranged.[11] The immediate preparations for the meeting went back to an encounter on a liner bound for the US. Whitaker had met Malley on board ship while he was en route to a meeting of the International Monetary Fund in Washington. Both had agreed to sound out their bosses back home about the possibility of a meeting between the two prime ministers.[12] Lemass jumped at the idea. Whitaker remembered:

> I knew O'Neill for a good while before the visit, that is why I was the channel for the invitation. The quickness of Lemass's response was notable. I had to remind him it might be an idea to have a word with [Minister for Foreign Affairs] Frank Aiken. 'I suppose so', he said, and rang him straight away. Aiken was a bit taken aback but fairly quickly agreed.[13]

O'Neill, although uneasy about his backbenchers, was also receptive, much to the surprise of some southern leaders, accustomed as they were to northern obduracy; O'Neill, an enlightened, if not always effectual, politician, was actively seeking to open doors between the two Irish states. Eventually, a note arrived from O'Neill through Malley and Whitaker that amounted to an invitation.

The meeting was a leap of faith for both men, and a brave one, particularly for O'Neill, who was in a much weaker position domestically. Lemass held the better hand, poker player that he was, but even he was taking an enormous gamble, and was trying to transcend or bypass a considerable amount of remembered history, bitterness and political passion. Admittedly, he had the advantage of being the prime minister of a sovereign country, and was also the undisputed leader of a highly organised political party, Fianna Fáil, a dominant party that he had played a major part in creating in the 1920s. He had recently inherited the leadership of the party from Eamon de Valera, legendary leader of Irish republican nationalism. O'Neill, by contrast, was the premier of a devolved government in a province of the UK, a province whose majority population had a collective psychology of siege and whose ruling Unionist Party was internally troubled. Furthermore, the Taoiseach had not only a united political party but also a consensual population behind him, whereas the North itself was riven, and within O'Neill's own party itself there were deep divisions and even hatreds behind the apparently monolithic front of Ulster Unionism. Eventually, this circumstance was to destroy O'Neill.

However, in 1965, this was all still in the future, and Lemass was exhibiting a considerable amount of empathy and political creativity. He came from a nationalist revolutionary tradition that had deep roots in Ireland; his family had a background of Dublin Parnellite politics, and there was a long family tradition of puritan hard work and successful artisanal and business enterprise. The militant Volunteer movement, a movement that culminated in the 1916 Rising and the ensuing struggle for independence, had swept up Lemass himself as a youth. However, as argued later in this book, his Parnellite and relatively liberal background seems to have set him apart from many of his Sinn Féin—later, Fianna Fáil—comrades. They tended to be bewildered by his pragmatism, his religious agnosticism, his disregard for many widely held orthodoxies and his mainly unspoken but quite obvious disregard for rural ways and society. Some were shocked by his lack of interest in the massive attempts of the new state to revive the Irish language as the spoken vernacular of the Irish people. He accepted the Irish-revival business as a means of boosting morale, always an obsession of his, but had to force himself to relearn it at the avuncular urging of de Valera. He was about to do something else unexpected: as prime minister and political heir to the rigidly anti-partitionist de Valera, he was, in effect, to recognise Northern Ireland. However, to placate northern nationalist feeling and to ensure that the northern minority did not feel that it was being sold out, he had to deny the reality of what he was doing. He was only partially successful. An aging man in his mid-60s and nearing the end of his political career, he possibly felt that it was time to clear up the unfinished business in the North, business he evidently felt to be irrelevant to the future of Ireland and damaging to the island's general developmental prospects.

Divided we stand

By the mid-1960s, the Irish cold war over partition and the disputes over the legitimacy of both Irish political entities had been going on, in one form or another, for over 40 years; Ireland had been partitioned by a British act of parliament in 1920 in the middle of the Irish War of Independence. For many Irish people in both parts of Ireland, the right to rule of the Stormont government was illegitimate; Republicans were fond of pointing out that no one in Ireland had voted for what they termed the 'Partition Act' of 1920. In the eyes of a significant and passionate Republican minority, the legitimacy of the new Irish Free State government of 1922 under the Anglo–Irish Treaty of 1921–2 was almost equally suspect. In the South a vicious little civil war had been fought between those who insisted on the continuing sovereignty of the half-imaginary Irish Republic declared in 1916 and 1919 and those who accepted the compromise Treaty of 1921 as the best deal that could be attained, a deal that could be improved upon peaceably in future. The pro-Treaty 'Free State' side easily won both the military conflict and the 26-county elections of June 1922 and August 1923. For a year afterward, Irish Army soldiers were posted outside ex-Unionist farmhouses in west Cork and elsewhere to ensure that no more 'burning out' happened. De Valera, putative leader of the Republican side but actually a virtual prisoner of the Republican diehards, declared that the Free State government was illegitimate and alleged that the Treaty had been signed under duress. Privately, he knew that the electorate was overwhelmingly against him and his political stance. He also must have gradually realised that the British could not wait to get out of 'Southern Ireland', as the Tommies, the Auxies and the Tans disappeared and the disbanded and pensioned-off Royal Irish Constabulary (RIC) left their barracks for looters to strip all over the 26-county area.

De Valera gradually drew certain political conclusions during the years 1923–6, some of them almost certainly prompted by sharp comments from Lemass. One was that nothing could be achieved through violence; another was that the way to power in Ireland was through the heart of the Irish voter. This second lesson he never forgot. In the short run, he set to creating a 'let's pretend' imaginary Republican administration, employing fellow anti-Treatyite leaders, among them a very young Séan Lemass. He held on to the control of American money in his capacity as 'President of the Irish Republic', even though he had been deposed by vote of the Second Dáil in January 1922 in favour of Arthur Griffith, the founder of the original Sinn Féin party back in 1904; Griffith was president of the Irish Republic from January through to the time of his death in August 1922. A few years later, de Valera formed, on the advice and urging of Lemass in particular, Fianna Fáil, a party that went on to be what political scientists term the natural governing party of the Irish state. De Valera's phenomenal charisma and Lemass's organisational energy eventually made Fianna Fáil an unprecedentedly successful Irish popular political entity. Lemass set to the apparently Sisyphean task of modernising and industrialising the agrarian Irish economy as minister for industry and commerce in the Fianna Fáil governments of 1932 onward.

In the North hideous pogroms between Catholics and Protestants accompanied the establishment of the northern state, resulting in Northern Ireland becoming a Unionist-dominated province within the UK. The northern polity became very much at odds with an increasingly nationalist and anti-partitionist Dublin state dominated eventually by de Valera and the Catholic Church to the south and west of Northern Ireland. In both jurisdictions religious minorities were subject to political subordination and discrimination. However, discrimination against Protestants in the South, although nasty, was minor compared with the wholesale discrimination against Catholics that occurred in the North. Furthermore, discrimination against the other guy was traditional in both parts of Ireland and on both sides of the religious fence. Another difference was that in the South there was a religiously instigated and extralegal attempt to marry Protestants out of existence, whereas in the North discrimination was more clearly state-driven.

In the South an anti-partitionist orthodoxy that laid claim to the North as the stolen and sundered 'Six Counties' became almost universally accepted. This irredentist mentality seemed at times to justify military action against what was seen as the Protestant and British local majority tyranny in the North. Even moderate opinion saw partition as evil and as an injustice, and it was blamed for Irish economic woes. In the North the siege mentality was reinforced by these developments, and the intransigence of Dublin also encouraged some northern Catholics not to engage with the northern regime. Catholics in Northern Ireland came to see the South as a Prester John country, hoping against hope that eventually the southerners would come to rescue them from their predicament. When Dublin behaved cautiously and moderately, it was seen by some as betrayal and sell-out.

Partition endured. It was reinforced mightily by Republican impossibilism after January 1922. More importantly, it was strengthened by the fact that Ulster, the northern province of Ireland, had, long before 1920, shown clear signs of developing in very different directions from the other three more agricultural and semi-feudal provinces on the island. This divergence occurred despite the existence of a common administrative system, good all-island communications and a compact geographical environment that both entities shared. The divergence also occurred in spite of Ireland's long existence as a cultural entity and even defied the existence of island-wide Protestant and Catholic ecclesiastical organisations, which were organised on a 32-county, all-Ireland basis. For a long time, even the Grand Orange Lodge of *Ireland* sat in Dublin rather than Belfast. Gaelic football and hurling were still organised on an all-Ireland basis after partition, as were international and domestic rugby. However, partition did have the effect of setting up two 'countries' in Ireland, to some extent reflected in two sets of social organisations. Two farming organisations emerged, and eventually there were two soccer teams for international purposes. Oddest of all, perhaps, were the three sets of cycling teams—one all-Ireland, one for Northern Ireland and one for the 26 counties only.

Partition therefore accelerated or aggravated a process of divergence that had previously existed, and did not artificially instigate it for the first time. Ulster was the only Irish province where a large British, non-Catholic population put down deep roots and became a settled and large community. The Ulster plantations of 1607 onwards were mainly Scots and English Borders in origin, and they proved very successful, while remaining culturally distinct from the majority of Irish people elsewhere on the island. Long before plantation, Antrim and Down had had intimate contact across the North Channel with south-western Scotland, the sea behaving as much as a large river as an arm of the sea. These contacts had prehistoric precedents, and in the first millennium, in Gaelic times, a joint eastern Ulster and western Scotland kingdom of Dál Ríada had flourished, ruled from its citadel at Dumbarton in Scotland. Even under landlordism, there had been the Ulster Custom, which rewarded tenants for improvements to their agrarian holdings, a proviso that did not exist in the other three provinces, where landlords and tenants were divided not only by religion but also by a land law that was highly exploitative. Again, the nine-county Ulster of British times was divided roughly half-and-half between Catholics and Protestants, the latter being mostly Presbyterians, whereas down in the South most Protestants were Church of Ireland, rather than Presbyterian, and were in a minority of well under 10%. Also, Ulster Protestants tended to be members of a large and classic Victorian working-class community, unlike their southern co-religionists, who were of all class backgrounds, with some bias towards relative wealth and privilege.

North and South, different before 1920, became more different afterwards because of their very different political histories, and have developed noticeably different identities. Within each area, the populations, simply by living together, have come to share common identities that exclude those outside for certain purposes. Protestants and Catholics in the North tended to see themselves as having much in common, much that was not shared by either the inhabitants of the Republic or by the peoples of Great Britain, even if what was shared often amounted only to an awareness of a common predicament.[14] Similarly, the people of the Republic came to see northerners as 'different', largely because they did not share the experience of independence, civil war and neutrality during the Second World War; nor did the northerners share the political education forced upon southerners by sovereignty. In particular, economic development, or the lack thereof, was a chronic obsession of southern leaders and of southern political debate, but northern development was really a concern of London. The South had sat out the Second World War as a terrified bystander, whereas northerners had participated openly in the battle for Britain's survival against Naziism. Men from both parts of Ireland fought on a volunteer basis in the ranks of the British forces, but southerners tended to keep quiet about it afterwards. Roughly equal absolute numbers of volunteers from both areas served. Oddly, five of the six Victoria Crosses awarded to Irishmen during the Second World War were won by southerners. All six were Catholics; the Irish situation was full of such ironies.[15] Paddy Finucane, a well-known Spitfire ace of the Battle of Britain who shot down five German planes and was killed over France in 1941, was the son of a man who had been 'out' in the Easter Rising. Southern Protestants threw in their lot with the new state and often became enthusiastic participants in democratic politics, opinion forming, the armed forces and public office, to an extent not generally possible for Catholics in the northern sub-polity. By and large, the inhabitants of the Republic forgot British rule, whereas northerners were always aware of it. Southerners thought rarely about the North, and to many northerners the South eventually became a picturesque irrelevance; to both, London remained for a long time the local *Weltstadt*, accepted by the Irish, at the assessment of that city's own inhabitants, as being the capital of the world. Confusingly, when any set of Irish, northerners or southerners, went to London, they were all lumped together by the uncaring English as 'Paddies', much to the annoyance of Unionists. To some northerners, southerners talked fast and thought slow; to some southerners, northerners were over-obsessed with each other. Despite having sympathy for the plight of northern Catholics, southerners for a long time envied northerners their higher standard of living, generated in part by the generous provisions of the British welfare state during the first decades after the Second World War. The southerners had a liking for the English that was in part derived from a feeling of equality with them; independence eventually eliminated the ancient sense of subordination. The opening up of Europe in the 1950s and the visit of John F. Kennedy to the Republic in 1963 intensified a sense in the Republic that the state had somehow arrived and that its post-war relative isolation was over. Northerners knew their destinies were controlled by a British government that was, if not exactly foreign, remote from both northern clans, geographically and psychologically. Again, the welfare state developed later, and in a rather different way, in the South.[16]

Like Spain and Portugal, or the partitioned German states during the period 1949–90, the two Irelands attempted to ignore each other, while at the same time being forced by propinquity and the interweaving of so many institutions and geographical facts of life to co-operate with each other. The Republic, which, after all, is not just the south of Ireland but all of the west and the lion's share of the east as well, came to pretend that it was Ireland *tout court*, while the North tried to represent the boundary between itself and the rest of the island as a wholly natural, obvious one with the immediate physical immediacy of a range of mountains or an arm of the sea. The North commonly labelled the Republic a 'foreign country', to unintended comic effect. For good measure, the Republic denied symbolic recognition to Northern Ireland and occasionally pretended that Great Britain was as remote and unfamiliar a country as Outer Mongolia. Even practical measures of co-operation, such as joint authority over the Foyle fisheries, the cross-border services of the Great Northern Railway bus and rail transport concern or the hydroelectric works on the Erne waters, took place quietly and without any public political rhetoric. Informal extradition of IRA suspects often occurred, suspects being handed quietly over from one jurisdiction to the other, commonly under cover of darkness at unfrequented border crossings. Eventually, this was ruled illegal by southern courts, but the two police forces quietly exchanged information quite frequently, when it was politically feasible. Top-level conferring, as distinct from extensive low-level co-operation, seems to have virtually never taken place between 1932 and the mid-1960s, an extraordinary circumstance in a compact island inhabited at that time by 4 million people. All of this made the official encounter of January 1965 of great symbolic and psychological importance.

Brief encounter: the thaw

In the 1950s and 1960s things had been changing: the influence of the mass media; of the relative, if partial, arrival of affluence; the coming of television and the impact of Vatican II on Irish Catholic 'group-think' had begun to erode the irredentist political orthodoxy created by de Valera and his ideologues. In the mid-1950s, voices were raised in the Republic against the doctrine of the 'Indivisible Island', and qualified defences of the Unionist tradition in Ireland were articulated by people of *nationalist* background, as distinct from contributors to the ex-Unionist Dublin *Irish Times*.[17] This paper always expressed a qualified sympathy with Ulster Unionism. The official anti-partitionist orthodoxy was more or less intact even as late as 1968–71, when the northern crisis erupted, but it had always had a certain flimsy, artificial and unpopular character to it, and only a passionate minority really took it seriously. Like so many of de Valera's doctrinal devices, it was designed to win votes at the margin of the electorate rather than to be a genuine attempt to understand everyday reality. As Lemass was wont to say privately, no one with any sense believes election promises. However, he also remarked once, 'the art of political propaganda is to say what most of the people are thinking'.[18] Patrick Hillery reminisced:

> [Lemass] on the North: there was a Parliamentary party meeting some time in '57–'59, after we had come back into government. The IRA campaign was on, and a lot of people were coming under pressure in the constituencies, as I was. Dev had called the meeting to pull things into line. At one stage a speaker suggested that 'peaceful means had failed'. Lemass was quick to respond, arguing strongly that 'peaceful means never got a chance'. He instanced a number of occasions over the years where possibilities had been missed; suggested it was almost as if Brookborough [*sic*] was in charge of the IRA—every time it looked as if we were gaining an advantage, the IRA would be summoned into action and everything would be jeopardised again.[19]

Lemass latched on to the European idea early, and in the 1950s 'Europe' started to become a concrete reality. As Taoiseach in 1961, he felt able to comment in almost traditional terms on the supremacy of political considerations over economic considerations:

> It would be a great error to underestimate the extent to which the full execution of the formal obligations of the Treaty [of Rome], even though they bear on economic matters, can affect the powers exercised by individual governments in a political sense, as this expression is generally understood. It is not believed [by the government] that political unity will grow, automatically, from economic

unity; rather it is believed that it is only on the basis of political agreement that a permanent solution of the economic problems can be founded.[20]

Northern Unionists began to see him as someone who was less 'impossible' than de Valera or even his younger fellow politicians in Fianna Fáil. Unlike many of his colleagues, Lemass saw through the absurdity of this self-defeating little cold war conducted by megaphone diplomacy. Northerners whom he trusted helped him evolve a very revisionist stance on partition. Whitaker was a later influence on him, as was Donal Barrington. Another informant was possibly an unexpected one: Ernest Blythe, northerner, Protestant, Cumann na nGaedheal minister for finance in the first Free State government and well-informed critic of southern attitudes towards the North. Blythe was also hated by Republicans for his rather bloodthirsty attitudes towards anti-government rebels in 1922–3. He had also been heavily involved in the acceptance of the existing partition line in 1925 in return for certain financial considerations, and famously termed it at the time 'a damned good bargain'. The Republicans, naturally, declared it to be another sell-out. In 1962 Blythe and Lemass corresponded with each other, and Blythe gave the Taoiseach a crash course in northern realities; sectarianism was a given in Northern Irish politics, he told Lemass. Dublin's posture of non-recognition, a posture that dated from 1937 rather than 1922 and was de Valera's creation, only made things worse. Dublin should unequivocally recognise the Northern Ireland regime, drop non-recognition completely and engage in free and equal co-operative policies. He went so far as to argue that the aggressive southern non-recognition of Northern Ireland, devised by de Valera in the 1930s to placate his IRA veterans, was the *cause* of northern sectarian politics, an argument that flies in the face of the matter-of-fact acceptance by W.T. Cosgrave's Dublin government of the northern refusal to come in to the Free State in late 1922. It also ignores the long resistance to Home Rule and the violent hostility to Catholic rights that characterised so much of Ulster politics dating back to the early nineteenth century. However, Blythe insisted quite cogently that any aggressive political action against Ulster Unionism was self-defeating and foolish:

> If at an early date we find ourselves able to abandon hostility and attempts at pressure, then even the Northern Nationalist party, which depends for its survival on the existence and exploitation of Catholic grievances, will not be able to keep general politico-religious segregation alive

and so will not be able to maintain Lord Brookeborough or his like permanently in power.[21]

This line was sympathised with quietly by what was possibly an unexpected figure: Eamon de Valera.[22] Lemass seems to have realised at least as early as the 1930s that Northern Ireland was here to stay in one form or another, and he seems to have had a pragmatic and unaggressive, but still nationalist, aspiration towards a federal Ireland with a self-governing Northern Ireland within it. He did, however, hew publicly to the traditional line that partition was an imposed injustice and was injurious to the economic development of both parts of Ireland, which he insisted on referring to as one nation divided between two states.[23] Also, he was so obsessed with developing the 26 counties and getting his state out of its agrarian stasis and into the modern world that much of the time he probably thought little about the North at all. A certain absent-minded schizophrenia towards the northern state persisted in his mind and certainly in his behaviour, conditioned as it partly was by his quite fixed opinion that politics was the art of the possible, and in a democracy that meant the ideas of other people commonly had precedence over one's own. If you wished to be a leader and you did not like the ideas of other people, it was your job as leader to change them through political argument. However, his underlying realism usually won out over traditional popular passions—passions that, to some extent at least, he certainly shared. He did, perhaps, like many southerners, underrate the implacability of Unionist sentiment towards any southern meddling in northern affairs or any question of a merger of the two Irish polities, but he was more receptive to such a perception than most of his fellow politicians in Fianna Fáil; he could change his mind. Writing to Blythe, he tried, perhaps defensively, to clarify his own thinking:

> I have never been fully able to understand what is meant by 'recognising the legitimacy of the Northern Government'. If this expression is intended to convey that they represent the majority in the Six-County area, this is no difficulty. If it means that the Northern Government is seen as having a permanent future, within an all-Ireland Constitution, this is not a difficulty either. If it means a judgement on their historical origins, this is a different matter. It seems to me that when Brookeborough speaks of recognition this is what he has in mind—acceptance of the two-nation theory, or at least a confession that, because of the religious division,

partition was only [the] right and practicable solution to the problem … without seeking to impose any pre-condition of acceptance of any historical theory, or advertence to the fact that, while we do not conceal our hope that co-operation will lead in time to an acceptance of the concept of unity, they for their part say this can never be. It is my belief that the [European] Common Market will compel co-operation on these terms.[24]

There is wishful thinking and a certain uncharacteristically contorted reasoning visible here, and some quite visible goodwill. However, he also, again rather defensively, tried to excuse northern Catholic truculence in the face of undoubted discrimination. It was, he told Blythe in December 1962:

too easy to find fault with the attitude of the Northern Nationalists. It would be expecting far too much of human nature not to expect them to express their resentment of their second-class status, and their desire to end it in the only way which at present seems possible by destroying the authority whose policy it is to sustain it. If the Northern Government had ever shown any disposition to want to treat them otherwise the position might have developed differently.[25]

Lemass, however, in the same breath, accepted the desirability of there being a separate parliamentary government in Northern Ireland. By the standards of the Republican subculture he came from, this was extremely moderate, and it is evident that Lemass had more or less internalised the proposition that partition was a reflection of Irish social, religious and political divisions and not some artificial division imposed on the unwilling Irish by the imperial British in 1920. These new revisionist views had been increasingly noisily expressed in the Republic in the late 1950s and early 1960s, and Blythe, in his extreme old age, found himself in the intellectual company of quite a few younger people, in particular, perhaps, Donal Barrington and Michael Sheehy.[26] In 1963 Lemass told his colleagues, with a characteristic impatience, that Northern Ireland, however artificial an entity it might be, existed with the consent of the vast majority of its inhab-itants.[27] A strong perception that Lemass was different from his older revolutionary colleagues seems to have prompted O'Neill's attempt to break the ice. The January 1965 meeting took place therefore in the context of a southern cultural orthodoxy which had held that the northern polity was il-legitimate and had no right to exist. Lemass therefore could be held to be breaking an unspoken but very strong taboo by going north. Interestingly, public and elite opinion in the Republic approved generally of this break with orthodoxy; the taboo was not held by a very wide section of public opinion, and further meetings between the two leaderships occurred over the next few years. Going to one such meeting in 1967, Taoiseach Jack Lynch, Lemass's successor, had snowballs thrown at him by Paisleyites, the latter thereby presumably trying to demonstrate their spiritual and cultural superiority. When Lemass got back to Dublin after the momentous encounter of January 1965, someone asked him on behalf of the press for a statement. He said, 'Tell them things will never be the same.'[28]

The South loved the Lemass–O'Neill démarche, and O'Neill was acclaimed and even declared 'Irishman of the Year' by southern popular newspapers. O'Neill was genuinely liked by southerners who had little understanding of his predicament, and an era of good feelings between North and South was enjoyed for a few short years. It was not to last, as everyone knows, and the rise of Ian Paisley on the Unionist side, coupled with the mobilisation of idealistic young people in the civil rights movement, culminated in sectarian violence and near civil war in Northern Ireland from 1969 on. The Irish civil rights movement, like so many things in Ireland, was modelled on American prototypes and applied to non-American situations that had very un-American political dynamics. The result was disaster. Lemass could not have foreseen this; he possibly did not realise how fragile the northern government was, based as it was on Unionist consent and nationalist passivity. Stormont was eventually destroyed by the partial withdrawal of that consent and the eventual violent end to passivity in the form of the Provisional IRA and other paramilitary forces on both sides of the sectarian divide. The Lemass–O'Neill meetings and their sequelae arguably helped to start a chain reaction involving both parts of Ireland, Britain and, eventually, the European Union (EU) and the US.

Some would argue further that the meeting of January 1965 was naive and even dangerous, triggering a breakdown into communal violence of the northern polity, a polity that was dangerously fragile, a fact that was not sufficiently realised by either leader. O'Neill certainly did not see it that way, and possibly saw the meeting as an attempt to head off a coming crisis. Long before 1965, Paisleyism had already mobilised and organised angry loyalist crowds in Belfast and elsewhere against any display of nationalist or Republican self-assertiveness. Paisley was provoked also by O'Neill's attempts to open doors to the Catholic minority in the Province, O'Neill remembered:

On 24 April [1964], just over a year after I had become Prime Minister, I took my first step in the direction of improving community relations. I visited a Catholic school in Ballymoney, County Antrim. And what is more, it emerged quite naturally as a result of my known wishes and attitudes. I was making one of my 'meet the people' tours and this visit was included in the schedule. Of course it stole the headlines. The Chairman of the Board of Governors, Canon Clenaghan, had been padre to the Connaught Rangers in the First World War … [a Belfast paper's] photographer waited outside the front door and when, an hour later, I emerged, with the aid of his telescopic lens, he made it look as if the crucifix was over my head. I was later shown how Paisley was able to make use of this picture in his own paper.[29]

O'Neill saw quite clearly that the northern chain reaction had started long before the meeting with Lemass and that it was the hard-line Protestants who had endangered their own people's historical future in Ireland. Years later he wrote with foreboding about the future of what he evidently thought of as his own people, his little platoon, he commented:

If Ulster does not survive, then historians may well show that it was the Protestant extremists, yearning for the days of the Protestant ascendancy, who lit the flame which blew us up. This, of course, was coupled with the fact that for far too long no effort had been made to make the minority feel that they were wanted or even appreciated.[30]

It could be argued that the Ulster explosion was inevitable, given the hardened attitudes of both sides and the fact that the stability of the Stormont system had relied upon Catholic passivity and Protestant complacency. The gradual replacement of the passivity by self-assertion expressed by a better-educated generation of leaders may have been aided and abetted by empty southern rhetoric, as suggested by Blythe, but this was somewhat beside the point; the North was inherently unstable. This new self-assertion shattered the complacency of the Protestant side and gave Paisley his chance to bring O'Neill and his moderate Unionist leadership down. A resumption of communal violence, possibly on the scale of the 1920s, as remembered by folk tradition, was very much expected in the summer of 1964 in Northern Ireland. Ordinary folk predicted that the whole thing was going to start again in a few years. And it had little to do with the South, other, of course, than the fact that the simple physical existence of the South conditioned the whole situation: it represented the hoped-for or dreaded possible alternative. It was the vague hope for one side (the nationalists) or the equally vague menace for the other (the Unionists), and it remained so, almost regardless of what the southern government did or did not do.[31] Southern anti-partitionist propaganda and partial tolerance of the IRA did not help, but silence on partition, total formal recognition of the Belfast government and immediate and draconian internment of all known IRA sympathisers would not have helped much either; the basic problem was internal to the North. It would have taken a decision by the Republic to sink beneath the surface of the Atlantic Ocean like Tír na nÓg to lessen the aspirations of one side or the paranoia of the other. For Northern Ireland, the Republic was the great green rhinoceros in the corner of the drawing room. Everyone knew it was there, and everyone pretended it was not.

Lemass did the right thing, although perhaps he did it by instinct rather than by some kind of prophetic insight into the coming disaster. What the Lemass–O'Neill meeting did was set up a kind of 'hotline' between the leaderships of the two Irish entities that did foster inter-elite mutual understanding. Meetings between ministers and senior officials on a one-to-one basis became routine. Belfast paranoia about the intentions of Dublin had, naturally, always been strong; just because you are paranoid does not mean you have not got enemies. Northern Unionist distrust of Dublin was partly based on a shrewd and realistic pessimism about Dublin's good intentions, but also partly on a naive cynicism. North–South meetings at least enabled both sides to build up gradually a more nuanced and sophisticated view of each other. Northerners needed to know that the IRA, for example, was as much the enemy of Dublin's democracy as it was of the northern polity. Similarly, southerners needed to understand the fragility of democratic and liberal values in the North; each side had to wake up to the other, rather than relying on fantasies of each other, as had been the case for far too long. In 1995 Paddy Doherty, a prominent leader of the old Nationalist Party, described Lemass as a man whom the northern situation had left 'emotionally committed but intellectually baffled'.[32] That was not a bad start for serious thinking about a problem that had long suffered from far too little serious thought and far too much unearned intellectual certainty. The Stormont meeting did also contribute greatly to the long evolution of North–South and British–Irish diplomacy that eventually, if slowly, wound down the 30-year-long murder campaigns in Ulster. Towards the end, this process not only involved Dublin, Belfast and London but also Washington and Brussels. It all started in the loos of Stormont.

Terence O'Neill and Lemass walking in the grounds of Stormont House following their historic meeting, 14 January 1965. Behind them from left to right are Ken Bloomfield, senior officer in the Northern Ireland civil service; Cecil Bateman; and T.K. Whitaker, secretary, Department of Finance. (Courtesy of Ken Bloomfield)

Jim Malley, private secretary to Terence O'Neill; Harold Black, Cabinet secretary; and Ken Bloomfield, *c.* 1965. Malley fought in the Second World War and received three gallantry decorations. He suffered ill-health due to damaging a lung during his repeated long flights in an unheated aircraft during the war. (Courtesy of Ken Bloomfield)

Cóip

Letter from Eamon de Valera to Lemass, 23 February 1961. In it, de Valera anticipates that objections might be raised to his proposed visit to Armagh Cathedral marking the beginning of the Patrician year. However, he feels that 'it would be much better to be prevented in that way than that we ourselves should default through anticipating difficulties'. (UCDA-OFM, P150/3497)

23rd February, 1961

A Thaoisigh, a chara,

The time has come when I must tell the Cardinal definitely whether I intend to be, or not to be, in Armagh on March 17th for the celebrations opening the Patrician Year.

I am now firmly of opinion that I should be there. The Cardinal, I know, desires my attendance, and should I fail to respond he may regard it as a slight.

The occasion is, of course, a great national one, and it would seem to be the President's duty to participate, if at all possible. Indeed, should the President not attend, the feeling would, I think, be widespread that he has been guilty of a dereliction. All sorts of questions would be raised publicly, and I do not think that adequate answers could be forthcoming.

The ceremonies will be religious, and my being present at them should not create any special difficulties, particularly as Protestants, no less than Catholics, honour St. Patrick as the National Apostle.

Should the unlikely however, happen, and the Northern authorities make objection to my entering the Six Counties, it would be much better to be prevented in that way than that we ourselves should default through anticipating difficulties and consequences which might never arise.

I have given consideration to the possibl effects of my attendance on the political relations between the two parts of the country, and I cannot see that my going to Armagh on this occasion could, in any way, be detrimental. Accordingly, I would propose that I tell the Cardinal, immediately, that it is my intention to be present: I would be glad to know, as soon as possible, that you agree, and that the necessary preliminar steps to inform the Northern authorities will be taken by the appropriate Government Department.

Le mór-mheas,

Do chara,

Sgd. Eamon de Valera

An Taoiseach Seán Lemass,
Áras an Rialtais,
Baile Átha Cliath.

23

*Minister,
I see it.
Ah
18/1/65.*

STORMONT CASTLE,

BELFAST, 4.

We have today discussed matters in which there may prove to be a degree of common interest, and have agreed to explore further what specific measures may be possible or desirable by way of practical consultation and co-operation. Our talks — which did not touch upon constitutional or political questions — have been conducted in a most amicable way, and we look forward to a further discussion in Dublin.

[signature: Seán Lemass]   *Terence O'Neill*

Thursday, January 14, 1965

I ascertained from Mr Whitaker that this document was essentially Stormont draft and that it was their idea that it should be on headed paper and signed. The document was done in duplicate.

*[initials]
14/1/65.*

Communiqué sent by T.K. Whitaker to undisclosed senior civil servants asking for feedback on the proposed areas of practical co-operation with Northern Ireland following the Lemass–O'Neill talks four days previously, 18 January 1965. (NAI, DFA, P363/1)

ROINN AIRGEADAIS.
(DEPARTMENT OF FINANCE)
BAILE ÁTHA CLIATH 2.
(DUBLIN 2)

URGENT

18 January, 1965.

Dear

    I enclose an extract from my report of the recent meeting between the Taoiseach and the Prime Minister of Northern Ireland.

    Amongst the possibilities of co-operation which were not specifically mentioned, but which had been noted beforehand from the summary made in the Taoiseach's Department following inter-departmental inquiries in September, 1963, were:

General Economic Matters:

    Periodic meetings between Finance officials on both sides and between representatives of Economic Councils to exchange information, experience and forecasts (as in Economic Policy Committee of OECD).   Particular attention to common objectives in regard to promotion of economic growth, attraction of foreign industries and capital, reduction of unemployment, regional development.

Local Services:

    Harmonising in contiguous areas of public road networks, housing, schools, regional water supply and sewerage facilities, industrial location, drainage, preservation of natural beauty (e.g. Lough Melvin, Erne, Foyle) and cooperation in surveys and research work related to physical planning.

Agriculture:

    Possibility of N.I. support for exclusion of butter exports to N.I. from British quota.   Possibility of processing of N.I. cows in our meat factories.

Customs Clearance:

    Further easing of cross-border movement.

Entertainment and Sport:

    Closer relationship between T.E. and U.T.V.   All-Ireland representation in international events.

    As the Taoiseach wishes to be in a position to send a complete list as soon as possible to Captain O'Neill, I should be grateful if you would indicate urgently what amendments or extensions to the points mentioned at the meeting, as supplemented above, are desirable.

                              Yours sincerely,

                              T. K. WHITAKER

25

Letter from T.K. Whitaker to Dr S. Ó Nualláin, secretary, Department of the
Taoiseach, 29 January 1965. He attaches to it an updated list of possibilities
for North–South co-operation for comment. (NAI, DFA, 96/3/16)

29 January, 1965.

Dear Ó Nualláin,

I attach an up-to-date list of possibilities of co-
operation between North and South based on inquiries from
Departments following the Taoiseach's meeting with the
Northern Premier. The Taoiseach, as you know, promised
to send Captain O'Neill such a list and it is submitted in
its present form for the Taoiseach's consideration. I am
personally doubtful about including item 18 (Sport). Some
draft sentences for a letter which might accompany the list,
when settled, are also enclosed for consideration.

There are likely to be various meetings - at Ministerial
and official levels - in addition to the return visit of
Captain O'Neill to Dublin and it seems important that early
arrangements be made to ensure that all concerned in these
contacts know what is happening in other fields and that there
is some central coordination to ensure both consistency of
approach and maintenance of the original impetus.

An interdepartmental committee of Secretaries, reporting
periodically to a Cabinet Committee of the corresponding
Ministers, may be the right solution, as it has so far worked
satisfactorily (I think) for problems concerning our external
trading and economic relations.

I am sending a copy of this letter and enclosures to
McCann and am asking him to let us know whether he has any
observations.

Yours sincerely,

T. K. WHITAKER

Dr. N. S. Ó Nualláin,
Secretary,
Department of the Taoiseach,
Upper Merrion Street,
DUBLIN, 2.

POSSIBILITIES OF COOPERATION AND CONSULTATION

1. General Economic Matters

Periodic meetings between Finance officials on both sides and between representatives of Economic Councils to exchange information, experience and forecasts (as in Economic Policy Committee of OECD). Particular attention to common objectives in regard to promotion of economic growth, attraction of foreign industries and capital, reduction of unemployment, regional development.

2. Physical Planning and Construction

Consultation at central and local levels on physical planning policies and practices, including regional planning and industrial location. Exchange of information in regard to planning surveys and research. Preservation of areas of natural beauty (e.g., Loughs Melvin, Erne and Foyle) and other natural amenities of tourist value. Harmonisation of policies and cooperation, where appropriate, in contiguous areas in relation to such matters as roads, road traffic, water and sewerage, housing, drainage and schools.

3. Administrative Problems

Consultation and cooperation in such matters as organisation and methods and training courses, etc.

4. Education

Cross-border interchange of pupils, scholarships and teachers, where convenience, economy and other circumstances render this appropriate. Educational research, particularly relating to teaching of languages and problems of mental handicap. Pooling of knowledge and experience in relation to school building.

5. Health Services

Cross-border arrangements (including sharing of cost) for hospital and specialist services, in case of road accidents, maternity, blood transfusions, etc., where convenience and urgency make this desirable.

6. Electricity

High tension connections; technical cooperation. Possible joint development of nuclear stations.

7. Peat

Cooperation in development of peat resources.

8. Transport

Existing cooperative relations to be continued and extended.

9. Tourism

Joint promotion abroad and greater interflow at home.

10. Forestry

Testing of timber grown under Irish conditions. Forward planning of industrial development in the timber-using sector.

11. Fisheries and Game

Sea fisheries policies and problems. Joint conservancy control of inland fisheries in appropriate cases. Cooperation in regard to rod and gun licences, open game seasons and game protection arrangements.

12. Agriculture

Firmer and wider basis for coordinated approach to research problems. Coordination of inter-area trade in livestock and other agricultural commodities, including butter. Cooperation in livestock and poultry improvement schemes.

28

13. Trade

Lowering of tariffs against goods of Northern Ireland manufacture.   Joint export promotion.   Joint participation in trade fairs.

14. Industry

Some joint promotion and at least sufficient coordination to reduce the risk of wasteful bidding against one another. Cooperation in such matters as training for industry, retraining and resettlement, industrial research and testing.   Exchange of views on industrial relations.

15. Harmonisation of Legislation in relation to Commerce

Prior consultation in relation to the introduction of legislation affecting commercial activities - Company Law, Business N ames, Hire Purchase, etc.

16. Justice

Further cooperation in such fields as reciprocal practising rights for lawyers, administration of charities by an all-Ireland Board, common legal journal.   Exchange of views on prison reform, probation system, etc.

17. Civil Defence, etc.

Continued cooperative approach to civil defence and allied matters.

18. Sport

All-Ireland representation in international events.

THE IRI

Price 6d. No. 34,087   DUBLIN, FRID

Premiers at Stormont Castle   LEM

Front page of the *Irish Times* reporting on the previous day's meeting at Stormont, 15 January 1965. (Courtesy of the *Irish Times*)

Mr. Lemass with Captain O'Neill in the grounds of Stormont Castle yesterday.

SS — O'NEILL MEETING WELCOMED

N.I. Premier to visit Dublin

By Our Political Correspondent

THROUGHOUT Ireland last night there was warm approval for the f
official meeting between the Taoiseach, Mr. Lemass, and the Northern Prin
Minister, Captain O'Neill. It took place in Stormont at about 1 p.m. and co
tinued at a luncheon later. Further talks will be held when Captain O'N
comes to Dublin. Both the Taoiseach and Captain O'Neill expressed the he
that it would open a new era of co-operation between the two States.

On his return to Dublin last night Mr. Lemass declared: "There is no question that
meeting was significant. Its significance should not be exaggerated. I think I can say tha
road block has been removed. How far the road may go is not yet known. It has been tr
said, however, that it is better to travel hopefully than to arrive.

"The practice of consultation and co-operation in matters of economic importance w
I feel certain, prove to be so useful that once started everybody will expect and welcome
continuation and extension."

Northern reaction was that a
new era in North-South co-operation
was marked when the Taoiseach,
in a symbolic gesture, "walked
through the gates of Stormont" to
a new recognition in the relations
between North and South. Inside
the gates he was greeted by the
Northern Premier and began a
meeting which was initiated through
the friendship between Captain
O'Neill and Mr. T. K. Whitaker,
Secretary of the Department of
Finance.

Indeed, the idea for North-South
co-operation was discussed in Tokyo
last October when Mr. Whitaker
and Captain O'Neill were delegates
to the World Bank. Subsequently
Captain O'Neill sent his invitation
to Mr. Lemass through Mr.
Whitaker and it was accepted
but all was done in an informal way
without any letters passing between
the statesmen.

The meeting is the very first
since the historic meeting of Mr. de
Valera and Sir James Craig in
Dublin 45 years ago before the
new Irish State was established and
when Mr. de Valera was President of
the Irish Republic, apart from meetings in London in 1925. Although
yesterday's meeting is symbolic of

THE COMMUNIQUE

The communiqué issued after yesterday's meeting betwee
Mr. Lemass and Captain O'Neill said: "We have to-d
discussed matters in which there may prove to be a degree
common interest, and have agreed to explore further wh
specific measures may be possible or desirable by way
practical consultation and co-operation. Our talks—which d
not touch upon constitutional or political questions—have be
conducted in a most amicable way, and we look forwa
to a future discussion in Dublin."

O'Neill outlines events

CAPTAIN O'NEILL said last night in a television interv
in Belfast, that there had been no pressure from
British Labour Government for him to meet Mr. Lemass, a
disclosed that he, himself, did not write directly to the Taoisea

Captain O'Neill said he had informed the British Government of
his decision to invite Mr. Lemass
and it had welcomed his move.

"I have attended six or seven
meetings of the World Bank," he
said, "and at these meetings I met
and became very friendly with
Mr. Whitaker, permanent head of

O'Neill added: "I, myself
pay a return visit to Dubl
Asked when this visit would t
place, he replied: "That depen

Asked if he and Mr. Len
agreed to differ politically,
co-operate in economic matt
Captain O'Neill said that
position was something like the

THE PRIME MINISTER CAPT. TERENCE O'NEILL HAS BROKEN HIS PLEDGE TO ULSTER AND WELCOMED IN SECRECY LEMASS OUR WOULD BE DESTROYER TO STORMONT

In order to justify himself he then has the brazen audacity to link those who fly the Union Jack with the I.R.A. murderers. The St. George's Unionist Association has invited Capt. O'Neill to Sandy Row. Capt. O'Neill and his henchman, Mr. James Baillie, have been reported as saying that they will defy the Protestants of Sandy Row.

MONSTER PROTESTANT DEMONSTRATION AND LOYALIST PROTEST MARCH

TO P.M.'S MEETING IN GLENGALL STREET, SANDY ROW,

ON THURSDAY NEXT, 25th FEBRUARY, 1965

EAST BELFAST march leaves Templemore Avenue at 7.30 p.m. sharp.
WEST BELFAST march leaves outside West Belfast Orange Hall, Shankill Road, at 7.30 p.m. sharp.
SANDY ROW march leaves Aughrim Street Hall at 7.30 p.m. sharp.
Demonstration converges at City Hall at 8.15 p.m. and marches to Glengall Street.

Protestants show O'Neill that he can't sell Ulster in secrecy to Lemass and Co.

Register your protest by joining in our ranks

NO SURRENDER

Organised by the Protestant Unionists

WHICH IS YOUR ROAD

UNITED KINGDOM | EIRE REPUBLIC

'Which is your road ... vote Unionist', 1953. Ulster Unionist Party election poster. (NLI, Ephemera Collection, POL/1950-60/1)

Left: 'The prime minister Capt. Terence O'Neill has broken his pledge to Ulster', c. January 1965. (Courtesy of Seán O'Connor)

VOTE UNIONIST

Issued by the Ulster Unionist Council, and printed by John Cleland & Son, Ltd.

TWO

Bildungsroman (1899–1924)

Still from 'Irish election result! President de Valera together with his entire Cabinet who have been returned to power with big majority', 1933. (© British Pathé)

⚙ Jackeen

John Francis Lemass, later known as Jack to his childhood friends and family and ultimately as public figure Seán Lemass, was born in Ballybrack, Co. Dublin, on 15 July 1899. He was the third child and second son of the family. A tragic event was to colour his entire emotional life: his elder brother by two years, Noel, was to be murdered viciously in 1923, after the Irish Civil War, on the bleak and windswept Featherbed Mountain, south of Dublin city in Co. Wicklow. The killing was reportedly the work of men from Oriel House, the Irish Free State's Special Branch, many of whom had been recruited from Michael Collins's notorious squad of hit men. Seán thought in later life that Noel had been killed because he had been mistaken for his brother; he was to name his only son after his dead brother. At the time of the killing, Jack was in the Curragh Prison Camp, and he was released on compassionate grounds because of the murder.[1] This compassion was ironically shown by the same Irish government whose nominal minions had committed the murder. A younger brother, Patrick, died in his teens, apparently of natural causes. His youngest surviving brother, Frank, became an accountant and railway administrator and was to be a companion in careers and in politics after 1923. Another boy, Bernard, died in infancy. His eldest sister was Alice, who became a medical doctor; she was to die in midlife of tuberculosis contracted in the line of duty. He also had two younger sisters, Claire and Mary Frances.[2]

The children were, after the fashion of the time, born close together: eight children, all born between 1897 and 1914, a period of eighteen years. John T. Lemass, the father, had inherited a hatter's shop on Capel Street in inner-city Dublin, and was a modestly prosperous and well-known businessman; hence the rented summer house in then-rural Ballybrack, south Co. Dublin. Capel Street had once been the main street of the city, and it still maintained something of that status as late as 1900, a status now almost forgotten a century on as the city centre has moved east and south. Even then, the street was a relatively prosperous island in the ocean of the Dublin slumdom of that time. John's wife, Frances Phelan, came from a broadly similar background of skilled worker-cum-businessman, her father being a horticulturalist who worked in the National Botanic Gardens in north Dublin city and also ran a florist's shop on Wicklow Street.[3] Her family had a Fenian background. The Fenians, or Irish Republican Brotherhood (IRB), were an underground organisation that was very widespread in Victorian Ireland; it was, at least in theory, devoted to organising an armed rebellion in Ireland against British rule. Frances, who lived to see her son become an established leader of the people in the late 1940s, had a powerful personality and strong political opinions. As a boy, Seán occasionally misspelled his middle name *Frances*.

The young Seán Lemass learned early the virtues of patriotism, along with hard work, skilled labour and systematic supervision of a workforce. It was said that the Christian Brothers at the O'Connell's Schools taught him the 'Irish Four R's'—reading, writing, 'rithmetic and rebellion—but it is to be suspected that his family background also gave him a good grounding in Irish political history from a mixture of revolutionary and Parnellite viewpoints; his mother's side thought of a national revolution in Ireland, while his father's side were veteran practitioners of constitutional nationalism.

Before 1916 he had, like many an other in that generation, already changed his given name to a more patriotic 'Seán'. He experimented briefly with a Gaelicised form of his surname but wisely soon abandoned the attempt. Like many other Republicans before him and since, Lemass had to come to terms with his twin inheritances of militarism and constitutionalism, and it took him over a decade to discard some of the wilder aspects of his Republican formation. Some people thought that he never grew out of militant Republicanism, and he probably agreed with them himself. Young Seán grew up on Capel Street and, although his father did take him on trips to different parts of the country, he remained very much a city boy all his life, with a fundamental disregard for rural attitudes, interests and values. His Parnellite background may have soured him permanently on farmers and farmers' interests, although he apparently never made such a point. As adolescents, he and Jimmy O'Dea, later to be the celebrated Dublin comedian, were best friends; a constant characteristic of Lemass all his life was a loyalty to his boyhood friends, to school friends and to old acquaintances who were uninvolved in political life. The two lads put their heads together at one stage and, as Philip P. Ryan reminisced, concocted a newspaper of sorts:

> The Lemass family had a hatter's shop almost opposite the O'Dea's in Capel Street, which is how the two young friends first met, and one of their first youthful ventures together was to produce an entirely handwritten publication for distribution among their friends. The funny bits and the serial were written by Jim while Jack [Seán] contributed the serious stuff.[4]

Later, Seán and Jim did a fair amount of amateur acting, in a popular tradition that was extant in a city always well-known for producing actors and playwrights over the previous two centuries. Lemass played, at one stage, the part of Sir Lucius O'Trigger in Richard Brinsley Sheridan's comedy *The rivals*. Later on, the pair kept up the friendship and went on excursions, in particular to Skerries, a well-known fishing port and watering hole north of the city on the coast of the Irish Sea. Skerries was also where the Lemass family holidayed, and was, later on, to be a haunt of Lemass in his decades as a political leader. In 1924 Jim was to be Seán's best man at his marriage to Kathleen Hughes, in a very different Ireland.[5] A darker connection was the fact that O'Dea, trained as an optician, identified the corpse of Noel Lemass by recognising a pair of glasses in his coat pocket.

Seán's grandfather, also named John Lemass, was from Co. Armagh and was also a hatter and outfitter. He had been an enthusiastic member of the Land League of 1879–81 and a devout follower of Charles Stewart Parnell, the charismatic and somewhat enigmatic nationalist leader of that time.[6] The Land League, which had branches all over Ireland and a headquarters in Dublin, was an extraordinarily successful organisation, co-ordinating the rent strikes and boycotts carried out by hundreds of thousands of agrarian tenants. Instructions went down the line from headquarters on O'Connell Street—about a half-mile to the east of the Lemass shop on Capel Street—to the local branch secretaries. The Land League headquarters regulated the rules of shunning and boycotting, discouraged the use of Luddite tactics such as smashing labour-saving farm machinery, forbade open violence and advocated the naming of persons to be shunned or 'boycotted'. The League was essentially a mass-membership political party on O'Connellite lines and the immediate ancestor of a string of mass parties set up in nationalist Ireland over the following generation; it became a classic model in Ireland for the means by which the great numbers of the ordinary people of the country could be welded into one organisational weapon with a view to taking and wielding political power.

Renamed the 'Irish National League' in 1882, the organisation dominated Irish popular politics for ten years after the triumphant successes of the Land League in the Land War of 1879–81. The League found itself acting not merely as an electoral committee but as local lawgiver, arbitrator, police force and supreme court. For a while, it came quite close to becoming a state within a state in British-ruled Ireland, and its example was one that was to inform directly the nascent underground Irish revolutionary state of 1919–22. That underground organisation similarly set up a state within a state, complete with postal system, land courts, general-purpose courts, local government apparatus, parliament, army and even a police force of sorts. In fact, the land courts were a traditional form of local arbitration tribunal dating back to times even before the Land League and very possibly based on the Whiteboy tradition of the eighteenth century.[7] Young Seán had nationalism, political organisation and Parnellism in his blood.

Publicans and shopkeepers commonly provided the local leadership of the League because, in general, such people had rather better educations than farmers and also because shops and pubs were, besides churches, the natural meeting places of country people. In a way, the pub became the centre of opposition to other sources of power, since landlords' agents and Catholic priests, as two sets of aspirant aristocrats in a democratising country, did not frequent them; the pub became the centre of a perpetual and rather popular opposition. The licensed trade was to gain considerable political power in Ireland, a power that has not faded away completely even in the twenty-first century.

Eventually, the League was to split and collapsed because of the embroilment of Parnell in a divorce case. In the subsequent general election of 1892 the rural areas of Ireland, with some significant exceptions, followed their priests in voting against the Protestant 'adulterer' and thus set up an enduring and very powerful political myth of the noble leader pulled down by the ungrateful and bigoted mob, led by its all-powerful priests. Parnell died shortly afterwards, thereby intensifying the image of the betrayed, tragic martyr. The myth of Parnell became grist to the mill of many Irish writers, including such very different ones as W.B. Yeats and James Joyce. By and large, Dublin and the other urban areas tended to stay loyal to the 'Uncrowned King of Ireland', and this reflected a classic town–country division within Irish nationalist opinion, which was to linger on into the twentieth century and affect subsequent generations' politics in many often unrecognised ways.[8] Bourgeois and working-class Dublin became Parnellite in contrast to the mainly anti-Parnellite countryside, whose farmers owed their property rights to Parnell's great movement; farmers were seen by Parnellite loyalists as priest-dominated ingrates. The Lemasses stayed staunchly Parnellite in the face of a massive anti-Parnellite farmers' vote.

Edward MacAonraoi, an old Gaelic Leaguer and civil servant who had served under Lemass in later years, remarked in his old age on Lemass's resemblance to Parnell, even in his personal relationships. Like Parnell, Lemass, he commented, had few personal friends or acquaintances and was possessed of 'the same inscrutability'.[9] He did not know his civil servants, MacAonraoi claimed, and kept his distance from them so as not to be accused of jobbery. He worked through his trusted and intellectually brilliant secretary of department, John Leydon. Parnell, rather similarly, did not know his members of parliament.[10] There is some exaggeration here; Lemass was indeed remote from many of his officials, but he was very conscious of exceptionally able, energetic and purposeful personalities. He tried to encourage such people and further their promotion. He also had many friends, but they were in business or outside politics completely.

The eldest John Lemass was elected to the City Council in 1885, and his son, Seán's father, continued in the same political tradition, but in a more quietly spoken and subdued fashion; he seems to have had a 'strong, silent' type of personality—quiet and kind, but firm. Again, Seán Lemass echoed his family background rather well in his personality, which was rather self-contained and sometimes rather stern, even forbidding and gruff. However, he actually seems to have separated his public and private sides rather sharply, stepping easily from one role to the other; in private he could be genial and entertaining, as many witnesses attest. Horgan quotes an anonymous eyewitness description of Lemass at work in the Department of Supplies during the Second World War as having:

> a human streak but I only really saw it once. A letter came
> in to him written on pages torn out of a school exercise
> book, by a boy at school at Westland Row. It was written
> at the request of the boy's mother, on behalf of his father,

a taxi driver whose petrol allocation had been revoked after he had been caught taking a party of golfers home from the Hermitage Golf Club. The father had gone to England to try and get work. The boy was trying to get a job as a messenger but his teacher had said that if he stayed at the school he would get a scholarship. The letter had come in that morning's mail, and as Lemass was passing through my office I showed it to him. His response was quite unprecedented. He asked for the file, and asked for a typist to come into his private office with him, and dictated a reply to the lad there and then. He told the lad to tell his father that he would restore his petrol allocation there and then. He was also to tell his mother that he was to remain at school. And he was to tell his father, also, that if he offended further, Lemass would have no mercy on him.[11]

The private persona briefly intruded on the public one. This characteristic separation of one's life into two hermetically sealed worlds was a common enough feature of the social culture of the artisan and middle classes of the time in Irish cities and towns, and looked strange and almost off-putting to country people, with their communal way of life and disregard for privacy—the open half door versus the closed hall door, or perhaps even *Gemeinschaft* versus *Gesellschaft*. Kevin Boland commented:

> My father [Gerald (Gerry) Boland] was joint honorary secretary of Fianna Fáil with Lemass and they worked very closely together. As it developed, however, Lemass became the headquarters man, my father the field man. Lemass had an abrupt manner—he didn't have the balance that was required for country people. He came to realise himself that he couldn't deal with the rural mind—it was too lackadaisical. My father had the patience for it—it took him three trips to get [Seán] Moylan [of the North Cork IRA] to join FF [in 1926–7]. The thing was that if you identified a key IRA man in any one locality and got him to join, then you had a ready-made organisation that came along with him.[12]

In answer to a question asked by Michael Mills in 1969 about his Republicanism, Lemass answered in terms of a strong Dublin Parnellite family tradition of electoral politics at an intensely local level, involving strong emotions and political passions of a kind that, as a child, he did not fully understand but that he certainly internalised subconsciously from the social environment around him. He also had a strong sense that modern people of the 1960s tended to read their history backwards:

> Well, when you are talking about a Republican tradition you are talking in terms of the 1960s in relation to the 1900s. My father was always a strong Nationalist and my grandfather had been a Parnellite member of Dublin Corporation, for a year or so anyway. My father was active in the Irish Party in his early years. Indeed my earliest political experience at that time was when there was a by-election in the constituency in which we lived and the Irish Party had nominated a candidate of whom the local Nationalist Party supporters disapproved. I won't mention names because there are people of his family still alive, but in these days there was no such thing as a constituency convention to nominate a candidate. The Party leaders nominated a candidate and they nominated a candidate on this occasion who was generally regarded as not being the most suitable person for election to Parliament.
>
> I remember the meeting being held in the back of my father's shop in Capel Street. Six or seven of the local traders were there. They were all strong Party supporters; and the long debate ended with the decision that for the first time in their lives they were going to vote against the Party, in support of an independent candidate who had been nominated to contest the seat against the Party candidate. They all went out of the shop in a group, like aristocrats walking to the guillotine, with their faces set and their fists clenched, pale and drawn-looking, determined to do this thing which was a mortal sin for anyone involved in politics in those days. But they did it; they voted against the Party. That was in 1906 or 1907 and it is the earliest political experience I can remember. But it does represent the sort of political atmosphere in which I grew up. But there was not a Republican tradition in that sense. My father was still a strong member of the Irish Parliamentary Party after I joined the Volunteers.[13]

This 'earliest political experience' occurred when he was seven or eight, when the Catholic Church understood you to have reached the use of reason. In the interview he went on immediately to reminisce about this momentary filial rebellion in fond terms; there was no real generational or ideological division between old Parnellite and young Sinn Féiner; but the constitutional idiom in Irish political history had been temporarily replaced by the insurrectionist one. Young Seán had been in the General Post Office (GPO) during the Easter Rising in 1916, and he was picked up by the police afterwards, but was let go on account of his youth. After the fighting in Dublin ceased, involving much loss of life and the shelling of the city centre by the British, he went home, to the Capel Street house a few yards away from the headquarters of the rebel Republic of Easter Week:

> When I got back home after [the] 1916 [Rising] I was very tired and I went to bed. I remember the next morning my father came into the bedroom with a great big green white and orange celluloid button in his lapel, which was his way of telling me he had come over to our side.[14]

The approval of the older generation was still fondly remembered by the young rebel in his own old age.

The man from God knows where

The family name seems to be Huguenot in origin, and was originally Lemaistre; at least that is both the family tradition and the folk opinion among his friends, colleagues and descendants in Dublin; it is also the opinion of MacLysaght's standard work on Irish surnames. The name has existed in Dublin and Carlow since the eighteenth century.[15] Lemass used to crack a family joke to the effect that they were all descended from French pirates. Physically, he certainly looked somewhat un-Irish. There is a photograph of the young Lemass in Volunteer uniform, dated around 1915, which resembles nothing more closely than pictures of young Italian conscripts fighting Austrian forces in the Alps at around that time.[16] His immediate ancestors came into Ireland from Scotland, and the hereditary skills of tailoring and millinery ran in the family for generations. Presumably, at some stage a Lemass converted to Catholicism, for Seán never regarded himself as anything other than a Catholic, although apparently one who became increasingly sceptical of religious belief systems as he grew older in body and colder of intellect. In a prison camp in 1920 he became unpopular, or at least distrusted, among northern Volunteers for refusing to go to Mass or participate in a collective rosary. He would stand apart and say out loud, apparently mocking the simple faith of his comrades, 'Oh God, if there is a God, save my soul, if I have a soul.'[17] However, his scepticism and nonconformity had its limits: all his life he attended Sunday mass and conformed to the rituals of the tribe. Not to do so would have been politically unwise and, perhaps, bad manners.[18]

His sceptical habit of mind extended to other realms of human concern, and he showed a marked ability all his life to change his mind when circumstances clearly demanded a rethink; in this, his habits of mind differed from the fanatical and semi-religious political mentality that dominated the minds of so many young IRA and Sinn Féiners of his era and later. Consistency, for him, was silly; you changed your mind when the evidence changed. His outlook was inherently empiricist and scientific. However, he always claimed an underlying consistency of general political outlook, while admitting a methodological agnosticism or eclecticism: objectives were unchanging, but means varied widely.

In both 1914 and 1915 he sat his Intermediate Certificate examination, emerging the second time with a very creditable string of honours in arithmetic, history, geometry, experimental science and French. He got passes in English, Latin and Irish. Horgan points to his ability at mathematics: 'On the basis of his 1915 results he won a first-class exhibition in the mathematical group of subjects, worth £15. Three of his classmates did the same, affording the school a remarkable 40% of the ten first-class exhibitions in the junior grade awarded in the country as a whole'.[19]

Despite his name change, there is rather little evidence of Lemass having any real interest in the Irish language or in the Gaelic League.[20] However, that did not prevent both Noel and Seán from being swept up into the Irish Volunteers as very young men: Seán joined up, lying about his age, at 15 years and some months. Local circumstance seems again to have been the trigger, and de Valera a very early influence:

> I was fifteen when I joined. I was not, in fact, eligible for membership. There was a man named Pat Mullen employed in my father's shop. He was a very active Volunteer and he was always trying to persuade me to

come along and join. I told him I didn't think I was old enough to join and he said—'Well you look a great deal older than you are and this will be a white lie anyway.' So he brought me along and I was accepted as a member of the Volunteers. I was a member of A Company of the 3rd Battalion, commanded at that time by a man named Sheehan, one of those who did not fight in 1916. He was one of the Bulmer Hobson group who felt the Rising was a mistake. He was followed by the famous Joe O'Connor—'Holy Joe' as he was known.

After I joined, de Valera was appointed the Battalion Commandant. The first time I saw de Valera was when he came down to a parade of our Company in York Street to address the Battalion. My impression of him was of a long, thin fellow with knee britches and a tweed hat. But he had, of course, enormous personal magnetism and the capacity to hold that crowd of Volunteers there while he addressed them at inordinate length as he always did. There was not a movement among the crowd until he had finished. It impressed me enormously, notwithstanding what I thought was his rather queer-looking appearance. [De Valera] had a theory, I remember, which even at that age I thought was a bit odd, about a tool which was to be capable of being used as a pike or as a trench digger. I must confess that I thought this was going a little bit far in bridging the gap in military technique. As far as I know, the tool never emerged. But, he had this simple approach to things: what have we to do? how can we do it? This was characteristic of him in politics later on. It was this capacity to talk to audiences in simple terms that gave him the tremendous influence he had. I have seen crowds of people standing in bitter cold and heavy rain while he talked for an hour-and-a-half or two hours about political matters in simple terms they could understand.[21]

De Valera, this strange man with the strange name, a name even stranger than 'Lemass', clearly had a huge impact on young Seán, a man who was later not to be easily influenced by other people; it was an odd, but mutually beneficial, alliance that worked. Perhaps this was in part, as he suggested himself, de Valera had a common touch and lacked the shyness that many detected in Lemass. Charles Haughey, his latter-day son-in-law, remarked that Lemass loved Dev 'with a kind of impatient fondness'.[22] When asked in 1969 who among Irish political figures had influenced him, Lemass had to repeat himself:

> I find this hard to answer. I suppose the only one was de Valera, to whom I was personally committed all the time he was head of the Party and of the Government. Nobody, except de Valera, has ever influenced me to any extent; at least to the extent of making me change my outlook on an important matter. He was the only one who ever did … [even when I was still very young] it would be de Valera. I had been associated with him before 1916, but not so much for a period afterwards. He was the one person who impressed me very much by the personal magnetism which he exercised to an extraordinary degree.[23]

Whether or not they had much to do with the Gaelic League, Eoin MacNeill, joint founder of that cultural organisation and also chief of staff of the Irish Volunteers, had no trouble recognising the two young Lemass lads on Easter Monday 1916, as they were out walking in the Dublin Mountains with Jimmy and Ken O'Dea, disappointed that the muster of the Volunteers had been called off, as it happened, by MacNeill. He sadly told the lads that a Rising had gone ahead under the leadership of Patrick Pearse and James Connolly, and that public buildings in Dublin were being taken over by the Volunteers and the Citizen Army. This news galvanised the Lemass boys, presumably contrary to MacNeill's intentions, and they rushed off to join in with what they seemingly still half expected to be simply an ordinary parade. They found themselves engaged in an actual fully fledged rebellion against the British authorities. Eventually, Seán made his way to the GPO and was apparently made adjutant to Pearse himself, a man he hero-worshipped, being, as he remarked much later in the same connection, a very impressionable young man. Evidently, a characteristically Lemassian scepticism about Pearse's militarist romanticism set in fairly early on.[24] At one stage he was posted on the roof of the GPO, firing off the odd shot from a shotgun. Later on, he said he hoped he had not killed anyone.

Lemass made little of his exploits during Easter Week, but evidently the possibility of death in the fighting and even execution for treason afterwards matured him very rapidly. He came to a realisation that something very big had happened and that he had almost unknowingly become part of a movement that would change Ireland forever. His formal education effectively terminated at that point; his father, although he had come over to what was increasingly, and inaccurately, being termed the Sinn Féin cause, wanted his son to complete his education with a professional qualification in accountancy or law. Noel took a different course: staying in work while remaining a member of the Volunteer movement, an organisation that was rapidly evolving into what was later to be termed the Old IRA.

Lemass was not heavily involved in active service until quite late on in the Anglo–Irish conflict, unlike Noel, who seems to have been more involved. However, on 21 November 1920, Seán was involved in the systematic killing of British agents in Dublin by Michael Collins's squad of hand-picked marksmen. The killings were, in part, a response to British successes in picking up or killing key IRA men, plus the occasional innocent bystander shot by the authorities because of a confusion of names. Lemass's name is not on any list of named members of Collins's squad; there are at least seventeen such names, as some people moved in and out of the list of the dozen or so active members. Hence the sobriquet for the squad: 'the Twelve Apostles'. However, Lemass was on active duty that day with his IRA battalion, so at a minimum it can be inferred that he did escort duty for one of the killers. A shroud of secrecy still hangs over the names of the perpetrators. Lemass himself fended off queries with curt remarks about how firing squads didn't have reunions. This itself sounds suspiciously like an admission; however, such a guarded admission would have heightened Lemass's political prestige and legitimacy in post-revolutionary Ireland. The men and women who had been 'out' in 1916–21 were admired. British intelligence named him as one of Collins's group. There is a persistent story, heard by myself as a young man, that Lemass was involved, actively or passively, in one of the killings on the south side of Dublin, that he handed his gun to a bystander, walked to a little-used workman's ferry, crossed the Liffey and walked home. By this simple subterfuge, he walked through the police and military cordons.[25]

My own doubts about his membership centre around the absence of his name from all of the known listings and the simple fact that, as a member of the squad, it would have been rather unlikely for him to have chosen the anti-Treaty side in 1922; those close to Collins followed him, with some ambivalence, into the Free State; admittedly, a few of them joined the irreconcilables who refused to accept even de Valera's constitutional order, the 'dictionary republic'. Again, Lemass said casually many years later that for him Collins was a remote senior figure: '... I met him, but I did not know him. He was far above my rank in those days.'[26] Michael Mills remembered that tears came to Lemass's eyes when, as an old man, he was asked about his involvement in the fighting of 1916–23; he desperately wanted it to be forgotten and forgiven.[27] There was not too much love lost between the squad members and ordinary Volunteers; the relationship seems to have resembled that between regular soldiers and guerrillas, or *francs-tireurs* as they were then known: regulars despised guerrillas. C.S. Andrews (known universally as 'Todd') commented on his own eyewitness involvement in an abortive attack on the same day; to his relief, the target was absent. Collins's men behaved, he said:

> like Black and Tans. In their search for papers they overturned furniture, pushing the occupants of the house around, and either through carelessness or malice set fire to a room in which there were children. [Company Captain] Coughlan was furious at their conduct. Having seen the children to safety he directed Kenny to bring two more members of the Company into the house so that we could form a bucket chain from the tap in the basement (the only tap in the house) to the first floor where the fire was becoming serious. Nearly half an hour was wasted putting out the fire before we were able to get out of the house, dump our 'dogs' [guns] in the waiting taxi (oddly enough the taxi-driver was not a member of the IRA) and disperse singly on foot.[28]

Lemass went to work part-time in his father's shop, proving to be quite innovative in his marketing strategies. During the War of Independence, often called the 'Tan Scrap' by veterans, he was certainly hardened in his political purpose by the uncompromising and brutal acts of both sides in the struggle. When the Anglo–Irish Truce arrived in July 1921, he was by no means a diehard purist, and seems to have wavered for a long time between the compromisers led by Collins and Cosgrave and the purists led by de Valera and Liam Lynch. In this, he was like many another. In early 1922 he served briefly as an instructor for the new police force, the Garda Síochána, being set up by the provisional government of Ireland, the predecessor of the Irish Free State. His leadership abilities had already been noticed, and by the pro-Treaty people. However, when his first pay cheque arrived, he noticed it was drawn on the provisional government rather than on the government of the Irish Republic, and he changed to the anti-Treaty side. This curious episode, displaying a legalism that was uncharacteristic of his later self, suggests that his Republicanism was somewhat marginal. Perhaps he could not stay away from his beloved de Valera and his pals in the Four Courts Garrison; like many others, he went with his peer group, a natural thing to do at age 23. He was in the Four Courts throughout the bombardment of June 1922, and he went on the run afterwards, having escaped from Free State custody with suspicious ease. Later, he was picked up and interned in the Curragh Camp. He attempted to escape again and was badly beaten by government soldiers. The limits, or even the pointlessness, of political violence were brought home to him by the Civil War that had followed the compromise Treaty settlement of 1922–3. The experience of being swept into violence by his peer group twice in ten years seems to have strengthened a natural self-sufficiency and determination not to be influenced decisively by anyone ever again.

Himself alone?

Lemass was commonly stereotyped as being a businessman manqué, and there is probably some truth in that proposition; certainly, his business background imparted to him a respect for business, enterprise, buying and selling, innovation and efficiency that lasted all his life. He accepted implicitly the assumptions of private enterprise and the dynamism of capitalism, while having a radical streak in the form of respect for the worker, whom he saw as having a common interest with the employer rather than having a necessary class enmity. His daughter-in-law remembered his family background as one of niceness, but also as one of toughness and coldness. Work was a pervasive ethic. Seán had something like a 'Joycean childhood', but certainly without the abject poverty of the actual Joyce family of that time. Maureen Haughey remembered her father describing a childhood where 'people would come in with fiddles etc. on a Sunday night, like a scene from *The Dead*; piano as well'.[29]

Despite his advocacy of state enterprise, he had an inborn preference for private enterprise; in Ireland, however, because there was so little private enterprise, he concluded that public enterprise would have to fill the gap, at least temporarily. There was also a solitary side to his character, which manifested itself in a certain self-sufficiency, a privacy and a thoughtfulness that was almost academic in character—a certain monkishness. He told Michael

Mills in 1969, in answer to a question about his not proceeding to do law as his parents wished him to, in reality a question about his curtailed education in general:

> I am not really able to answer this question. I don't know. I often thought when I was actively involved in political work dealing with the most contrary element in life, that's human beings, you know, that the ideal situation would be to be a sort of research chemist up in the top back room of some university not dealing with human beings at all but dealing with inert materials and knowing that you could establish absolute truth in relation to these materials and not have any opinions about the truth. But this was merely a reaction from the experiences of those times [of 1916–23].[30]

He made a similar remark to T.K. Whitaker, fantasising wistfully about being an atomic scientist or something of that sort.[31] James Ryan quoted him as reminiscing, 'When at school the only thing I got real pleasure from was working out problems in Euclid, problems in mathematics'.[32] Again, his wife recalled him saying at one stage that if he had not become a politician, he 'would have opted to live a hermetic life and would have been perfectly happy to spend his days working out complex mathematical problems'.[33] He remarked to Seamus Brady, apparently in the early 1960s, 'I would like to have been away from all worldly things like politics. To be in a hut in the mountains surrounded by books on mathematics and working out problems of physics. With such a life I could be very happy'.[34]

As he suggested himself, these were probably the wistful daydreams of a rather workaholic man beset continually by pressing practical problems involving large numbers of powerful, articulate and, sometimes, aggressive people, like any busy public man. His most generous periods of isolation and leisure seem to have been granted to him as a guest of the British and, later, the Irish nation at two prison camps. In the British prison camp at Ballykinlar, Co. Down, in 1920–1 he was sometimes seen as stand-offish, as he was always reading, particularly on economics. In the Irish government's prison camp at the Curragh in 1922–3, he seems to have hit the books more seriously, the camp serving, as such camps often had before and would serve again, as universities for guerrillas trying to think their way out of their political quandaries. He devoured books that he had sent in regularly from outside. He was sometimes twitted because of this unusual studiousness, and also on account of his unusual demeanour and appearance. Lemass was nicknamed 'the Jewman' because of his dark complexion and teased as 'Charlie Chaplin' because of his toothbrush moustache. Constance Markievicz referred to him as 'Mephistopheles', presumably because of his dark complexion, brown eyes, sleek black hair and moustache.[35] He also had a wolfish grin and an occasionally ferocious sense of humour.

However, he was mainly remembered as sitting in a corner ploughing through books dealing mainly with economics and history; Horgan suggests that his real intellectual and emotional formation occurred around this period in the Curragh, when he was gradually shaking off his militarism and thinking of getting married. He was also coming to the conclusion that Ireland's problems were as much economic as political. His appearance was always immaculate; to be well dressed was to keep up one's own morale and that of others around one—this was his openly expressed attitude.[36] He was seen as a serious young fellow, even something of what a later generation might describe as an 'anorak'. One comrade remembered, 'in Tintown [Curragh Camp] all the lads were larking around. Lemass would be sitting in a corner reading books on economics. [He was] known as "the little Jewman". Soldiers guarding them [the prisoners] were paid on Wednesdays: [after which] he'd take money off them at cards'.[37]

Although a nervous speaker as a young man, he persevered, and was to become one of the most incisive, aggressive and well-prepared public speakers of his generation. He could destroy an ill-prepared opponent with a devastating, almost brutal, well-informed and cutting remark that ranged facts and figures with chilling accuracy against some vague generalisation. This effectiveness overcame a somewhat stiff, even wooden, style of diction that echoed his underlying shyness. He had an extraordinary memory, like many of the top political administrators of twentieth-century Ireland; Michael Collins and Garret FitzGerald come to mind among others. Lemass is seen by some as having been a man with a mission; Liam Skinner, a biographer who veered occasionally towards the hagiographic but who was well-informed, claimed that Lemass saw himself from early on as having a vocation to pull Ireland into the modern world: 'As a Minister, he was guided by the unshakeable conviction that the work he was doing was peculiarly his—because he had deliberately fitted himself for it—and that he could do it better than any one else.'[38]

To some of his colleagues, he seemed solitary, even remote, but he did have firm friends, in particular Kathleen Hughes, who wrote to him from 1916 until their marriage in 1924. Their two families had known each other from the Skerries holidays in pre-war days. Kathleen described herself as being of a placid, non-worrying disposition, certainly a qualification for being Lemass's 'best pal', as several people described the relationship. Kathleen was very religious and, also unlike Seán, could write a good letter in Irish. Haughey remembered that Lemass 'adored her'.[39] Several people reminisced that she had an extraordinary charm and a lack of any pretension.[40] Her father did not really approve of young Lemass, and was, if anything, a bit pro-British.[41] 'That boy is always on the run; he'll never be able to make a home for you' was her father's perception of the 25-year old ex-gunman.[42] Kathleen smoked cigarettes, but only in private, because at that time respectable women did not smoke on the street. She seems to have had a huge stabilising influence on him, and she certainly accepted his part-time domesticity and the fact that he had a job which demanded his attention almost literally 24 hours a day. But then, she was already familiar with his non-stop work habits. He turned into a devoted family man and father, often going home for lunch during working hours, a common practice in the small and compact city that Dublin was at that time.

Lemass also held on to his school friends into later life and, characteristically, observed a rather strict separation between his professional colleagues and his personal friendships. He was known for his loyalty to old friends, a loyalty that survived his rise to national and international fame in later years. Kevin Boland pointed to the importance for Lemass of his old comrades in the Four Courts during the crisis of June 1922, many of them fierce Republicans with a somewhat shaky relationship to the reigning constitutional order, even in its de Valeran form. Lemass's real legitimacy in their eyes was his national and military record, not his democratic status as Irish prime minister. Kevin Boland reminisced:

> The Four Courts Garrison remained the core of Lemass's strength (organisation) in Dublin, until they began to disappear. There was an annual mass for the Four Courts Garrison in Dublin Castle and one year [Seán Lemass's son] Noel Lemass went down [in the early 1960s] and told the secretary, 'Skinner' Reilly, that he was there to represent the Taoiseach. Reilly said fiercely: 'You're not here to represent the Taoiseach. You're here to represent your father. There's no-one here to represent the Taoiseach.'[43]

One of the Four Courts Garrison, Hugh Early, was to become his ministerial Garda driver for many years after 1932.[44]

An interviewer in 1953 commented on his personality: 'A pipe lies in an ashtray made of the piston head of an airplane ... kindliness of his light brown eyes set in innumerable crowsfeet [*sic*], the warm voice'.[45] De Valera, with whom Lemass had been politically close all their adult lives, admitted at one stage that he had never quite been able to size up his younger colleague. In part, this was due to de Valera's lack of any interest in economics or any real grasp of economic issues. Lemass, on the other hand, had a passionate obsession with economic development as the only real key to Ireland's historical and social problems and shared little of de Valera's interest in culture or the Irish language. Whitaker remembered, in the 1990s:

> In 1956–57 Seán Francis Lemass was laid up and inactive for some months; [I] went to see him in hospital. 'Dev wants me to use this time to brush up on my Irish. But I'd prefer it if you sent me some books on economics' [he said]—he got Sayers on banking, stuff on development economics, and by Lewis, the Jamaican. He had been reading about the US division of powers [at the time].[46]

Michael Hayes, admittedly a biased observer because he had been pro-Treaty, commented years later on de Valera's lack of interest in what anyone else had to say. Furthermore, 'He never at any point in his career up to [retirement in] 1959 showed any close acquaintance with the hard realities and details of any Irish financial or economic problem'.[47] The relationship between the two leaders was to be an odd, and perhaps classic, mixture of friendship, mutual fondness and intellectual and temperamental distance, a mutual dependence pact that each tacitly observed. To this writer, the working partnership was not unlike Henry Luce's classic partnership between the rock and the wild man. Alternatively, perhaps it resembled the relationship between the yogi and the commissar or between Don Quixote and Sancho Panza: that between the dreamer and the practical man, each utterly dependent on the other, and each aware of the fact that he could not operate without the other. Furthermore, each had a bit of the other in him; each could also be pretty cunning when necessary, although their styles contrasted starkly. Dev dreamed in public but could be very practical indeed, and Lemass had his own dreams but generally kept them to himself. He confined himself fairly determinedly to means, leaving the ends implicit but fairly obvious.

In the 1960s Hayes described the relationship in acerbic but rather shrewd terms. Free State leaders like Kevin O'Higgins had assumed that de Valera would fade out of politics because of the dreamlike unrealities of his political position and style in the late 1920s and early 1930s. Hayes commented:

> That was their great mistake. He was capable of lasting much longer and I think for that Lemass deserves great credit, much more than he has ever got. Lemass did what Kevin O'Higgins refused to allow, what J.J. [Walsh] tried to do. He supplied the bread and butter argument while de Valera supplied Kathleen Ní Houlihan with green robes.[48]

Lemass and his brother Noel, c. 1902. (Courtesy of Seán O'Connor)

Lemass relaxing with two of his daughters, Maureen and Peggy, 1940s. (Courtesy of Seán O'Connor)

Lemass kisses Kathleen goodbye at Dublin Airport, 29 August 1952.
(© Lensmen Photographic Archive)

TO THE

Irish National Volunteers.

❦❦❦❦❦

You are in arms for the defence of your country. It is for you to consider what the obligation which you have freely laid upon yourselves entails. At this moment your country is threatened by enemies more powerful and more hostile than any who have attacked her in the past. Their victory would mean the complete conquest of Ireland, the end of her claims to be a self-governing nation, and her subjugation to the rank of a conquered German Colony. Nothing stands between your enemies and an invasion of your country but the Allied Forces both on land and sea. If they are defeated no Volunteer force however good will keep back the doom of Ireland. Do you want it to be said that the Irish Volunteers left their kinsmen and their allies to do the fighting on the plains of Belgium and France?

You do not! As Irishmen you are too proud to allow others to do that which falls to you Volunteers as a duty.

One of your Committee, Professor KETTLE, has already joined the Irish Brigade, many of your comrades are already in its ranks. Ireland expects you to follow their example. The place to defend your Country is on the battlefields of Europe.

Men of Ireland do not fail your Motherland.

'To the Irish National Volunteers', c. 1914. Handbill used by the Volunteers to encourage enlistment in the British Army with the aim of achieving Home Rule at the end of the First World War. (NLI, Ephemera Collection, POL/1910-20/15)

Rúnaide S. ᵿ Cómairle
Cumann Aᵫᵬ Cᵬaoᵬ
Cómairle Ceanntair Stiᵬᵬáin Greᵬn

sinn féin.

I, Sean Lemass.

accept the Constitution of Sınn Féın.

Lemass's card indicating his acceptance of the Sinn Féin constitution, c. 1916. (Courtesy of Seán O'Connor)

Following page: 'Do you want to be free?', c. 1922. Pro-Treaty handbill urging the electorate to vote for pro-Treaty Sinn Féin. (NLI, Ephemera Collection, POL/1920-30/26)

DO YOU WANT TO BE FREE?

NATIONALLY
To govern yourself, in your own way, for your own good.

COMMERCIALLY
To develop and protect your Industries, by tariffs if necessary.

SOCIALLY
To deal with your own problems in your own way.

INDIVIDUALLY
To hold in peace; to acquire in justice; to pursue happiness.

THEN VOTE FOR THE TREATY

IRISH PAPER, IRISH INK, IRISH TRADE UNION LABOUR.

ORDER UNDER REGULATION NO. 14 B. OF THE RESTORATION OF ORDER IN IRELAND REGULATIONS.

WHEREAS on the recommendation of a Competent Military Authority, appointed under the Restoration of Order in Ireland Regulations, it appears to me that for securing the restoration and maintenance of Order in Ireland it is expedient that **Noel Dennis Lemass** of **2.Capel Street,** in the County of **the City of Dublin** should, in view of the fact that he is a person suspected of acting, having acted, and being about to act in a manner prejudicial to the restoration and maintenance of Order in Ireland, be subjected to such obligations and restrictions as are hereinafter mentioned :

Now I HEREBY ORDER that the said **Noel Dennis Lemass** shall be interned in **Ballykinlar Camp or Curragh Camp** and shall be subject to all the rules and conditions applicable to persons there interned and shall remain there until further orders.

If within seven days from the date on which this Order is served on the said

Noel Dennis Lemass

he shall submit to me any representations against the provisions of this Order, such representation will be referred to the Advisory Committee specially appointed for the purpose of advising me in connection with Orders made under the above-mentioned Regulation and presided over by a Judge of the High Court, and will be duly considered by the Committee. If I am satisfied by the report of the said Committee that this Order may be revoked or varied without injury to the restoration and maintenance of Order in Ireland I will revoke or vary this Order by a further Order in writing under my hand. Failing such revocation or variation this Order shall remain in force.

2nd June,1921.

IRELAND OVER ALL

IRELAND'S OWN REPUBLICAN NEWS SHEET

No. 1.   **MARCH 11th, 1924.**   Price 1d.

THE SOUTH DUBLIN BYE-ELECTION

The citizens of South Dublin are given to-morrow a splendid opportunity of striking a telling blow, not alone for their country, but for their own future prosperity. If they but consider for a moment the fruits of the Treaty, there can be little doubt as to how their votes will be recorded. When they were asked to vote for the acceptance of this iniquitous measure, which designedly attempted to undo the work of Pearse and Connolly, they were told that the acceptance of the Treaty meant the commencement of an era of splendid prosperity for the Irish people. Has it done so?

Starvation reigns on the Western seaboard, from Donegal to Kerry, and that in a country that was once able to support eight million people and that to-day cannot support four million.

The Old Age Pensioners are having their pensions cut down, some by one shilling, some by two shillings per week.

The Poor Law Relief has become almost a thing of the Past.

The Teachers' salaries are being docked. Grants made from Free State Government sources have appended to them conditions designed to pull down the wages of the working man.

In every way the conditions of the workers of the nation have been disimproved; and this is being done whilst the upper classes, the Pro-British Party, are being nursed and petted as they have never been before.

Every landlord, whose estates were built up by the blood and sweat of the Irish people, who cleared the lands in the old days of the peasantry and sent to their deaths in the coffin ships, who flattened with the battering-ram the cottages that at one time plentifully covered the plains and hill-sides of Ireland, who filled the slums of our city with the unfortunates whom they refused to let live on the lands that was theirs and their fathers' for countless generations; every one of these landlords has now become once again a power in the land under the protection of the Free State, and from their position in the Senate are dictating the capitalist policy of the Free State Government.

Nay! The very tools of the Free State, the men who joined its army to crush the Republic, are now suffering for their treachery. They are slung out of the army they served so faithfully, sent out to walk the streets without a chance of finding employment, whilst men are retained whose only claim to retention is that they are German officers or that they distinguished themselves fighting England's battles on the Continent of Europe.

Such are the fruits of the Treaty; but it has had even more serious results. It brought us Civil War when it was boosted as being the road to Peace. It brought us English Domination when it was claimed as a stepping-stone to the Republic. It has given us a government whose sole concern is their own jobs and salaries, when we were told it would give us a government whose sole interest would be the welfare of the Irish people.

Surely the people of Dublin must have the blindfold removed from their eyes by this. Do they stand for the stealing of the pensions of their aged poor wherewith to pay the enormous salaries of the Pro-British Ministers? Do they stand for the starvation of the common people in order to find money to rebuild the burned mansions of the landlords, their centuries old enemies? Do they stand for the exploiting of the many in the interests of the few? If they do, let them vote to-morrow for the Free State Candidate. If they do not, let them vote 1 for Sean Lemass and thus striking a death-blow to knavery and corruption and the victory blow for Ireland's Independence and Prosperity!

THE FREEMASON RING

Ascendency Party's Grip on the Free State.

Facts that Speak.

Our people do not as yet seem to have sufficiently realised the grip which Freemasonry has established over the Free State. An analysis of the personnel of the Senate indicates the extent to which the beaten Ascendency Party have re-established themselves under Mr. Figgis's Constitution. Let us take the 30 Senators appointed by President Cosgrave. With one exception they are all entirely ignorant of the language of Ireland. All except 13 of the 30 are Freemasons. One of the 30 took an active part in the War of Independence on the Irish side. Selected from a territory where five out of six are Catholics, 23 of the 30 belong to the remaining one-sixth. So is the tail able to wag the dog!

The following are "President" Cosgrave's nominations in the Senate:—

Sir John Bagwell, Imperialist and Freemason. His Brittanic Majesty's Deputy Lieutenant.

The Rt. Hon. H. G. Burgess, Imperialist and Freemason. One of His Brittanic Majesty's Privy Councillors in Dublin Castle.

The Dowager Countess of Desart, Imperialist.

The Earl of Dunraven, Imperialist and Freemason. His Brittanic Majesty's Lieutenant for County Limerick; Privy Councillor in Dublin Castle.

Mr. J. C. Dowdall, Imperialist.

Sir Thomas Esmonde, joined the Sinn Fein movement in 1907 and ran away when the Party threatened his expulsion.

Sir Nugent Everard, Imperialist and Freemason.

Mr. Edmond J. Eyre, Imperialist and Freemason.

Mr. Martin Fitzgerald, Successor to the "Sham Squire" in the "Freeman's Journal." His offer to drive President De Valera out of public life in December, 1921, by a campaign of personal slander, refused by the late Arthur Griffith.

Dr. Oliver St. John Gogarty.

Mr. John P. Goodbody, Imperialist.

Mr. Henry Guiness, Imperialist and Freemason.

Lord Glenavy, better known as Sir James Campbell, Castle-hack and Freemason, ex-Tory, Solicitor-General, ex-Liberal Attorney-General, ex-Unionist M.P., the Lord Chancellor, who, in 1919, was one of the signatories to the Dublin Castle Proclamation proclaiming the Sinn Fein movement, the Gaelic League, the Irish Volunteers and Cumann na mBan.

Captain Greer, Imperialist and Freemason.

The Earl of Granard, Castle Catholic and Imperialist. His Brittanic Majesty's Lieutenant for County Longford. Ex-Lord-in-waiting to King Edward, the Peacemaker, and ex-Minister of the Horse to the English Royal Household.

Mr. Benjamin Haughton, Imperialist.

The Marquis of Headfort, Imperialist and Freemason. His Brittanic Majesty's Deputy Lieutenant for County Meath.

Mr. Andrew Jameson, Imperialist and Freemason.

Mr. Arthur Jackson, Imperialist and Freemason. His Brittanic Majesty's Deputy Lieutenant for County Sligo.

Sir John Keane, Imperialist and Freemason. His Brittanic Majesty's Deputy Lieutenant for County Waterford.

The Earl of Kerry, Imperialist and Freemason. Heir to the Marquis of Lansdowne, the bitterest and most anti-Irish of the landlords.

Sir Bryan Mahon, Imperialist and Freemason. His Brittanic Majesty's Privy Councillor in Dublin Castle. Commander-in-Chief of the English Forces in Ireland from 1916 to 1918.

The Earl of Mayo, Imperialist and Freemason. His Brittanic Majesty's Deputy Lieutenant in Mayo, and Privy Councillor in Dublin Castle.

Sir James Moran, Imperialist and West-British Catholic.

Mrs. Wyse-Power. The only member of the "Senate" who worked in the Sinn Fein movement. Formerly a Republican.

Sir Horace Plunkett, Imperialist and Freemason. Denounced frequently by the late Mr. Arthur Griffiths as a British spy. In the early nineties made his bitter attack on Catholicism which called forth the late Monsignor O'Riordan's reply: "Catholicity and Progress."

Mr. W. B. Yeats. Formerly a Separatist, which creed he relinquished on getting a pension from the British Government, when he ceased to have any further interest in Irish Nationalism.

The Earl of Wicklow, Imperialist and Freemason.

Colonel Hutchinson Poe, Imperialist and Freemason.

Dr. George Sigerson. The only worthy member of an Irish Senate. Is it any wonder that he tendered his resignation of the hybrid body with which his name should never have been associated?

THE FREE STATE ARMY MUTINY

Matters look decidedly desperate for the Free State just now. Dissensions amongst the Ministers has been followed by mutiny in its army. The cause of the mutiny, according to the "Evening Telegraph" of Saturday night last, is that certain army officers, disgusted with the Pro-British attitude of the Free State Government, addressed a letter to the heads of the Free State pointing out that the Treaty was not being used in the best interests of the Irish people. For writing this letter they are now on the run, hunted for high and low by the Free State Blood Hounds. As long as these men served the Free State and obeyed its vicious orders, they were petted and pampered. The moment they dared to express an honest opinion of their masters, they have to take to the hills.

The lesson is one that ought to be taken to heart by all. Treachery to a nation must be paid for sooner or later; and the men of the Free State Army, now on the run, betrayed their own comrades of the Four Courts and are now paying for it. If they were really deceived into attacking the Republicans by insidious Free State propaganda, we now sympathise with them. If they served their masters for the sake of English gold, we can only say they are receiving their deserts. It is, however, heartening to Republicans to see their enemy's camp thus dissolving early like a mist under the rays of the rising sun. Freedom's Day is coming fast.

THE RELEASE OF JOSEPH DOWLING.

A striking example of the might of the re-born Sinn Fein Movement is afforded by the release of Joseph Dowling from his captivity in England. This veteran fighter had been lying in an English dungeon for six long years and would be rotting there to-day if he were depending on the Free State to liberate him. But his Republican comrades determined to have him. The Standing Committee of Sinn Fein forwarded a resolution to Ramsay MacDonald demanding the immediate release of his prisoner. MacDonald acknowledged the resolution stating the matter would be at once seen to, and almost immediately the prison doors were flung open and Joseph Dowling was able to stand on Dublin soil last Wednesday night and receive the welcome of thirty thousand of Dublin's citizens.

So has the first round been won. Now for the next.

WHAT THE PEOPLE ARE SAYING.

That Mr. Cosgrave excelled himself in College Street on Sunday last.

* * *

That he added the utmost dignity to the "Free State" by criticising the colours of the young ladies' hats.

* * *

That only for his guard of D.M.P., he would have been the victim of a forcible expression of the Will of the People.

* * *

That his fellow orators were anything but dignified during the proceedings.

* * *

That Mr. O'Mara did not improve his election chances by flinging paper Balls at his audience.

* * *

That General Mulcahy's favourite song since the Mutiny is: "I'm afraid to go home in the dark."

* * *

That a warrant has been issued for the arrest of Parnell's Ghost which has lately taken to haunting the Viceregal Lodge.

* * *

That many men, who had Republicans on the run, are now on the run themselves.

Vote I — SEAN LEMASS

J. T. Lemass,

Hatter and Outfitter,

2 & 3, CAPEL STREET (One door from Grattan Bridge)
DUBLIN.

9/7/23   192

M _Lord Mayor O'neill_

My Dear Lord Mayor,

Could you find out for me the whereabouts of my son Noel D. Lemass. He returned to Ireland a few days ago after an absence of Eight months and was arrested in Exchequer St on Sunday July 3. He was in the Company of Mr. Devine of the Corporation at the time as I have not heard from him I am anxious about him. Will you kindly do what you can for me and oblige J.T. Lemass

---

Letter from J.T. Lemass (Seán's father) to the Lord Mayor of Dublin, 9 July 1923. Mr Lemass expresses his concern regarding the whereabouts of his son, Noel, and asks the Lord Mayor to do what he can to locate him. Noel was abducted in Dublin in July of that year by Free State Army forces and his mutilated body was found in the Dublin Mountains on 12 October 1923. (Courtesy of Seán O'Connor)

NOEL LEMASS

with an unsurpassable record of

IRISH VALOUR

has been brutally murdered by agents of the "Free" State.

The mangled body of this Republican Patriot has been found on the lonely hillside in such a shocking condition as goes to prove that the victim was, before death, subjected to diabolical torture.

Why was Noel Lemass murdered? Because he refused to violate his oath of allegiance to the Irish Republic. Because he refused to " be faithful to King George of England." Because he refused his support to the " Free " State Government, and thus helped to prevent Ireland from becoming a mockery in the eyes of the other nations. That is why Noel Lemass has been tortured to death.

Electors of South Dublin show your disapproval of all such hellish acts by recording your

VOTE FOR
MICHAEL O'MULLANE

the SINN FEIN CANDIDATE, who stands for the principles of TONE, EMMET, PEARSE, MacSWINEY, BRUGHA, MELLOWS and NOEL LEMASS.

Published and issued by JOSEPH CLARKE, T.C., Agent for MICHAEL O'MULLANE. Committee Rooms, 25 Aungier Street.

Handbill soliciting support for Michael O'Mullane in the 1925 by-election in Dublin South. It mentions the death of Noel Lemass. The coroner's report published in the *Irish Times* described the murder as something which 'suggested a barbarism of which the most pitiless savage would be ashamed', see *Irish Times*, 16 October 1923, 5. (NLI, Irish Large Books Collection, 300, p.37)

OGLAIGH NA hEIREANN

DUBLIN BRIGADE CONVENTION

. . TO BE HELD AT . .

41 PARNELL SQUARE

On the 15th March, 1922, at 7.30 p.m.

Admit *Lieut Seán Lemass*

as Delegate of 6 Coy. 2nd Battn.

Coy. Capt. Signature

Bn. Comdts. ,,

Bde. Comdts ,,

Lemass's invitation to the Dublin Brigade convention of Óglaigh na hÉireann, March 1922. (Courtesy of Seán O'Connor)

Following page: Lemass's military service certificate valid under the Military Service Pensions Act of 1934, 19 March 1943. (Courtesy of Seán O'Connor)

Military Service

SERVICE

In the matter of the application of.............. *Sián F. Lema*

for a Service Certificate in accordance with the terms of the Military S

WHEREAS the Minister for Defence has taken into consideration

THIS IS TO CERTIFY that the said .... *Sián*

has rendered Service in the Forces and during the periods as set out a

Service Period prescribed in the Act.

1. The week commencing on the 23rd day of April, 1916 ....
2. The period comprising :—
   - (*a*) the period commencing on the 1st day of April, 1916, and ending on April, 1916, and ....
   - (*b*) the period commencing on the 30th day of April, 1916, and ending March, 1917 ....

3. The period commencing on the 1st day of April, 1917, and ending on the 31st day

4. The period commencing on the 1st day of April, 1918, and ending on the 31st day

5. The period commencing on the 1st day of April, 1919, and ending on the 31st day

6. The period commencing on the 1st day of April, 1920, and ending on the 31st day

7. The period commencing on the 1st day of April, 1921, and ending on the 11th day

8. The period commencing on the 12th day of July, 1921, and ending on the 30th day

9. The period commencing on the 1st day of July, 1922, and ending on the 31st day

10. The period commencing on the 1st day of April, 1923, and ending on the 30th day of S

AND THAT for the purpose of the Act the grade of rank of the

Dated t

ICATE.

Palmerston Rd„ Rathmines Dublin

sions Act, 1934, and the Regulations made thereunder,

of the Referee appointed under the Act on the application,

mass.

Forces in which Active Service was rendered.	Duration of Active Service during each of the prescribed periods as established to the satisfaction of the Referee.
IRISH VOLUNTEERS	$\frac{5}{7}$ of ENTIRE PERIOD
IRISH VOLUNTEERS	$\frac{1}{2}$ of ENTIRE PERIOD
IRISH VOLUNTEERS	$\frac{1}{6}$ of ENTIRE PERIOD
IRISH VOLUNTEERS	$\frac{1}{4}$ of ENTIRE PERIOD
Oglaigh na h-Eireann.	$\frac{1}{2}$ of ENTIRE PERIOD
Oglaigh na h-Eireann.	$\frac{2}{3}$ of ENTIRE PERIOD
Oglaigh na h-Eireann.	ENTIRE PERIOD
Oglaigh na h-Eireann.	ENTIRE PERIOD
Oglaigh na h-Eireann.	ENTIRE PERIOD
Oglaigh na h-Eireann.	ENTIRE PERIOD

cant is Grade .... *D*

19 day of *March 1943*

Rúnaidhe. Roinn Cosanta

MAKE IT CLEAR

that the Defeatists speak only for themselves

GIVE FIANNA FÁIL
A CLEAR MAJORITY

FODHLA PRINTING CO., LTD., DUBLIN.

THREE

Revolutionist to constitutionalist

'Make it clear that the Defeatists only speak for themselves', *c.* 1933. Fianna Fáil election poster. (NLI, Ephemera Collection, POL/1930-40/9)

✺ A pre-political culture

Lemass grew up into a world of great empires—empires on the verge of dissolution, but not evidently doomed. It was also a world at war and in revolution; the Boer War was raging at the time of his birth, and was widely seen in Ireland as the first small crack in the mighty and apparently monolithic edifice that was the British imperial superpower of the time. The world war of 1914–18 was the beginning of the end for the British Empire and was also the beginning of what has been the greatest military, social and technological convulsion the world has ever seen, lasting from 1914 to 1950, resulting in a world that was, by the standards of 1900, almost unrecognisable. Anyone born around 1900 felt in old age, if they ever got there, that they had seen and survived Armageddon, and wondered if the world could survive any new violent transformation on the lines of that which they had witnessed in the first half of the twentieth century. Revolutions and *coups d'état* came to be regarded as almost everyday and even legitimate phenomena in Europe, and the idea of a constitutional democratic order was one that had, as yet, little broad appeal in many countries; resistance to democratisation had both right-wing and left-wing guises. Even relatively peaceful little Ireland at times seemed to be no exception to this generalisation. Todd Andrews drew a vivid picture of his own pre-political mentality on the occasion of the signing of the Anglo–Irish Treaty and its subsequent ratification by Dáil Éireann in January 1922:

> Since the days of the Irish Party and John E. Redmond, the word 'politician' was never applied to a member of the Movement. It was a word of ill-repute. Now, nearly all the members of the Dáil overnight became in my eyes 'politicians'; a distinction was rapidly being drawn between 'the politicians' and the [Irish Republican] Army. In the critical situation now developing my hopes were pinned on the unity of the IRA being maintained and on the IRA effectively taking control of the institutions of Government. I fully sympathised with De Valera when he remarked 'I have only seen politics within the last three weeks or month. It is the first time I have seen them and I am sick to the heart of them.' I was even more in sympathy with him when earlier he pointed out that the control of the Army was not affected by the political situation. I was a reasonably well-informed member of the IRA but the dichotomy between the old Dáil, the new Provisional Government and new Parliament with, at the back of it all, the Sinn Féin organisation and its coming Ard Fheis, left me in such a state of confusion that I decided that the only clear authoritative element in the situation was the Army.[1]

According to his older self, young Andrews was not only sceptical about politicians but did not fully understand, or believe in, the principles of liberal democracy. He viewed journalists as hired liars who committed wholesale libel on noble leaders like de Valera and brave warriors like Liam Lynch. The new semi-independent Ireland of the Treaty was going to be taken over by fat cats, gombeen men, university graduates, professors, snobbish 'West Britons' and all those who had contributed little or nothing to the fight for freedom. These were people who cared nothing for the dream of an independent Irish Republic with a spiritual and cultural authenticity that neither British-ruled nor Free State Ireland could boast. To the minds of many young IRA men, the army of the Republic had as much, or even more, political legitimacy as that of Dáil Éireann; after all, the Volunteers pre-dated the Dáil by about six years, a point that Andrews did not make, but that influenced much thinking at that crucial time. The Free State was being accepted by the people because it represented law and order and safe enjoyment of one's property, rather than representing authentically any true Irish political liberation. For some, the army *was* the Republic and the true vanguard of the Irish people in revolt. Michael Hayes, in the context of conversations he had had with Gerry Boland, prominent anti-Treatyite, in the mid-1960s as two old veterans, reminisced:

> It is to be remembered that the [Irish Republican] Army was an unpaid volunteer force which was in existence before the Dáil and which, as a condition to coming under its jurisdiction had insisted on all the members of the Dáil taking an oath of allegiance to the Republic.[2]

Collins and de Valera had tried to fix the numbers of pro- and anti-Treaty Dáil deputies before the election of June 1922 in an agreement labelled the 'pact'. Hayes noted that the anti-Treaty elements, dominated by the IRA and outnumbered in the Dáil, tried to represent the vote as a victory for the 'coalition government', agreed to opportunistically by Collins before the pact election in June and repudiated by him on the eve of the vote. The anti-Treatyites knew that the people were pro-Treaty, which is why they agreed in the pact to freeze the numbers of deputies at pre-election proportions. Collins agreed to the pact to persuade the IRA not to sabotage the poll. What happened, of course, is that the electorate, generally fairly free of IRA intimidation because of Collins's trick, commonly voted for pro-Treaty Sinn Féin or, more crucially, for Labour or Farmers' Party candidates, thereby wrecking the pact and making de Valera and company look foolish. The IRA also tried to represent the pro-Treatyites as a minority, which they evidently were not.[3] Andrews commented:

> In the spring of 1922 the idea of a military dictatorship in itself had not at all the frightening connotations it has now. Mussolini had not marched on Rome, the word 'Fascist' to the limited few who had ever heard of it had no untowards significance. Hitler had only begun the long haul to power, while Stalin had not yet undertaken the liquidation of the Kulaks or the show trials of the Old Bolsheviks. Equally, democracy had not been, as it since has been, elevated to the position of a goddess in the public mind. 'The democratic process' were words which would have fallen on uncomprehending ears in the Ireland of 1922. What the people understood by military dictatorship, as propounded by Rory O'Connor, was that they were liable to be pushed

around at the whim of young IRA commanders. Discipline was rapidly deteriorating in the local units of the IRA. People began to feel unsafe in the enjoyment of their property and their freedom of movement.[4]

Andrews possibly exaggerated the non-democratic mentality of his peers, extending his own pre-political mentality to others perhaps older and slightly more worldly wise than he was, by his own very honest account. De Valera and others certainly grasped quickly that the people wanted peace and, if permitted, would vote for it, whether or not they put a philosophical value on the right to vote; Dev said repeatedly in 1922 that the people would vote against his cause if permitted to do so. However, many veteran fighters felt caught in a quandary. To their minds, democracy was going to mean an elected government that accepted subordination to British policies and symbols. To take up arms against such a government, on the other hand, looked like fighting the Irish people, a people sometimes seen as slavish and apathetic. Faced with such a choice, they were politically paralysed, and it took years for some of them to think their way out of the impasse. Some gave up in disgust or despair, while others took refuge in political impossibilism and became part of a sect rather than a political party. Others again retreated to the religious life; 1923 saw a huge surge in vocations.

Seán O'Faoláin argued that the entire Republican position, and its insistence that the Second Dáil still existed despite the partition of Ireland and the election of a Third Dáil on 16 June 1922 *with Republican consent*, was consistent with a turn of mind that was a clerical mixture of legalism and theology.[5] The phrase of the time was 'Dev in the political wilderness'— between a Republic that did not exist and a Free State that was regarded as unacceptable ideologically. On top of that politics of disappointment was the bitterness and hatred generated by the vicious little Civil War of 1922–3, in which at least 2,000 were killed. O'Faoláin's eyewitness account of the defeated Republicans is vivid:

> These febrile, fractious, bitter, hungry-eyed ex-freedom-fighters were now in every sense out of a job; shabbily dressed, wearing old hats that one liked to think had once been grazed by bullets, their ankle-length overcoats stuffed with manifestos and pamphlets, their mouths thin with enmity and resolve, and one guessed at empty pockets, perhaps even empty stomachs, and wondered how or on what, in God's name, they and theirs lived.[6]

Personal suffering and grief, rarely spoken about later, fuelled many; some wanted vengeance, while others stifled such impulses, knowing their self-destructive effects. Many, however, merely followed the gang of brothers into one side or the other. A personal ambition, blasted by electoral and military defeat, fired many. R.M. Fox wrote:

> The civil war left its trail of dark passions. In by-lanes and alleys assassins lurked, the scenes of their handiwork marked now by little stone crosses to show where victims had met their death. Reprisals and counter-reprisals succeeded each other in a tragic circle of despair.
>
> The climax came when Noel Lemass—an active Republican—was dragged through the streets of Dublin in broad daylight, his body afterwards being discovered, gnawed by rats, in a gloomy, desolate spot known as the Featherbed, up in the Dublin mountains.
>
> At the funeral of Noel Lemass the Irish Republican Army marched through the city for the first time since its military defeat. Thousands were in prison, others were harried and hunted through the country. But that day they came in, no one knew from where. I saw them marching along the street—a silent, sombre army. No music kept time to the tramp of their feet—that scraping, dragging tramp which beat out the 'Dead March' for their murdered comrade. Their faces were stern and tragic, their eyes and mouths bitter. There were countrymen who seemed to bring the clay of the fields in with them, the atmosphere of bog and marshland. They looked neither to the right nor left, but marched straight on. It was a silent army, but—as I looked at it—it did not seem to be a defeated one.
>
> A granite memorial was unveiled out on the Featherbed where the body was found. Here the elements joined to give a Macbeth-like sullenness of tragedy to the scene. The wind howled and shrieked. Men and women fought their way in the teeth of its blast. A dark mist rolled over the bog so that the memorial was blotted out. People threaded their way carefully along the path, holding hands, stumbling past holes filled with brown bog water, to the place of mournful ceremony.[7]

This was the emotional legacy, and the political potential, that young people like Lemass had to deal with. The Republicans came home from defeat, with terrible memories in many cases, uncertain of what to do next, if anything. Many realised slowly, however, that the Treaty settlement was seen as insufficient by the general public and that, given peace, many people would vote for a furtherance of separatism by incremental means; although few of the Republicans would admit it, a version of Michael Collins's 'stepping stones' argument, to the effect that the Treaty was only a first instalment, gradually gripped their minds. As Collins had said, the Treaty gave them the freedom to achieve freedom. In an important little book that was published in Dublin in 1924 and not reprinted until 1998, a prominent pro-Treaty figure, P.S. O'Hegarty, predicted almost exactly what the future constitutional evolution of the country into complete formal independence would involve: formal symbols of subordination such as the Oath of Allegiance, the right of appeal to the Privy Council or university seats in the Dáil would wither away, and complete Republican independence would follow in time. His only major inaccuracy was his depiction of the ending of partition as inevitable as well.[8] A gradual consensus emerged among the majority that the defeated Republicans should seek what was termed 'an intermediate objective'.

Lemass and the discovery of politics

Lemass described many years later an abstentionist Sinn Féin that refused to take seats in Dáil Éireann on the grounds that the Second Dáil had never been dissolved and therefore still existed in some ghostly form. He reminisced:

> at this time [in 1923] there was a great deal of discussion going on as to what we were going to do. There were those who argued that there was nothing to do but fight as soon as we were ready to fight and overthrow the Free State and its troops. This was completely unrealistic because the opportunity for a successful campaign of that kind did not exist. There were others in favour of turning to political action and, of course, there was a great deal of searching for what we used to call 'the intermediate objective', recog-

nising that we could not get the people at one go to vote for the overthrow of everything that had been set up [by the Free State] and accept a Republican Government.

The abolition of the Oath was eventually selected as this intermediate objective and to make this campaign effective we had to say that if the Oath was removed we would take our places in the Dáil. The I.R.A. Executive Council were being urged at this stage to agree to this change in policy. The meeting at which this was finally settled was in Bulloch Castle in Dalkey [on 14 November 1925], which was then owned by a man named Maguire and the meeting went on for several hours. I was there representing the Shadow Government as Minister for Defence urging the Army Council to accept our policy. Frank Aiken and several officers of the Volunteers who were also Dáil Deputies were present, too. But it was not agreed to and the Army then decided that its allegiance to the Shadow Government would be withdrawn and that the Army Council would be the only authority they would recognise in this regard. The Shadow Government then went out of existence, and I ceased to be Minister for Defence. The Sinn Féin Ard Fheis then met [in 1926] and Mr. De Valera's motion on this new policy [of eliminating the oath] was defeated by three or four votes. We withdrew from Sinn Féin and began to organise the Fianna Fáil Party. There was, I gather, some form of Shadow Government, becoming more and more shadowy, with Arthur O'Connor as its President, but it ultimately faded away altogether.[9]

There is some foreshortening of history going on here, but there is an underlying accuracy. In November 1924 Lemass campaigned in a by-election to the Fourth Dáil on an abstentionist but reasonably radical ticket. His propaganda leaflet emphasised free education, 'including free books and luncheon' for children and a generous scholarship system aimed at able children of poor families who otherwise would have had to drop out of school early. This would enable 'the child of the poorest Irishman' to go to university 'if sufficiently brilliant', while (an interesting touch) the parents would be recouped for the loss of the child's labour during his or her education. The leaflet also touted 'The protection of our Industries by the imposition of adequate tariffs, with proper safeguards against profiteering'. Ireland was to be rebuilt 'not from the top down, but from the bottom up'. 'Vote for Lemass and social justice.' Healthy abuse was heaped on his Treatyite opponent.[10]

Lemass won very handily in south Dublin. He did not take his Dáil seat but instead became a member of Comhairle na dTeachtaí, the assembly of the surviving members of the anti-Treatyite minority of the Second Dáil, which imagined itself to be the Irish government. De Valera appointed him as minister for defence in his Republican 'government'. In this role, he engineered a successful breakout of Republican prisoners from Mountjoy Jail. This was probably his last semi-revolutionary act, as he began to outgrow his fairly wild and woolly youth; he got married that year, which almost certainly steadied him up. At some stage, he virtually asked his putative prime minister whether he was minister of defence or a common criminal. At Comhairle na dTeachtaí Lemass said:

> I was never a member of the 2nd Dáil but I was a member of this body and I held a position on the Executive as the Head of the Department of Defence. In that position, I sanctioned certain military acts, for example, the raid on Mountjoy in November last. I think it is most astounding suggesting that my action needs any ratification from this Body. I think that we should resent that very much. These acts were just as valid then as they are now. I, as one of this Body in giving my action to this act gave it all the justification needed ... It is suggested now that these acts were invalid at the time? ... When you said that such acts sanctioned by Comhairle na dTeachtaí required validation, does that mean that any acts that I did as Minister for Defence were not valid?[11]

The absurdity of the Republican position had dawned on many people, and Free State informers prophesied the birth of what became Fianna Fáil early in 1926, a month before the split actually occurred. They had hinted at such a rift from mid-1924 onward.[12] Lemass had a strong sense of reality. He could see, as a businessman's son could easily see, that standing on prin-ciples and legalisms that were infinitely arguable had its practical limits. The founding of Fianna Fáil by the large minority of delegates who walked away from Sinn Féin in 1926 freed the new party of a 'collection of not merely dedicated people but of various cranks of one kind or another'. The image of Sinn Féin in the minds of the public was being ruined by the public behaviour of this 'galaxy of cranks', he remembered decades later.[13] Interestingly, the split seems to have been reasonably amicable; afterwards, the Sinn Féin paper, *An Phoblacht*, was happy to give houseroom to rather self-flattering material sent in from the new party, a party that was eventually to swallow up what was left of Sinn Féin; even in the months after the split, Dev's new departure seemed to be gaining majority support within the Republican body of public opinion, and it was clearly also mobilising support from thousands of Republican veterans who had not been attracted to abstentionist Sinn Féin. Sinn Féin almost seems to have had a death wish. As we shall see, as so often in Irish politics, the split was partly generational, and Lemass was to put himself squarely at the head of the younger genera-tion, and not for the last time. Interestingly, he used the historical analogy of the forgotten causes of the French Revolution in speaking of the quandary Republicans found themselves in by the mid-1920s:

> It was assumed, of course, that the Ard Fheis [of 1926], which rejected de Valera's policy represented the majority of Sinn Féin opinion throughout the country. But when we started to organise Fianna Fáil we found this was not so. Within a year of the first Fianna Fáil executive being set up we had a nationwide organisation, the strongest in the country, fully geared for action with Cumainn and County Executives everywhere. The speed with which the Fianna Fáil organisation came into being, from a group sitting in Dublin to a nationwide organisation extending to every parish in the country was quite phenomenal. Now, this represented first of all the desire of the republican community in the country to have a programme of action that looked sensible and to which they could commit themselves again. It was a recognition that if we did not get organised on a political basis with political aims we were going to disappear like the Jacobins, exercising no influence at all on the course of events in Ireland. It is quite a remarkable story, you know. Fianna Fáil was founded in 1926; it fought the general election in 1927 and won fifty-odd seats, and in the next general election became the Government. This, I think, represented the situation much more accurately than ever in the country before.[14]

Like Dev, Lemass realised that the people had wanted peace so desperately in 1922 they were prepared to accept Collins's argument that the Treaty was a stepping stone to freedom—that it gave the Irish the freedom to achieve freedom. But he further realised that people still harboured the old Republican aspirations and that the Free State could indeed be regarded simply as a stepping stone, to be left behind eventually. Those in Sinn Féin who were incapable of 'accepting anything except the whole of the Republican demand' found that they did not represent anyone at all, 'and they virtually disappeared in the next decade'.[15] The fact that this was the prospect before them dawned on many Sinn Féiners. Articles appeared in *An Phoblacht* documenting the steady and solid progress towards complete practical independence that was being made by Ireland's role model, Canada, in the mid-1920s.[16] Sinn Féin was not so much splitting as melting into thin air because of the unreality of its ideas.

As early as 4 May 1925 Lemass proposed himself as chairman of a special committee of the party to reorganise Dublin city and county.[17] He also wrote several neophyte articles for *An Phoblacht* between 1924 and 1926, berating the party's activists and its leaders for inefficiency and inactivity, his rhetoric becoming more pointed and impatient as the years wore on. He sensed that the party was falling apart even before the fateful Ard Fheis of 1926, partly because of the policies of non-recognition and abstentionism. In July 1925 the secretary of Donegal Comhairle Ceanntair *wrote* to the general secretary of Sinn Féin to say that he was emigrating to the US:

> Sinn Féin is not popular enough for the people to join and you will find that this Comhairle Ceanntair consists of very little more than *Myself* … funds cannot be raised here. So much so that anyone in business and depending on the public could not employ an ex-prisoner or he would loose [*sic*] his trade.[18]

Eamonn Donnelly sent in a general report at the same time, saying more or less the same thing: 'Since my last report … the general state of apathy still remains'. Economic depression and the emigration of activists were the usual explanations offered by locals. The organisation was unhealthy. Leinster was not too bad, but Longford was hopeless. 'Some efforts' were being made in Westmeath, Meath and Louth, Laois and Offaly were so-so, but nothing was being done in Wexford. South Kilkenny and Carlow were better, and Dublin city and county were being reorganised. However, 'all over Connaught there seems to be a general wave of depression'. Galway was the best of a bad lot in the western province, with emigration to America being the general explanation for the lack of activity in this province. Cork city's Sinn Féin organisation was 'in a hopeless plight'. Kerry was coming on, but the other Munster county organisations scarcely existed; they were just about there. In Free State Ulster the organisations were inadequate.[19] In November 1925 a report on the Sinn Féin organisation for the Ard Fheis gloomily informed the leadership that the number of registered branches had decreased from 1,500 in 1923 to 707 in 1924.[20]

Lemass was evidently well aware of this situation; in what was to become a characteristic piece of behaviour, he gradually came around to the view that it was pointless to throw good money after bad. Sinn Féin was finished, and, to use a suitably Parnellite term, a new departure was necessary; as a good, if perhaps unconscious, Parnellite, Lemass duly provided one. In late 1925 he stirred up a historically significant controversy in the pages of *An Phoblacht*. At the time he was still chairman of the committee on reorganisation of the Dublin branches of the party, and he had become acutely aware of the parlous state of the rank and file. By September 1925 his deep unease was being communicated even through the bland officialese of his routine reports on reorganisation. Many branches had become inactive, and he felt that 'a few energetic individuals scattered throughout the county could change the existing state of affairs within a few months'.[21] A week later, he went public with a feature article:

> I have attempted to set out hereunder certain impressions I have formed about the Sinn Féin organisation in Dublin, and to make suggestions arising out of them. During the past four months, as Chairman of the Dublin Reorganisation Committee, I have inspected at close quarters the working of several Cumann [*sic*] and Comhairle Ceanntair in the city and county and I have had a unique opportunity of studying existing conditions and of forming opinions as to the causes of them. Believing that these views will be of interest to those whom they concern, I set them down here …
>
> It is a sure sign of decay in a political organisation when the members of it devote the major portion of their time and energy to discussing trivial points of rules or of procedure instead of to more useful activities. That this sign is unmistakeably present in Dublin [Sinn Féin] cannot be

denied. In each one of the three constituencies there are 'disputes' in existence all revolving around the interpretation of some rule or another in the scheme of organisation. One such dispute in the North City has already lasted nearly twelve months, and more energy and time has been wasted over it than would have been required to build up the organisation in that area to its old-time efficiency. None of the disputants seem big enough to abandon the petty points of vantage they may have gained and to sink their differences for the sake of the common cause.

Rules are only a means to an end. If they are ineffective they can be abandoned. There is work to be done for Ireland at every hand: work that will well repay the doing of it. But the important thing is TO DO IT, not merely to follow the correct procedure in attempting it. Those who would have you come back from the firing line to examine the red tape leading up to it are greater impediments to success than the enemy in front of you. Ignore them. They will still be squabbling like old women over some forgotten section of the Constitution while you are carrying the flag to victory.

There is a real danger to the organisation in the tendency that exists to elect the older members of Cumainn to the positions on the officer boards. There are in Dublin a large number of middle-aged men and women, who have given valuable service to the Movement in the past and who, because of that, are invariably elected to fill the most important positions. Unfortunately, these people, as is natural, are so tied up with precedents and experiences, that they are incapable of giving an active lead when it is needed. It is easy to sit on a committee and give the members of it the benefit of an experience ranging over ten or twenty years, but the vigour and originality necessary for success will not be there. If the movement is to survive, these people must be taught to stand down and to give the younger men a chance. Those who, from motives of personal pride, persist in holding on to office long after their period of utility is over, must be removed. There is no other remedy. Sinn Féin must be rejuvenated if it is to live.

To the young people in the Cumainn I say with all seriousness: Take Control. The future is yours, and if our organisation is to have a future also, you must command it. In a few weeks now all the officers of the organisation will be re-elected. That will be your chance. If Republicanism in your area has lost ground in the last twelve months, if your Cumann has become weak and ineffective, it is those outgoing officers who are responsible. Keep them out. Put men and women into the positions who are young and active and who are not afraid to take chances. Make the pace for the movement.

Headquarters has been waiting for a sign from you that you are ready and willing to move forward from the present position. Heretofore that sign has not been given. Give it now.[22]

Lemass deliberately defined the coming split as generational, and he quite openly sided with the young against the old, with those born in the twentieth century against those born in the nineteenth. He lambasted the older Sinn Féiners as engaging in vacuous argument, and as lacking in energy and organisational ability. Inevitably, feelings were hurt. Maighréad Bean Uí Bhuachalla, clearly stung, wrote in to rebut his argument in a way that simply proved his point. She argued that the older Sinn Féiners had valuable experience, that they were younger than these young people when they first became interested in Irish nationality, and that they 'began by laying the foundation of an intellectual and spiritual knowledge of the meaning of freedom'. Unlike the modern young, they were not flung into the movement unthinking, but had made a great personal choice. Too many young people were more interested in 'jazz' dancing than in the noble cause. Their outlook was not Gaelic enough, and they needed the older people to teach them.[23] The following week, someone by the name of 'Fingan' sympathised with this cautiously, but pointed out also that the young men that they had were not up to the required standard because the right types were not joining the party. He made the key point, evidently understood by Lemass, that the ex-internees—IRA veterans all—should be in Sinn Féin, but very few of them were attracted to it: 'there is a notion that one retires from being a patriot at thirty'.[24] Fundamentally, he was agreeing with Lemass's unspoken but obvious programme of getting the IRA ex-prisoners into the ranks of the party. Simultaneously, Lemass fired a second broadside.

For the previous year, Sinn Féin had been punching well below its real potential strength. The party had suffered reverses and disappointments, and had only its own leadership to blame, he argued. In September Lemass openly urged his fellow young people to take over the party:

During the past twelve months Sinn Féin has failed to influence the life of the nation to any degree commensurate with its strength. The roseate hopes we held at the time of the last Ard Fheis have all been disappointed. In places where the Republican spirit is strong, we have merely held our own; in other places we have lost ground…

It is useless to deny facts, when these facts are obvious to everyone, even to our opponents. A thorough examination of our present position is essential to success. Our failure in 1924 is due to causes which can be discovered and removed. Now is the time to discover wherein lies our weakness…

We will not be able to achieve a revolution in Ireland by the methods of a mutual benefit society. We must compel the people to consider our doctrines by forcing attention to our actions. Action is wanted—useful action in every phase of our national life. Wherever there is something to be done that will increase the stock of happiness in the nation: Sinn Féin must do it. Wherever a wrong is being perpetrated: Sinn Féin must be found defending the right. Whenever the rights of the common Irish people are assailed by private or by public interests: Sinn Féin must be the spear-point of the people's resistance…

I am convinced that the cause of the weakness in every branch of our organisation, high and low, is incompetent leadership. Headquarters has, time and again, attempted to promote activities, but failed to get the results they expected because, in between them and the rank and file, there were a number of honorary officers who were either incapable or unwilling of performing the duties of the positions to which they accepted election. If Sinn Féin is to be fired with new life, to be fit to undertake the tremendous task in front of it, it must have leaders who are not afraid to lead. It must have officers elected for their ability and not for their reputations—young men and women who are willing and anxious to win their laurels by hard, unselfish work. Judged by results, the older men have failed, so let us give the younger men their chance now. At, and after, the Ard Fheis the ordinary members of the organisation will get their opportunity. Let them examine carefully the activities—and inactivities—of those whom, twelve months ago, they placed in positions of responsibility, and weed out the 'duds'—alike those who have outlived their utility and those who were always useless.

The success of the Republican movement and the rejuvenation of Sinn Féin are so closely connected that they are practically the same thing. We have a policy which, in spite of our critics, is capable of bringing victory, if developed in full. In the hands of young and active men it can be made real and live. In 1924 we touched the bottom of the depression that followed the civil war: from now on we will go upward and forward. With a fighting policy and a fighting organisation we can win, if we will try hard enough.[25]

These fighting words, addressed as much to the alleged gerontocracy in the party as to anyone else, brought some anger again. The following week, Patrick O'Shea, secretary of the Seán MacDiarmada Cumann, in a long apologia for the establishment, complained bitterly about the aggressive and irregular behaviour of some younger new members. His attack on Lemass veered, quite revealingly, into an *argumentum ad hominem*:

> Mr. Lemass considers old members are a menace when elected to position[s] on officer-boards, but good service and increasing age and wisdom are not a justification for their extinction, and we believe the majority of the organisation would prefer to entrust their destinies to tried men and women even in preference to younger people like Mr. Lemass, of whose personality we were totally oblivious until the brutal murder of his late dear brother brought him on the horizon of the National movement.[26]

The following week the paper carried a piece by the secretary of the Erskine Childers Cumann rebuking O'Shea and arguing that Lemass had a point and was indeed a young man, but one known for his dedicated and

splendid work for the cause. The editor then closed the entire correspondence, on the apparent grounds that it was all getting a bit personal.
Simultaneously, in the same issue, Lemass unleashed a third broadside. The
coming Ard Fheis would be critical to the future of the movement: 'There
is something in the air that tells us we have reached a parting of the ways.
One way leads to victory, and the other to defeat, but there are no signposts
to guide us'. He urged that there was to be no more laying the blame on
either 'Suffolk Street' (anti-Treaty Sinn Féin) or 'Merrion Street' (pro-Treaty
Cumann na nGaedheal in government in the Free State). He went on to
urge hard work, dedication, optimism and, in particular, a throwing off of
the terrible apathy that dogged Irish political culture. He was to repeat these
themes, in terms somewhat resembling the rhetoric of moral rearmament,
many times over the next 40 years.[27] The Free State government's observers
saw the shift quite clearly. A report in late October 1925 commented:

> Lemass is one of De Valera's strongest supporters, and he
> has also the support of the majority of the military section.
> Lemass is on the re-organisation Committee, and he is
> endeavouring to supplant the present Committees of the
> Sinn Féin Cumann in the North side [of Dublin], by
> members of the Military section, or, as he terms it, infusing
> young and new blood into the organisation. This is the
> reason for the ill-feeling against Lemass in the North side,
> as the 'old bloods' refuse to be supplanted, and new and
> rival Cumanns are springing up … there are now two
> Erskine Childers Cumanns in the North side.[28]

In January 1926 Lemass proposed that the abolition of the oath be made
a condition for Republicans' taking their seats in the Free State Dáil.[29] This
seems to have caused a final furore, as even this modest proposal was an
assault on the taboo-dominated thinking of so many Sinn Féiners. The
March special Ard Fheis turned down the proposal, and Sinn Féin split yet
again; it has even been suggested that some of the seceders voted against the
motion so as to consign Sinn Féin to a political wilderness of its own
creation and clear the ground for a new party, Fianna Fáil. This was allegedly
engineered by Gerry Boland, who went around the hall ensuring that those
who opposed Dev's putative motion did indeed do so.[30] Reportedly, Dev
remarked after his reputed defeat in the vote that he would retire from
politics, and it was then that Lemass sprung the idea of a new party on
him.[31] There are certain problems with this narrative; rumours of a new

party had been current for months prior to the special Ard Fheis, and Lemass had reportedly already run the idea of a new party past Dev and Boland, even going over to the leader's house at Cross Avenue, Blackrock, to push the idea. It is hard to believe, after Lemass's very public attack on Sinn Féin's leadership, that de Valera was unaware of his intentions. Furthermore, Dev had a habit of muttering about resigning from politics, perhaps partly a posture of disinterest and partly to disguise his addiction to political power, but in particular to mobilise sympathy and support for some new departure. He behaved the same way after hearing of the signing of the Treaty in December 1921. His pose as the innocent abroad was often quite brilliantly done, and generated great respect and affection. However, he was a very crafty political operator; even his simulated self-pity was mobilised to generate sympathy and affection. There was something indescribably clerical about his political style. His own version of the incident flatters both men and is subtly self-serving:

> On that day in March 1926, I happened to be walking out of the Rathmines Town Hall with Seán Lemass. I had just resigned as president of Sinn Féin and I said to him, 'Well Seán, I have done my best, but I have been beaten. Now this is the end for me. I am leaving public life.' Seán was shocked to hear me saying this, and he said: 'But you are not going to leave us now, Dev, at this stage … we must form a new organisation … it is the only way forward.' We discussed it further and at last I told him I could not but agree with his logic and said I would do all the necessary things.[32]

It is doubtful that Lemass was actually shocked at all, or that de Valera had any real intention of going back to school-teaching. Another intriguingly different version of this story was recounted by de Valera in 1949:

> Mr Lemass had that rare combination in him of being not only an idealist but a realist of the first order. It was Seán Lemass who first came to me and said: 'Surely you are not going to stop there. Surely you are going now, having put that policy before the people and believing in it, to found another organisation whose aim will be the execution of that policy?'
> I personally adopted towards him always a sort of fatherly attitude as I felt I was much older than he was. He was the Benjamin, so to speak, of the Cabinet.[33]

De Valera's son Vivion confirms the intuition that little was 'sprung' by Lemass on the Chief. Charles Haughey remembered, 'Vivion told me that

Lemass was the one who went out to Cross Avenue and told Dev "We have to form a political party; we have to get into politics."[34] The new party was to be called 'Fianna Fáil', Dev thought. Lemass, true to his disregard for neo-Gaelic nostalgia, wanted it to be called 'The Republican Party'. The resulting compromise reflected the curiously harmonious symbiosis of de Valera's functional sentimentality and Lemass's unsentimental functionalism: 'Fianna Fáil: The Republican Party'. James Ryan felt that the name had been forced on them by de Valera.[35] The term 'Fianna Fáil' is a romantic phrase invented for the Irish Volunteers by either Eoin MacNeill or an tAthair Peadar Ó Laoghaire (Father Peter O'Leary), and it means literally 'Soldiers of Destiny', echoing the romantic Gaelic past of the fianna of Fionn Mac Cumhaill and identifying the new party as the army of Ireland. Ó Laoghaire was the author of *Mo scéal féin*, a very popular, and quite vivid, autobiographical account in Irish of the lingering death of the Irish language in rural Ireland in the nineteenth century. 'Fianna Fáil' is one of the titles of the Irish armed forces, and every Irish soldier has an 'FF' badge on his cap. No one ever sued Dev for copyright, and that master politician was very adept at pinching other people's ideological clothing. Dev suggested with a smile that its greatest virtue was its endless ambivalences of meaning. Rather like 'Sinn Féin', it is a phrase that is almost impossible to translate accurately into English.

The new party was founded in the La Scala Theatre on Prince's Street, off O'Connell Street, on 16 May 1926. Dev, with his usual assumed modesty hiding a strong, even steely, sense of his own importance, described himself quite manipulatively as 'a private and with a private's liberty'.[36] Lemass and Boland became the honorary secretaries of the party. De Valera drafted the rules of the new organisation, deriving its semi-military structures from the prototype of the Irish Volunteers, much as the Sinn Féin of 1918 had been modelled on the Volunteers, and all three organisations had been modelled on Parnell's party.[37] The veterans of the prison camps showed up at the theatre; the ex-guerrillas were joined by teachers, civil servants, small businessmen, journalists, neo-Gaelic enthusiasts, students, feminists, small farmers, farm labourers, urban workers and many other humble, underprivileged but energetic and ambitious people, all seeing in Fianna Fáil their hope of a future for themselves or, at least, for their children. Kevin Boland wrote from family memory:

> They didn't just leave the La Scala. They marched out, heads held high, humming snatches of Civil War songs, back on course to the Republic clearly charted by President [sic] de Valera. … With their feet firmly planted on the road to being

'a nation once again', they scattered to the four corners of the twenty-six counties, the Free State, to light the flame in their own parishes and pave the way for the writing of Emmet's epitaph.[38]

Richard Dunphy has argued convincingly that Fianna Fáil was not a Sinn Féin under new leadership but fundamentally a different type of organisation, under semi-military discipline and almost obsessively voter-directed. Money collected from Irish–Americans dwarfed the amounts collected locally in Ireland and gave the new party the energy and means to finance a modern, card-carrying mass-membership party.[39]

The fact that the core of the new party was derived from the ruins of the defeated IRA of 1922–3 gave the new organisation much of its cohesion, internal discipline and respect for authority, combined with an attractive highly egalitarian style. The guerrillas of the defeated IRA wished for a way out of the dead end they found themselves in. In July 1923 de Valera sent a letter to all camps and prisons, urging that they be converted into miniature universities: 'The language, the history, the economics of our country can be taught and studied ... I give Education, Temperance, Organisation as your motto'.[40] As early as late 1923 prisoners in Newbridge Military Prison Camp were being taught courses in constitutional law, local government and Irish history under the auspices of a well-known Dáil civil servant, Dan O'Donovan, who ended up in the anti-Treaty ranks and tried to teach his comrades how to win in peacetime what they had lost in battle. He and other lecturers suggested that the victory of W.T. Cosgrave could actually be reversed by peaceful means under the rules of Free State democracy. Non-violent penetration of the local government representative apparatus, in particular, would, in the long term, deliver the country into their hands; capture the local councils and you will have the Dáil drop into your laps soon enough, was the message. The prisoners were particularly taken with the use of multi-seat constituencies and proportional representation by means of the single transferable vote (PR-STV), a system that is so super-fair that it appeared so even to Republican prisoners. It was dawning on their minds that Free State democracy was not as unfair and rigged as they had been led to believe by Republican propagandists. PR-STV had a powerful effect in giving the new and struggling little state legitimacy; elections were free and fair, and slowly realised to be so. The true genesis of what became Fianna Fáil occurred in the Free State's prison camps, as young guerrillas learnt the ABC of democratic politics.[41] Strangely, the fairness of the Irish electoral system did not grant forgiveness to its designers.

Fianna Fáil and the creation
of Republican politics

The first Fianna Fáil cumann was founded by Thomas Lincoln Mullins on 12 April 1926, a month ahead of the party's formal launching, and acted as an indicator of its potential popular appeal. Mullins was afterwards to be public relations officer and, later, general secretary of Fianna Fáil for many years between the 1940s and the 1970s. Born in New York of west-Cork Fenian stock, Mullins was named by his father after Abraham Lincoln. His Christian name was supposed to be Lincoln, but the priest at the registration hastily scribbled in 'Thomas'. He grew up in west Cork and inherited an American radicalism, but he was politically somewhat universalist: he was a lifelong admirer not only of Lincoln but also of the Soviet Union.[42] Better informed was his complete contempt for all post-1923 IRA successor organisations on the grounds of their political stupidity.[43] One of his proudest memories in old age was his early urging of the recognition in Catholic Ireland of the Soviet Union.[44] He also supported the idea of officially honouring Irishmen who had fallen in combat in the British Army during the world wars, a generous idea that was heresy to extreme Republicans. This somewhat inchoate mixture of radicalism, perception of politics as class war by other means, disillusion with romantic violence and an underlying generous, egalitarian liberalism characterised much of the early Fianna Fáil. Not only did some admire Joseph Stalin but some, such as Dan Breen, also admired Adolf Hitler—any radical in a storm of steel. Breen, incidentally, also jumped the gun and took the oath seven months before de Valera did.

James Ryan remembered something else: the youthful enthusiasm and administrative energy of the young men and women who found themselves in the movement, as they themselves termed it. The very words 'political party' were still distrusted. The building of Fianna Fáil was rapid and, in its way, revolutionary. 'Dr. Jim Ryan has related that for six years none of them were at home during weekends.'[45] Seán MacEntee independently made a nearly identical reminiscence.[46] The same almost fanatical dedication to political work consumed Lemass during the early years and his years in the Department of Industry and Commerce. Michael McInerney, writing in 1974, reported:

> Seán Lemass told a story of building the party in Donegal, talking to a farmer named [Neil] Blaney who was working on top of a haystack, urging him to come back after the despair

of civil war. As he waited for the farmer's hesitating decision he noticed a bare-foot young fellow running round the field. It was the future Minister for Agriculture! A start was made there and everywhere else and Lemass candidly admitted Fianna Fáil was built on the Old I.R.A.[47]

Blaney Junior remembered the incident independently:

My father and Lemass were not meeting for the first time. I recollect that my father also knew Lemass's brother Noel. As a child I recall the arrival of a motorcar in our area was still something of a novelty. Lemass got out of the car and made his way to the field where my father was saving hay. I still remember this impressive man wearing a cap and walking, what I considered to be the long way round, to where my father was working. He never discussed with me what he and Lemass talked about.[48]

Seán MacEntee, veteran Republican from Belfast, remembered:

For more than five years hardly any of us were at home for a single night or any week-end. Lemass bought up four or five second-hand Ford cars, 'old bangers', and with them we toured every parish in the country founding Fianna Fáil branches on the solid basis of Old I.R.A. and Sinn Féin members.[49]

Fianna Fáil took a considerable chunk out of Sinn Féin. Dunphy points out that many Sinn Féin Cumainn went over bodily to Fianna Fáil and that 17 of Sinn Féin's 37 Standing Committee members went over to the new party. Twenty-one of Sinn Féin's 47 TDs went over as well.[50] But this was a continuity only at a superficial level. De Valera's new party was a genuinely distinct entity, derived more from the Old IRA and the internees of 1922–3 than from the Sinn Féin cadres. Within a year, a pretty serious organisation had been set up, based systematically on polling districts at local and Dáil constituency level, the latter being far wider than the former local government level. Even nowadays, many Irish people sometimes refer to Fianna Fáil political loyalty as being essentially religious in quality. Certainly, in the 1920s de Valera was a focus for loyalty and even reverence that partook somewhat of the passion normally associated with folk religion. Fianna Fáil became a centrist party in a small and mainly rural country, a party that evolved a quasi-monopoly of state political power that was, after 1932, only sporadically challenged by a rather disorganised set of smaller opposition parties. From the beginning, Fianna Fáil set to organising itself as a true mass political party, relying on the votes, energies and resources of large numbers of minor people, rather than on the efforts and influence of local notables. In this, it was true to the tradition of the Parnellite and O'Connellite parties of the nineteenth century. More immediately, it evolved out of the Volunteer tradition and the mass mobilisation associated with the Sinn Féin of the 1918 'khaki election'.

Lemass, with his apparently endless energy, was at the centre of this, building on his reorganisation of the Dublin Sinn Féin Cumainn that became the nucleus of the new party in 1926–7. Dressed neatly in bowler hat and suit, complete with bow tie and wing-collar shirt, he drove around the country in an old Ford Tin Lizzie. De Valera—known to many of a later generation only as a blind, old man—was in his forties with plenty of energy, and he did a lot of driving as well, cajoling local veterans and leaders to join their old leader once again in what was seen as the collective search for a wider freedom.

De Valera held for a year to his public stance that the party's elected TDs would enter the Free State Dáil, but only if the Oath of Allegiance were abolished. This year provided a breathing space while the party was being built up. It was evident, however, that sooner or later they would go in to the Free State Dáil, oath or no oath. In June 1927 the new party did well, scooping up much of Sinn Féin's vote and gaining 26% of the total vote and 44 seats in a Dáil of 153 seats. Lemass won his seat in South Dublin easily. A few weeks later, Kevin O'Higgins was assassinated by a group of 'red' IRA dissidents in an incident so spontaneous and random that the police were completely baffled. Uinseann MacEoin casually threw away the scoop of the century in a long footnote in his classic biography of IRA man Harry White:

> In July 1927, on a Sunday morning at Cross Avenue, Blackrock, accompanied by Billy Gannon, one of Collins' squad, and another man (believed to be Tim Coughlan of Rathmines, who was himself shot dead six months later by undercover man Seán Harling at Woodpark Lodge, Dartry Road; we will avenge Tim Coughlan, said Seán MacEntee), he shot Kevin O'Higgins, Minister for Justice in the Free State. They were on their way to play a gaelic football match and merely stopped off in Cross Avenue. It was an operation said to have been considered by George Gilmore (the brains of the movement, Paddy Brown says of George) but discarded by him. Doyle and Gannon got there first. Briefly held for a hold

up at Kenny's, the builders in Donnycarney, in the mid twenties, unobtrusive and slight, Doyle survived on [IRA] HQ staff until 1944. Liam Burke can recall one afternoon in 1942, walking in Glasnevin cemetery, Archie [Doyle] pointed at a grave, remarking *there he is six feet down*. It was his only reference to the episode. Years later, he gave Harry [White] as a memento a short Webley: *This is the one that shot O'Higgins*, he confided in him.[51]

Things had gone too far; these gunmen, whether Free State or Republican, were a liability to Fianna Fáil, with whose leaders they had been associated by personal friendship or old comradeship. Malicious rumours were spread by prominent Fianna Fáil leaders that the Gardaí planned the assassination because they had been refused a pay rise. Others pointed the finger at prominent Republican dissenter Seán MacBride. Others again suspected the leadership of the new party, who must indeed have had an inkling of who did it, while being apparently quite unconnected with it themselves. By 1927 it was still not quite clear who was still a gunman and who had reinvented himself as a constitutional politician. Reality was descending on the Republicans. De Valera and his followers realised that they had to go in to the Free State Dáil, as Cosgrave used the pretext of the assassination to pass an act forcing all candidates for election to take their seats under the oath or forfeit the right to stand for election. Dev decided to swallow the oath, partly under casuist clerical advice that a forced oath was not binding on one's conscience, and partly on the grounds that, while signing the paper containing the oath, he was merely registering his acceptance of a seat while openly denying that he was taking an oath. Fianna Fáil entered the Dáil in August 1927, and in the subsequent election of September in that extraordinary year the party got 35% of the vote and 57 seats.[52] Fianna Fáil was already coasting home in a brilliantly conceived revival and remobilisation of popular opinion copper-fastened by the votes of farmers, farmers' sons and the small working class of the time; it is commonly forgotten that farming was the occupation of about 60% of the workforce back then, much of it subsistence or near-subsistence in character.

Lemass rapidly became deservedly famous for his organisational ability and energy. As Brian Farrell has argued, his performance as a parliamentarian has tended to be neglected.[53] However, one of his earlier contributions has become almost proverbial in the literature, and deserves somewhat closer examination than it is sometimes given. In a debate on the status of political and criminal prisoners instigated by Fianna Fáil in the Dáil on 21 March

1928, the young Lemass crossed swords with railwayman William Davin of the Labour Party, who wished to know, in a relatively sympathetic mood, if the Fianna Fáil party was actually going to adhere to constitutional methods in future. The Fianna Fáil proposal was that a select committee of the House would review the cases of Republican prisoners and activists with a view to amnesty. Davin remarked:

> I cannot decide for myself, as a result of the discussion [in the Dáil], as to who is a criminal offender or a political offender, or a semi-criminal or semi-political offender. That is for the [proposed select] Committee to do. I believe it would be a good day's work for the Dáil and will save a good deal of discussion to set up this Committee, and I hope to learn, as a result of the Committee's deliberations, the real meaning of constitutional activity as interpreted by Fianna Fáil.

Lemass, evidently stung, responded spontaneously with a phrase that was to enter into the memory of Irish popular political culture:

> I think it would be right to inform Deputy Davin that Fianna Fáil is a slightly constitutional party. We are perhaps open to the definition of a constitutional party, but before anything we are a Republican party. We have adopted the method of political agitation to achieve our end, because we believe, in the present circumstances, that method is best in the interests of the nation and of the Republican movement, and for no other reason ... Five years ago the methods we adopted were not the methods we have adopted now. Five years ago we were on the defensive, and perhaps in time we may recoup our strength sufficiently to go on the offensive. Our object is to establish a Republican Government in Ireland. If that can be done by the present methods we have we will be very pleased, but if not we would not confine ourselves to them.[54]

He was not quite yet the convinced constitutionalist, confronted as he was by a constitutional order that had not only an oath of fidelity to the British Crown in it but also a Senate dominated by pro-Treaty and ex-Unionist opinion, with considerable delaying powers on the democratic Lower House (the Dáil) and six seats reserved in the Dáil for the (mainly conservative and privileged) graduates of the two major universities in the state. However, it is clear that he had turned a constitutional corner and that he increasingly feared violence as a politics or anti-politics of unreason; he was not just appealing to the government to show mercy: he was also acting as advocate for popular political opinion, which was still wavering between sympathy for the traditional 'men on their keeping' (on the run from the police) and the democratic political order that was developing in Ireland. For Fianna Fáil to work, he and his colleagues were going to have to walk a fine line between Republican radicalism and the demands of civil society, a society that was quietly but relentlessly pushing the Republicans away from the gun and into democratic politics, or 'war by other means', to use an Irish inversion of one of Clausewitz's famous quotes. He passionately defended the men who had carried out his orders to engineer the Mountjoy breakout and, in effect, asked for an amnesty in this key Dáil speech:

> I do not want to go to prison. I am not inviting the Government to arrest me and put me on trial. Surely in this year, 1928, it is possible to draw a veil over events that happened in 1925. A lot of water has flown under the Liffey bridges since then. Many developments occurred in the political life of this country since then, and the situation which now exists bears no resemblance to the situation in 1925. I think, if those on the Government Benches, who spoke of the need of co-operation and the need for unity of effort amongst all parties meant one iota of what they said they would see the advisability of that incident, at any rate, being forgotten and of those connected with it, either members of the rescue party or prisoners rescued, being allowed to return to their homes. If it is punishment you want I think that those who took part in it have been punished enough. A man cannot be three years on the run, away from his home and family, living from hand to mouth on the countryside, without meeting with considerable hardship. If it is merely a desire to punish which is animating the Government, they can rest assured that that desire has been gratified. If they want to make unity of effort possible they must remember that the men on the run are a constant source of danger to that achievement. They are desperate. They are being hunted down like madmen, like lunatics at large, preaching the gospel of desperation. They are carrying the creed of violence into the homes they visit and amongst the people they meet and finally, sooner or later, if the Government persist in their present policy that creed of violence, that spark of violence which they are fanning to flame, will burst into flame, and this country will be driven back to the position it was in a few years ago.[55]

The sorcerer was warning everyone about the apprentice, and doing so with great sincerity. However, he did not get the amnesty he begged for yet. Lemass had chosen to go on the constitutional road, and had internalised the propositions that violence in politics was futile and that political despair and bitterness would, if encouraged and not assuaged by wise political action, consume the country. This was at the root of his later willingness to speak with, argue with, and cooperate with people who, from the Republican point of view, had Republican blood, and possibly even his brother's blood, on their hands. It was also true that he was thinking constitutionally, thinking of winning the hearts of the electorate and, of course, being Lemass, thinking of economics. By 1930 the new party was expecting a 1931 election. It actually occurred in early 1932. Lemass wrote to the Chief in January 1930:

> On the whole, prospects look good, however. I do not mean to imply that we are certain of a majority. I think that a great number of people are now on the ditch and will drop on our side if we play our cards rightly during the next six or twelve months.[56]

Consistent from the beginning, he urged the importance of a party newspaper on Dev a few weeks later.[57]

Free State soldier standing at a window during the Civil War, 1922. (NLI, INDH340)

Fighting at Nelson's Pillar during the Civil War, 1922. (NLI, INDH209)

Lemass carried shoulder high by supporters after election victory, November 1924. (UCDA, P176/1278)

Lemass addressing a crowd in Dublin, 10 July 1943.
(© Haywood Magee/Getty Images)

26. 9. 22

Dpt: Communications

To A. C.S.

1. To acknowledge your 482/A.

2. It would be much better of course if time-sheets could be printed and I am trying to get them done. I enclose a copy of those we are using now. It contains all the data necessary but is much too big.

3. I have noted the delay. The Post at Wicklow is apparently not working and. as I guessed, Ferns is also slow. I am sending a girl to re-organise this line and get it working properly.

4. I do not think it advisable to have a communications officer in each area. The work would be small and the adjt could easily do it. I could send to the adjt. of each brigade a list of the posts in his area and a general outline of the whole system. He could then be made responsible for the maintenance of the lines and to make changes where necessary and also to organise alternative routes.

Sheehan

D/Comm (Command)

Dept. Communication   2. 10. 22

To: H.A.&.S.

The following is report for this dept for last week.

Lines: All working fairly satisfactorily. The Wexford line, which was slow has improved and recent time sheets show no unreasonable delay. A test dispatch to 7.g.H.Q. by road took eight days. There is some delay on Dundalk line between Dundalk and Drogheda and I am investigating it.

Railways: We have now men on all lines, except D.S.E.R., who take dispatches and dispatches can be delivered by rail to: Belfast. Dundalk. Sligo, Longford, Athlone, Kildare, Limerick Junct. Mallow etc.

Enemy. Commns. I have gained some information about these and as sending instructions to command units which should had their interruption.

Dispatch of propaganda. We have this week delivered parcels of propaganda to 3rd and 4th Western divs.

Visual and Pigeon Commns. Nothing to report.

Cost of dept. for week   £14 : 1 : 11

                    Aiken
                    D/Commn (command)

STOP PRESS.

POBLACHT NA h-EIREANN

A Diary from the Four Courts.

JUNE 28th, 1922.

The following has been received from Father Albert at the Four Courts:—

3.40 a.m.	Ultimatum delivered.
4.20	War opened.
5.15	First Irish Republican soldier wounded.
5.15	Daly sent message: " When will you come out with your hands up?"
	Reply from O/C: " When you come for me."
	Daly: " Any chance of negotiations?"
	Reply O/C: " When your men retire."
5.40	Second man wounded.
7.40	Third man wounded.
8.40	Young Republican soldier said boldly: " We are still going strong."
8.40	We are being fired on from the Tower of St. Michan's Protestant Church, St. Audoen's, High Street, and the Medical Mission, Chancery Place. It is well to remember that from the same Medical Mission the soldiers of the Irish Republic were fired on in 1916.
	One of the boys remarked: " We are fighting the same enemy. They have only a different uniform."
12.30 p.m.	The fire was so heavy and so deafening that it was almost impossible for the priest who was hearing confessions to carry out his duties.
	The firing was carried on furiously for $7\frac{1}{2}$ hours.
	We have been heartened by the girls of Cumann na mBan and nurses and doctors who are here unselfishly giving their services to the wounded.
	After the Ultimatum was delivered to the Irish Republican soldiers, the boys all knelt down and recited a decade of the Rosary in Irish, placing themselves and their cause under the protection of the Blessed Virgin and all the patriot martyrs of the Irish Republic.

THE TREATY
GIVES IRELAND

1. A PARLIAMENT RESPONSIBLE TO THE IRISH PEOPLE ALONE.

2. A GOVERNMENT RESPONSIBLE TO THAT PARLIAMENT.

3. DEMOCRATIC CONTROL OF ALL LEGISLATIVE AFFAIRS.

4. POWER TO MAKE LAWS FOR EVERY DEPARTMENT OF IRISH LIFE.

5. AN IRISH LEGAL SYSTEM CONTROLLED BY IRISHMEN.

6. AN IRISH ARMY.

7. AN IRISH POLICE FORCE.

8. COMPLETE FINANCIAL FREEDOM.

9. A NATIONAL FLAG.

10. FREEDOM OF OPINION.

11. COMPLETE CONTROL OF IRISH EDUCATION.

12. COMPLETE CONTROL OF HER LAND SYSTEMS.

13. POWER AND FREEDOM TO DEVELOP HER RESOURCES AND INDUSTRIES.

14. A DEMOCRATIC CONSTITUTION.

15. A STATE ORGANISATION TO EXPRESS THE MIND AND WILL OF THE NATION.

16. HER RIGHTFUL PLACE AS A NATION AMONG NATIONS.

DUBLIN CASTLE HAS FALLEN !
BRITISH BUREAUCRACY IS IN THE DUST !
IS THIS VICTORY OR DEFEAT ?

SUPPORT THE TREATY

'The Treaty gives Ireland', c. 1922. Free State pro-Treaty poster. It proclaims, 'Dublin Castle has fallen! British bureaucracy is in the dust!' (NLI, Ephemera Collection, POL/1920-30/2)

PROCLAMATION

OFFER OF AMNESTY

(I.) Bearing in mind the acceptance by Liam Deasy of an immediate and unconditional surrender of all arms and men, and knowing that the reasons dictating to him that acceptance must weigh also with many leaders, and many of the rank and file, who have found themselves led step by step into a destruction that they never intended, but which has been the sequel of the line of policy adopted by those to whom they looked for leadership,

(2.) **NOTICE IS HEREBY GIVEN** that with a view to facilitating such a surrender the Government are prepared to offer amnesty to all persons now in arms against the Government who, on or before Sunday, 18th February, 1923, surrender with arms to any Officer of the National Forces or through any intermediary.

Risteard O Maolchatha, General,
Commander-in-Chief.

Dublin,
8th February, 1923.

66

HUGHES
The Foreman Spy!

HUGHES
of the notorious
Civilian Defence Force!

HUGHES of Oriel House!

People of Dublin!
DO YOU WANT THIS MAN
AS YOUR REPRESENTATIVE?

VOTE FOR
LEMASS

'Hughes the foreman spy!', 1924. Handbill soliciting support for Lemass in the 1924 by-election. It refers to his Cumann na nGaedheal opponent, Seamus Hughes, November 1924. (NLI, Ephemera Collection, LO P117 (66))

Left: 'Proclamation (R. Mulcahy) Offer of Amnesty', 1923. (NLI, Ephemera Collection, POL/1920-30/25)

Nov: 1924

'Seán Lemass stands for', November 1924. Handbill used when campaigning for Lemass in the 1924 by-election outlining his policies. (NLI, Ephemera Collection, LO P117 (65))

SEAN LEMASS

STANDS FOR

1. The re-uniting of the civil population of Ireland under the banner of the Irish Republic.

2. The administration of Ireland in the interests of the Irish people without any dictation from, or consultation with the Government of the British Empire.

3. The protection of our Industries by the imposition of adequate tariffs, with proper safeguards against profiteering.

4. The rebuilding of Ireland, not from the top down, but from the bottom up, that is, the making, first of all, of a contented foundation of Irish workmen, properly paid, properly housed, and enjoying their legitimate share of the profits derived from the results of their own labours.

5. Free education, including free books and luncheon, for children, and a proper system of scholarships, not alone enabling the child of the poorest Irishman to reach the University if sufficiently brilliant, but recouping his poor parents for the loss of his services to them during the period of his education for the State.

All these things can be achieved without the firing of another shot. England recognises now that Ireland is lost to her, if the Irish themselves only desire it ; and the English people will not allow a penny of their money or a single English life to be sacrificed in the reconquest of our island.

VOTE FOR LEMASS
AND SOCIAL JUSTICE

Published and issued by Joseph Clarke, 110 St. Stephen's Green, Dublin, Agent for SEAN LEMASS, and printed at the Wood Printing Works, Ltd.. Dublin. 2120.

MR. DE VALERA AND THE OATH.

LEGAL BARRIERS TO GO.

Mr. de Valera had a great reception when he addressed a largely attended meeting of Fianna Fail (Republican Party) at La Scala Theatre, Dublin, on Sunday. An overflow meeting of about a thousand was held outside.

In opening the indoor meeting, Mr. de Valera declared that he came there as president of nothing, but simply as a private and a Republican.

Madame Markievicz, who presided, announced that the meeting had been called " to start a new attack on the usurping Government of this island."

Mr. de Valera, who had a cordial reception, said that he felt that he would not be doing his duty to the rank and file of Republicans or to the Irish nation if he were to contemplate allowing Republicanism to be put into the position in which it would appear to be merely nominalistic formalism. The freeing of the nation was not an easy task, and could not be performed except with the enthusiasm and vigour coming from the passionate feeling of the nation. That passionate feeling could never be aroused if they were to move away from realities.

In the onward march of their movement they should act as a military commander, who, when given a task, felt that it was his duty to make sure of the exact position and strength of the enemy as well as his own. When the boys the other day rescued Jack Keogh they did not bury their heads in the sand when they set about the job. They, too, should not allow themselves to be hypnotised. Shouting unity was not enough, and some means would have to be found to bring the people together again, so that they would proceed along the same lines and not pull in opposite directions. Divided in two, the Imperial forces were bound to defeat them.

'Mr de Valera and the oath', *Irish Times*, 22 May 1926, 6. Report on the founding of Fianna Fáil the previous Sunday. (Courtesy of the *Irish Times*)

FIANNA FÁIL

(REPUBLICAN PARTY)

HEAD OFFICES:

13 UP. MOUNT STREET,

DUBLIN

Phone Nos.—Dublin 61551 and 61552.

An Coisde Gnotha—Oifigigh :

ÉAMON DE VALERA, T.D., Uachtaran.

P. Ó RUITHLEIS, T.D. ⎫
SEÁN T. Ó CEALLAIGH, T.D. ⎬ Leas-Uach.

SEÁN LEMASS, T.D. ⎫
GEARÓID Ó BEOLÁIN, T.D. ⎬ Rún Onór.

AN DOCTÚIR S. Ó RIAIN, T.D. ⎫
SEÁN MAC AN tSAOI, T.D. ⎬ Cisdeóirí.

Ceann Áṅur:

13 Sṁáiṁ an ṁóta, uaċ..

baile áta cliat

13adh Eanair, 1930.

Eamon de Valera, Esqr., T.D.

Dear Chief:-

I received your New Year Card and thank you for the good wishes.

I am very glad to know that you are optimistic concerning your prospects of doing what you went over for. I note you think that it will take you longer than you anticipated. I believe you should try to get the job finished in any case. It is the most important thing we have on hands, and no work done here would compensate for failure there. The Dail programme for February will not be very exciting. There are reasons, however, why you should try to get back for it as early as your work there permits.

I do not think that Sean MacEntee, T.D., or I should go across now. It would be unwise in view of the situation here I mean that the general political exodus to the States last year has aroused considerable comment, and unless circumstances there were very favourable our intended visit should be abandoned or, at least, postponed. Of course, if by going there we could get the wherewithall to fight the next General Election the effect here would be profitably ignored.

There is a lot of talk "about" an Election. The Political Correspondents have all being announcing it for this year and the Government have been equally voluble in asserting that they are going their full term. I believe we can expec it about June 1931. The Government can go to 1932 but will probably not do so as the Eucharistic Congress will be meeting here in that year.

114

Our most serious difficulty now is finance. We
cannot see how we are going to meet the estimated expenditure
until May next when the 1930 Collection is due. Our
estimated revenue is about £250 short. We have to stop the
present Collection this month or we will ruin the prospects
of the May Collection. We had to knock off ten of the
Organisers at the end of last month without notice, because
we had not enough to pay their allowances. The result was
not good. Things have got a little easier since. If we
could get a windfall of about £500 now it would help us over
the most difficult period.

The event of the moment is the arrival of the Papal
Nuncio. The interest aroused is much less than I anticipated
despite the efforts of the Newspapers. Our refusal to attend
the Government's "Social functions" in his honour is being
misrepresented to some extent, but appears to be generally
understood nevertheless. We are attending the Solemn
Reception in the Pro-Cathedral, of course.

The "left-wing" is making some progress at our
expense mainly in consequence of the general annoyance
of the C.I.D. Tactics, and the lack of movement in the
political situation. The sale of "An Phoblacht" is
increasing and we may loose some of our younger members
which will be serious. We must emphasise the Republican
basis of our policy this year to a greater extent than
heretofore.

The Organisation is keeping surprisingly good, and
anxious for activity. We are doing our best to give it. I
believe we will have a very good machine to fight the next
Election - much better than in 1927. Cork is holepess, of
course, and the Organiser in your Constituency must have died.
We have not heard from him in any case. If he is doing any
work he is very modest about it. On the whole, prospects
look good, however. I do not mean to imply that we are
certain of a majority. I think that a great number of people
are now on the ditch and will drop on our side if we play
our cards rightly during the next six or twelve months.

I will write again if anything happens worth writing
about. Best wishes, Is mise,

FIANNA FÁIL

(REPUBLICAN PARTY)

HEAD OFFICES:

**13 UP. MOUNT STREET,
DUBLIN**

Phone Nos.—Dublin 61551 and 61552.

An Coisde Gnotha—Oifigigh :

ÉAMON DE VALERA, T.D., Uachtaran.
P. Ó RUITHLEIS, T.D. } Leas-Uach.
SEÁN T. Ó CEALLAIGH, T.D.
SEÁN LEMASS, T.D. } Rún Onór.
GEARÓID Ó BEOLÁIN, T.D.
AN DOCTÚIR S. Ó RIAIN, T.D. } Cisdeóirí.
SEÁN MAC AN tSAOI, T.D.

Ceann Áṁur:

13 Sṁáiᵭ an ṁóᴛa, uaᴄ

baile Áᴛa Cliaᴛ

10adh Marta, 1930.

Eamon de Valera, T.D.,
Pennsylvania Hotel,
New York City, U.S.A.

A Chara:-

    I was glad to get yours of the 15th ultimo per Tadhg
Crowley, and to know that you are keeping well, although not over
optimistic concerning the success of your task there. The job of
putting the Newspaper project across in the circumstances describ
by you cannot be easy, but I hope that by the time this reaches
you the major difficulties will have been overcome.   It is
becoming more and more obvious here that we are only beating the
air without a press behind us.   The "Irish Independent" has
become more definitely hostile and than ever, and its power to do
harm amongst our own people is being repeatedly demonstrated. Ou
success at the next Election will be measured by your success now
This fact is widely understood and, therefore, the very announcem
that the United States quota has been subscribed will produce a
psychological reaction which will make victory easier.

    Everything is O.K. here.   The Organisation is alive
and active, and there is evident a greater willingness to underta
the work of propaganda and collection, than heretofore.   I
attribute this to the feeling of confidence created by the
certainty of growing public support.   In some districts, notably
Tirconaill, a veritable landslide in our favour appears to be
occuring and prominent Government supporters have been announcing
their conversion in increasing numbers.   Our success in Tirconai
has been greatly assisted by the support of the "Derry Journal"
and constitutes another instance of the power of the Press. We
are walking the tight-rope financially, of course, but so far
have managed to carry on.

Letter from Lemass to de Valera, 10 March 1930. He discusses the need for the 'Newspaper project' to get off the ground as soon as possible due to the hostility to the party of the *Irish Independent*. (UCDA-OFM, P150/3497)

- 2 -

I think I can say we have done well in the Dail this Session. There has been only one debate in which I feel we did not come out best. The biggest matter we have had to deal with was the Greater Dublin Bill, the Committee stage of which will be taken during the week after next. We won all the honours in the Second reading debate as even the "Independent" admitted. At one stage it looked as if we might defeat the Government, but they closured the Debate at the wrong time and caught us with ten absentees (mainly, sick of course). Our attendance has not been good. The Closure referred to above lead to a scene and we tabled a Motion of censure on the Ceann Comhairle, which gave Flinn a chance of getting some of his own back. This week we are taking the Report of the Imperial Conference Committee of last year and there may be some liveliness.

The most interesting situation has arisen in the Flour-Milling Industry. Rank (the British Combine) has acquired some Mills and now control thirty per cent of our capacity. The "Independent" has been campaigning against this development and has produced a situation favourable to our policy, which is now being advocated from the most unexpected quarters. On quite a number of economic issues we are obviously leading public opinion.

There are some difficulties, however, which cannot be tackled until you are home again but, on the whole, you need have no concern. Although I hope your stay there will not be prolonged after Easter, you need not hesitate if by doing so the success of your drive will be assured.

Hoping you and Sean will keep in good health.

Is mise do chara,

117

WE HAVE PEACE

REAL PEACE—NOT THE PEACE OF AN ELECTION CATCH-CRY

FIANNA FAIL, the Party salvaged by Mr. De Valera from the wreck of the Civil War—the Party whose record is uniquely a record of disturbance and shelter or assistance to disturbers of the peace—the Party that six months ago marched to Bodenstown in the ranks of the self-styled I.R.A.—have begun to spread their customary election smoke-screen. Mr. Lemass, ex-Minister for Defence in the remnant of defeated warriors who only five years ago still claimed the power of life and death over Irish citizens, now "declares officially" that the Fianna Fail policy "is one which will lead to permanent peace in this island."

Fianna Fail spokesmen still pursue the policy of saying what they don't mean and meaning what they don't say.

PEACE: By liberating the gunmen.

PEACE: By removing the only bulwark that stands between the citizen and those whom Mr. de Valera calls "Brave but misguided men."

PEACE: By legitimising the activities of Saor Eire and the I.R.A.; the Communists and the terrorists.

PEACE: By destroying the Treaty and provoking renewed trouble with England.

PEACE: By destroying the credit of the people.

Fianna Fail don't want peace. They want all the votes they can beg, borrow, or entice—TO GET THEIR REVENGE. Mr. Lemass says we misrepresent them. It isn't possible to misrepresent a party which blares with five contradictory voices at the same time. He says we have given no indication of our own policy.

OUR POLICY and OUR RECORD are written clearly across the bright face of a Reconstructed Ireland.

THEIR POLICY and THEIR RECORD are happily buried amid the ruins made by them, on which we have had to reconstruct.

That is why they have the effrontery to talk about Peace.

Vote for the Party that says what it means and means what it says.

ENSURE THE CONTINUANCE OF PEACE
BY VOTING FOR
THE GOVERNMENT PARTY

Published by Cumann na nGaedheal, 5 Parnell Square, Dublin.   Printed by the Temple Press, Temple Bar, Dublin

'We have peace—real peace', 1933. Cumann na nGaedheal election poster. (NLI, Ephemera Collection, POL/1930-40/29)

'Mr Cosgrave will think more about the unemployed', 1932. Fianna Fáil election poster. (NLI, Ephemera Collection, POL/1930-40/3)

GALLAHER'S
WAS A
REAL FACTORY
and Fianna Fail closed it down

VOTE FOR
CUMANN NA nGAEDHEA
AND GOOD EMPLOYMENT

FOUR

Political economist

'Gallahers was a real factory', *c.* 1932. Cumann na nGaedheal election poster. Gallaher's factory in the East Wall closed a little over a year after opening blaming the harsh duty rate imposed by the Fianna Fáil government in the May 1932 budget. (NLI, Ephemera Collection, POL/1930-40/30)

Student of a
dismal science

Liam Skinner was struck by Lemass's fixed conviction that he should be the architect and builder of the new state's economy, and by how he set out deliberately to become exactly that. He was also impressed by Lemass's equally fixed determination to equip himself intellectually for the job.[1] As we have seen, Lemass was fascinated by economics all his life, as he was by the allied subjects of history and politics. His leisure reading was, by contrast, pretty lowbrow: thrillers and books on the wild west, although he also enjoyed historical fiction. His interest in economics dated back to his teenage years, probably building on his schoolboy strengths in mathematics, history and English. He agreed later that it was only in the Curragh Prison Camp that he turned to serious study. Ballykinlar was, by contrast, 'a year of games and reading'.[2] As we have seen, he spent the years 1923–6 organising Dublin for political action as a role model for the rest of the country, and he gradually concluded that Sinn Féin's abstentionism and idealistic doctrinaire style were bankrupt.

De Valera did inherit from the older party a version of Griffithian protectionism and isolationism, a tradition going back to the eighteenth century and Jonathan Swift. He added cultural isolation and linguistic change to the list. Furthermore, to ensure electoral success, he also added the withholding of annuities payable by farmers to the British government in repayment of government purchasing of their landholdings under the Land Acts. In 1926 de Valera clearly nailed these ideological colours publicly to his mast: 'Ireland free, Ireland Gaelic, Ireland self-supporting, and as far as possible, self-contained economically—these are the aims which the new national organisation Fianna Fáil purposes to secure'.[3]

In harmony with this general vision, at the age of 30 Lemass was able to produce, for the young Fianna Fáil party leadership of 1929–30, an economic programme or prospectus that prefigured the policies that he was to preside over for the next 30 years. It was never published.[4] The document consists of 33 pages of typescript. The copy in Frank Gallagher's papers in the National Library of Ireland is not signed, but is ascribed to Lemass around 1929 or 1930 in what is apparently Gallagher's handwriting. The paper concerns itself with the Irish economic situation as it was two or three years before de Valera's party swept into power, and with the circumstances of post-war protectionism and depression in Europe. He offered a free-trader's paradoxical defence of protectionism:

> In recent years there has taken place a number of international Conferences of Financiers, Manufacturers, Economists and Statesmen, who met to consider the general trend of world economic development. From each of these gatherings there have come repeated and emphatic recommendations in favour of the systematic reduction or total abolition of all tariffs and other artificial restrictions on trade. There seems to be a definite movement in influential quarters in support of the idea of an international Economic policy, overriding and replacing the various and generally conflicting, National policies now in operation. The French Foreign Minister, M. Briand, has by his speeches started men thinking of the possibilities of a United States of Europe, and, as a first step to this end, the feasibility of a European Customs Union is even now being discussed by many practical businessmen. The case put forward by the International Bankers and Industrialists in support for their appeal for change from the present system is very strong. They point to the high level of prosperity now existing in the United States of America, and claim that it is due to the complete absence of trade restrictions and prohibitions in a vast area, with a huge

population, which is almost totally self-dependent in the matters of supplies of food and the new materials of industry. They assert that equally prosperous conditions can be produced in Europe, or throughout the whole world, if unlimited freedom of trade is permitted. They argue that the existence of a multitude of Customs barriers has raised the costs of production, depressed the general standard of living, and leads to a wasteful use of the world's capital resources and consequently, to abnormally high rates of interest.

Throughout Europe, where the number of Customs Units has increased from twenty to twenty-seven since the Peace Treaties, Tariffs are in most cases higher today than they were before the war, and show a tendency to increase.[5]

Whereas something close to a free-trade area had existed in Europe west of the Russian frontier before the First World War, Europe was now divided into more than two dozen customs units, tariffs were much higher and on the increase, and protectionism reigned supreme. Lemass observed that this was due to excessive industrial capacity generated by war-time production, which was now struggling to survive in peacetime and putting political pressure on the states to increase protective tariffs. The European nations, despite a general wish for free trade among financiers, were engaged in a continent-wide zero-sum game of beggar-my-neighbour. Lemass agreed that, in principle, a free-trade area was superior to what existed, and looked with wistful approval at the faraway huge continental market of the US, where the cost of living was very high but the standard of living was even higher. He essentially argued that such an American continent-wide solution was not on offer because of the realities of post-war European politics. Free trade would, in the real world, 'destroy the possibilities of remunerative employment for more than half our people'.[6] He apparently did not yet sense that a new European war was on the way, but he did see that the world around Ireland was a cold and dangerous place, where a small nation would do well to rely on its own resources as much as possible. Also, in the real world there were nations that, like Ireland, did not want to be squeezed into being a monocrop economy by the operation of an extreme version of the law of comparative advantage. That was exactly what had happened to Ireland under the Union with Britain of 1800–1922, which had had the effect of turning the island into a huge cattle ranch, condemned to import virtually all manufactured goods from the bigger and industrialised economy next door. Everything produced in Ireland could be produced more cheaply in Britain—the only, and fatal, major exception being cattle.[7] Lemass did not quite make this point, but he must have been well aware that the skills to produce other things had long since died out and been forgotten in the deindustrialisation of Ireland under the Union in the nineteenth century. Irish pastoral agriculture was very inefficient and gave little employment relative to productivity, whereas tillage would generate far more employment without necessarily displacing cattle farming, he argued. Nations and nation states, wanting to assert their individual identities and prosperity, would not go away, and would not accede easily to an international free market in the foreseeable future.

The country needed an industrial revolution to undo the effects of the long nineteenth century, he claimed. Protection over a wide range of manufactured products was the only means the party had of bringing such a revolution about. The country had some tariff barriers, but needed far more. Quite absurdly, Ireland even imported food, cement, building materials and agricultural tools. If these goods were replaced by Irish manufactures, the unemployment problem would be solved at a stroke, he asserted. There were problems: a lack of skilled workers was a big difficulty, and Lemass remarked rather innocently that he could not understand why the government was dragging its feet with the full implementation of the proposals for a full-blown technical education system put forward by a special commission. It is now known that the reason for the foot-dragging was the hostility of the bishops towards any system of education that they could not control.[8]

A general problem was the national inferiority complex, he believed. The country also needed a central bank. In addition, he felt that, in the long run, partition would have to be abolished to allow a general all-island tackling of common economic problems; he saw clearly that the longer partition lasted, the harder it would be to reverse, because vested interests in its maintenance would build up. He was not yet fully sensitive to the popular strength of partitionist unionism in Northern Ireland.

National self-sufficiency was the most important item in his list of the national interests. The independence of Ireland was achieved out of patriotic zeal, but also it was achieved by men and women who had a vision of an Ireland that was prosperous as well as free. 'Our object is to secure the highest possible standard of living for the greatest number of human beings in Ireland.'[9] If emigration was not stopped, the country would die. 'The goal of our efforts should be to keep the Irish people in Ireland and provide prosperity for them here. Everything else, even cheap living or accepted notions about efficiency, must be sacrificed to that end.'[10] Tariffs over a wide range of goods would have to be introduced; unemployment would thus be abolished:

> The absorption of 50,000 people, now idle, into remunerative employment would result in an increase in the value of the available market and provide scope for further development. The impetus thus given to the industrial machine, together with the improvement in Agriculture following on the adoption of a more progressive policy would set the Nation marching on the road to prosperity.[11]

He concluded the position paper in terms of a very nationalist rhetoric:

> In the course of this paper I have endeavoured to show that the economic policy which, in operation, will prove most beneficial to our people is that which is based on the recognition of our nationhood and which is primarily designed to protect National interests. The chief of these interests is, and should, be the achievement of economic self-sufficiency, and to that end, the preservation of our population, the improvement of the general standard of living, and the abolition of the twin evils of Emigration and Unemployment. I have endeavoured also to show that the object is attainable, but only by a courageous application of the methods which Economic Nationalism has devised and is now being used throughout Europe.[12]

He finally commented that the pro-Treaty government had been too faint-hearted, and that the Irish spirit of nationality and a collective wish that the Irish nation might live were themselves the greatest assets the country had. The document had a true revolutionary's unquestioning faith in the power of the state, in the right hands, to tackle and solve virtually any problem faced by the people. He was to have a rude awakening.

However, his argument also had a basic thrust that might be best summarised in the aphorism 'if you can't beat them, join them'; everyone else is using tariffs, and the Irish would have to tariff back, at least for some years. Nation states were not going to go away, and until a 'United States of Europe' arrived on the scene, everyone was stuck with them. Nations wished to preserve 'their distinct and separate existences', and could not be ignored as a matter of practical politics. The 'spirit of nationality' was a great force for good and evil in the world, he felt.[13] It is unclear how long he envisaged the fully blown across-the-board tariff system to last, but it seems likely he did not envisage a period longer than ten years, and hoped for a short-term shot in the arm for the economy before moving to an export-driven economy. In reality, the regime lasted over 30 years, with export drives and the gradual dismantling of tariff barriers only really starting in the 1950s. The programme enunciated by Lemass in 1929–30 was more or less that which Fianna Fáil implemented in 1932 under his stewardship. Tariff walls were erected against British products, and government was bent to assisting local concerns to engage in import substitute industrialisation (ISI) in a small home market of only 3 million people. Arthur Griffith and others had spoken of Listian tariff-protected economies that had been successful, most conspicuously nineteenth-century Germany after the *Zollverein*, but Germany was a much larger country with a far larger protected market in which to develop its economy. The US had operated an aggressive tariff system during its developmental stage as well; again, it was a huge country with a large and rapidly growing workforce and market. Ironically, although Irish protection had some success in building up a core of native industries of a wider range than hitherto, its real success seems to have been to get the country through the privations of the Second World War. There is also some incidental evidence that Lemass was willing to start winding down protectionism in the late 1930s, but the war intervened. Certainly, he lost his initial enthusiasm for tariff-driven development rather quickly. Todd Andrews was convinced that protection had been forced on Lemass by circumstance. James Ryan commented a generation later, 'Trade would have been freed up in 1938 if it hadn't been for the war.'[14] Another factor in aggravating the situation was the British riposte to the withholding of annuity payments: a trade tariff war (the 'Economic War') that lasted for half the decade and caused great damage to the cattle trade. That damage was done mainly to class opponents of Fianna Fáil and, if anything, strengthened Fianna Fáil's political position electorally. However, it certainly did the economy no good.

Lord protector

Combined with protectionism, under Lemass a determined programme of state-led and even state-run industrialisation was set about. John Leydon, a civil servant four years older than his new boss, had been offered the job of secretary of the Department of Industry and Commerce by William Cosgrave as a midnight appointment when Cumann na nGaedheal went out of power in 1932, and he turned it down. Already recognised as a brilliant civil servant, Leydon was promptly offered the post by Lemass when he came into office. Leydon accepted, and he and Lemass became an enduring partnership. A small man usually dressed in a black suit and hat, vaguely clerical in manner, Leydon was the son of a small farmer from Roscommon and had been a novice in Maynooth Seminary for two years before deciding he had no religious vocation. He served as secretary of industry and commerce until 1939, transferring then to the emergency Department of Supplies—a temporary war-time annex—and going back to the parent department in 1945. Lemass, commonly described even by opponents as an exceptionally able administrator, used to refer to Leydon as the most able man he had ever met.[15]

For some time in the early 1930s Lemass continued to remain in the constitutional shadowland of a Republicanism that was gradually coming to terms with Free State democracy. He continued, while in power, to declare the Senate, for example, as having a faulty constitutional status. However, his questioning of the political legitimacy of the Free State became increasingly muted; by 1938, to get the Treaty Ports returned from the UK, he was to sign up to amendments to the Treaty of 1921, thereby apparently giving that legal instrument some retrospective recognition. He was under heavily armed guard in the mid-1930s; elements of the renascent IRA of the time were believed to have considered his assassination, pre-sumably for what they considered his constitutional backsliding.[16] However, he had feelers out to the pro-Treaty people even before Fianna Fáil came to power. Michael Hayes wrote:

> [De Valera] was obliged in the nature of things to come and see me now and again [in my capacity as Ceann Comhairle/Speaker of Dáil] in my office but he never saluted me in the corridor. Others, like Lemass and MacEntee were quite cordial, but when in company with de Valera they looked away, which is one of the most disgusting things that I remember, even including some of the disgusting things of the Civil War. The [Fianna Fáil] backbenchers mostly—to their credit—ignored this kind of policy and mingled with their fellow-members from the same constituency and from other constituencies.[17]

Those who had fought the British were more conciliatory than those who had only post-Treaty fighting experience, he felt.[18] Hayes does not say so, but his sketch suggests the complete political dependence of Lemass and MacEntee on de Valera at that time.

Lemass received an unexpected intellectual ally for his protectionist programme in the form of John Maynard Keynes, who gave the first Finlay Lecture at UCD in 1933. Derived from the famous economist's own *Times* journalism, it expressed sympathy for policies aimed at national self-sufficiency and avoidance of the dangers of extreme economic globalisation. He expressed scepticism about an international economic system which resembled a 'parody of an accountant's nightmare'. Robert Skidelsky comments:

> For Keynes to appear in Dublin as an economic nationalist pleased the [Fianna Fáil] Irish government, but annoyed the British ... Keynes had a long private talk with de Valera, 'who impressed me distinctly favourably ... I was very glad to find that his mind was moving away from his insane wheat schemes to peat proposals which are at any rate harmless and might quite conceivably turn out well.' Cosgrave, on the other hand, was 'such a nineteenth century liberal!'[19]

An unavoidable side effect of the country's withdrawal from the British market in 1932 was the concentration of considerable economic and social power in the hands of local bureaucratic officials, politicians, businessmen and the chief executive officers of the new semi-state bodies and state-aided industries. A lot of well-connected people became rich. Imported goods were subjected to a complex system of quotas and *ad valorem* tariffs, and a licensing system was introduced as well. Inevitably, the country was filled with local monopolies, each necessarily wielding political influence and becoming, to use Lemass's own phrase, a 'vested interest'.[20] Between 1932 and 1948, approximately 100 new and separate industries were established, and nearly 1,000 new factories were built; 80,000 jobs were created, of a new and unprecedented variety.[21] It has been argued that this exaggerates the progress. Lemass himself defended his policy in 1937:

> Industrial progress has been so rapid in the last few years that mistakes were nearly inevitable, but I do not admit that they were either numerous or serious. During that time, I acted on the principle that the only way to avert

mistakes was to do nothing. As I did not intend to do nothing, I discounted the mistakes in advance.[22]

During his two decades of tenure at the Department of Industry and Commerce, including his war-time stint in the Department of Supplies, Lemass, with Leydon, was responsible for the creation of nearly 30 state boards presiding over an extraordinary range of parastatal organisations. They included a tourist board, Bord na Móna, Aer Lingus, the Sugar Company and Córas Iompair Éireann (CIE; Irish Transport Company)—an amalgamation of the Great Southern Railways (GSR) company with the long moribund canal systems and several private bus companies. The GSR had itself been an amalgamation of 30 smaller companies. During the war years, the statification of the economy increased. An emergency merchant shipping company, Irish Shipping Ltd, cobbled together from ships stranded in neutral ports or salvaged from breakers' yards in Dublin, Arklow and Cork, succeeded in keeping a minimum of essential supplies coming into the country. Irish Shipping could not get insurance for its ships, so it set up its own insurance company. Incredibly, it made a profit over the war years. Even farmers were forced to increase tillage at the expense of cattle grazing. However, one happy result of this policy was that bread was never rationed during this period. Last-minute stockpiling of fuel and essential foods paid off handsomely during what was quaintly termed 'the Emergency' of 1939–45.[23] However, during his years in the Department of Supplies, Lemass had the opportunity to visit many of the new plants that had mushroomed under the protectionist system, and he was dismayed at the ineffectiveness of the system that had been brought in with such fanfare and at such a public sacrifice. He apparently started to be privately disillusioned about protectionism at that time.[24] However, he had had his doubts about it from the beginning; he looked upon it as a Hobson's choice. His Department of Industry and Commerce of 1,000 civil servants was the largest in the state and was run, by all accounts, with great efficiency and energy. Tadhg Ó Cearbhaill, who worked with Lemass for years, reminisced:

> Lemass was always conscious of risk, but believed also that nobody was wiser for delaying a decision. They could always be changed if a 'new situation' arose, even though he might have created the new situation concerned. Even in the case of protection, import quotas were for only six months at a time. The Department [of Industry and

Commerce] was very responsive; policy failures would be reported up; it was a crack regiment.[25]

Lemass developed a folk reputation on foot of his extraordinary record in Supplies during the war years. His ability to improvise from very unpromising materials became almost proverbial. Monsignor Paddy Browne (Pádraig de Brún) of University College Galway, a well-loved and wise scholar of the period, put it in an appropriately folksy way:

> He kept the bit and the sup in our mouths, he kept our
> fires burning and our lamps lighting, he kept our lorries
> and buses and cars (some of our cars anyway) on the roads,
> he kept, almost by miracle, our trains running a couple of
> times a week, he kept up a supply of food and necessaries
> between town and town, and between town and country.[26]

Dublin folksong had a similar, if more sardonic, take on him (turf was regarded as a bogman's fuel by coal-loving jackeens):

> Bless them all! Bless them all!
> The long, the short and the tall,
> Bless Mr. Lemass above in the Dáil,
> He gave us the turf, sure it won't burn at all!

Despite the privations of war-time, Lemass was already thinking ahead in a very ambitious, even visionary, way. In 1943, for example, he raised the question of the country getting involved, after the war ended, in the manufacture of aeroplanes on a small scale.[27]

By 1946, P.L. MacEvoy, president of the Federation of Irish Manufacturers, felt able to complain of the possibly irreversible socialisation of the economy under the management of Lemass and the growing oligarchic and politicised character of the country's business leadership:

> Equally disturbing is the apparently narrow panel from
> which the directors of these companies and boards are
> chosen. Indeed, some names occur with such regularity as
> to leave the impression that services rendered in other
> capacities rather than business ability are the reasons why
> certain individuals are chosen.[28]

MacEvoy thought it even worse that civil servants were commonly appointed to these boards, because, he felt, a good civil servant could not be independently minded. He also thought that the civil service had a strong grip on Irish trade and industry and that the civil servants had come to think of themselves as indispensable and often fancied themselves as experts:

> For that reason, if for no other, he [i.e. the civil servant] will try to keep the grip on our affairs after the [war-time] conditions which caused his interference have passed. He forgets that scarcity and a consequent rising market compensated for delays and indecision inherent in bureaucratic control. In a normal competitive market such delays and indecision would be sufficient to ruin any industry or trade, and consequently that control cannot be tolerated.[29]

Lemass was a philosophical believer in private enterprise, but, paradoxically, he believed that Ireland, in his time, was incapable of developing a modern private-enterprise economy. He defended this opinion by an appeal to history. Skinner put it succinctly, paraphrasing Lemass speaking in January 1946:

> The reason for doubt about our people's attitude [to risk-taking enterprise] he attributed to historical reasons. For too long a period in our history, our people were bereft of the opportunity of enterprise in economic spheres, and compelled to wait until other nations had moved ahead before being allowed to follow.[30]

Irish people had been denied the skill of entrepreneurship not by some Weberian absence of the Protestant ethic and the spirit of capitalism but by imperialism, by an extreme form of comparative advantage that had morphed into comparative disadvantage, and by simple indifference and neglect on the part of faraway political masters.

Air travel was a particular enthusiasm of Lemass. He was, in many ways, the founder of what became Aer Lingus ('Air Fleet') in the mid-1930s, and he pushed its expansion after the war, getting the company to buy Douglas DC-3 and Vickers Viking airliners for the British and Continental services. He was also very much in favour of an Irish-run transatlantic service, and he engineered the purchase of five Lockheed Constellation aircraft for the Atlantic run in 1946–7. The Constellation was virtually the only large commercial aircraft capable of making the run safely at that time. This project was closed down by the incoming inter-party government in 1948, and the airliners were sold to the British Overseas Airways Corporation. The British could not believe their luck as they exchanged depreciating sterling for the almighty and desperately scarce dollars that the Irish had apparently thrown away. Shortly afterwards, the new chassis- and engine-building project set in train for CIE at the Inchicore works in west Dublin was closed down, with the jigs and other equipment being sold back to Leyland Motors Ltd and other concerns in England.

Lemass made his usual comment on reverses of this kind. Instead of arguing profit and loss, he, in effect, argued for training and education on the job. Some of the capital invested in developing the skills of the Irish workforce had been lost, he felt, by these closures. The central need of the Irish economy was to increase the proportion of workforce jobs that involved high degrees of training and technical knowledge.[31] Implicitly, he saw the workforce as undereducated, yokelised and ill-trained, but intelligent, willing and of a great, if unrealised, potential. Lemass saw his industrialisation programme as being partly educational and conceived it as being a gigantic on-the-job training programme for the entire workforce. Without using the phrase, he was really pushing for investment in human capital on a large scale; economic activity became an educational experience. This cut across conventional economists' short-term profit-and-loss styles of thinking. He was also very much a man of his time; state-led industrialisation had apparently been very successful in the Soviet Union and Nazi Germany, and Roosevelt's US had also engaged in similar experiments. Sweden was another much-touted role model of those years. His idea of parastatal on-the-job education may also have been seen by him as a way of avoiding clerical obstructionism in the mainline educational and training system.

Possibly, he never thought about it this way, but his stance is reminiscent of Alexander Hamilton, who used the emergent American federal government to build up the infrastructure for an American industrial revolution in the 1790s; perhaps Lemass was a Hamiltonian. Despite his policies not being all that unorthodox by the standards of his historical epoch, he certainly did not have things his own way. Not only did he have a barrage of aggressive criticism coming from Fine Gael, but he had enemies inside his own camp. Gerald Boland, joint honorary secretary with Lemass of Fianna Fáil since the founding in 1926, did not think much of Lemassian ISI. Kevin Boland reminisced:

> My father had a very sarcastic tongue. Above all he didn't agree with Lemass's industrial policy, setting up all these little factories everywhere making inferior goods and huge

profits. Later it became personal. He [Boland] believed more in industry based on fish, food and farming. He was particularly opposed to the CKD car assembly business as a fake 'industry' producing an inferior article for which you paid double the price. He used to refer scornfully to 'back-lane factories'. He didn't see why we should, for instance, attempt to beat places like Sheffield at their own game—although ironically Newbridge Cutlery was one of the successes. I remember that we paid for it during the war, trying to shave with the razor blades that were made here.[32]

In actuality, back-lane factories were sometimes important and successful enterprises in post-war Ireland.

A puritan among clientelists

Lemass presided over a federation of local monopolies, protected by legislation essentially devised by him. Jack McQuillan, a veteran Clann na Poblachta TD in Roscommon for many years and a man of left-wing views, knew Lemass quite well. He saw that Lemass was sometimes disliked for good reason. Lemass despised favouritism; '[he] was quite unpopular among many FF TDs, in particular those … who built their political fortunes on patronage and jobbery'. He thought that Lemass had little confidence in such people doing much to salvage rural Ireland.[33] On the other hand, his beloved semi-state bodies were subject to similar infections. Lemass tried to shelter them from Dáil supervision so as to keep them out of the clientelist networks of the Fianna Fáil party, or any other party for that matter. McQuillan, who admired Lemass, reminisced:

while L[emass] didn't believe in jobbery and wanted to shield the operations of the semi-states from the Dáil for this very reason, many of the FF people appointed to boards etc. operated them as fiefdoms. L[emass] … actually tried through procedure and privileges to prevent questions about semi-states being raised in the House.[34]

As early as 1949, the *Irish Independent* commented editorially about Lemass's dilemma; personally quite puritanical and honest, even naive, about financial matters, he was, while in office, surrounded by people who saw him as a powerful person who could be a source of great profit to them. In late 1947, for instance, he wrote a note to Gerry Boland, minister for justice, concerning one Frank Dunne of Limerick, who was boasting locally about political influence in getting import licences from Industry and Commerce; he had never applied for one, or received one, and was a prominent local member of Fianna Fáil.[35] In 1948 this dilemma had been inherited by Daniel Morrissey, who was then sitting in Lemass's seat as minister for industry and commerce. The *Irish Independent* commented:

> There is something slightly amusing in the attitude of a Government which, while itself setting up monopolies on the grand scale, at the same time initiates an enquiry into other alleged monopolies. From the point of view of the public, there is little to choose between a combination created by means of nationalisation and one brought into being by arrangements between commercial enterprises. Both, as a rule, take little heed of the interests of the consumer, who undoubtedly would be better served by the operation of healthy competition.[36]

Lemass was almost haunted by the pervasive personalism of Irish political culture, and went out of his way to try to set a counter-example by his own personal behaviour. Quite deliberately trying not to know the names of his own civil servants was only one example of this attempt to swim against the cultural tide. His daughter Sheila remembered:

> [He was] very opposed to jobbery and corruption in relation to members of his family. When boxes of tea came during the war he'd make us send them back. He was unhappy with the appointment of Jack O'Brien [husband of Peggy Lemass] as his Aide de Camp, although it was for good reasons. Family learned quickly enough not to come to him to ask him to intercede for them even though he'd do it quickly enough for others![37]

A crash of an Aer Lingus DC-3 airliner in Wales in 1952 impelled Lemass to insist on flying by DC-3 himself so as to instil confidence in air travel and in the specific aircraft type.[38] In 1958 Lemass had to court extreme unpopularity inside the Fianna Fáil parliamentary party by enforcing meritocratic hiring practices in his beloved Aer Lingus. The chairman of the company, Jeremiah (Jerry) Dempsey, a veteran administrator in the airline and in Irish Shipping during the war years, circulated the Fianna Fáil parliamentary party, essentially telling them that canvassing would disqualify. Dempsey was a key ally of Lemass from early on as reported by a party member:

> lively debate [occurred] on [a] letter from Aer Lingus to each member of the [parliamentary] party warning them not to recommend any person for employment with Aer Lingus. An Tánaiste [Lemass] explained that he felt no obligation to defend Aer Lingus in regard to the action of its Chairman in this instance but stated that any disqualifications of candidates who applied for positions in the service of Aer Lingus were due to the breach by them of an undertaking given by each applicant in his (or her) application form not to use influence, political or otherwise [in the course of their application]. It emerged from the discussion that the majority of the party strongly resented the letter but no decision was taken on the motion.[39]

Tadhg Ó Cearbhaill remembered that Lemass was not hostile to the leaders of the industries that had been set up under his protectionist system, even though they tended to form a bloc that would defend the protectionist system long after it had outlived its usefulness. On the contrary, he felt a loyalty to them and considered himself responsible for their welfare, the well-being of their workers and the projects that they tended:

> On protection, he had a sense of loyalty to those who had set up industries under protection, and was sensitive to the danger that with the dismantling of protection they might lose the all-important home market. He could have been thinking of people like Joe McGrath, Joe Griffin, Barney O'Driscoll of Nenagh and Vincent Crowley...
>
> Between '51 and '54 he loosened up on ownership policy, but gingerly. At the same time he began to encourage exports; and he was coming to the conclusion that one of the keys to progress was technical know-how which could be imported from abroad. Irish Management Institute established 1952; John Leydon involved? The Government also spent a lot on apprenticeship training at around this time.[40]

A gradual consensus emerged among leaders in the 1950s that 'something would have to be done', as the country was slipping further and further behind the recovering economies of Western Europe. An early turning point was Lemass's abortive attempt in 1947–8 to get governmental control of tendencies towards economic monopoly so as to nip them in the bud. Whitaker remembered, 'I had the impression that Lemass was already converted [to free trade]. 1947 was critical—the Industrial Efficiency Bill. After that a complete change of mind'.[41] Lemass himself reminisced rather understatedly in the 1960s that 'Our general assumption that pre-war development policies would still be applicable to the post-war situation died slowly'.[42]

A further turning point was the arrival of Marshall Aid and American economic experts in 1945, with the idea of a drive towards European free trade finally looking like a real prospect. From Lemass's point of view, and perhaps from the country's also, a crucial circumstance was Fianna Fáil's loss of power in early 1948, to be followed by a series of alternating governments until 1957. This was caused mainly by the emergence of a 'New Republican Party' in the form of Clann na Poblachta, led by Seán MacBride, son of Maud Gonne and 1916 martyr John MacBride. The release of IRA internees in 1945 provided a miniature reprise of Lemass's transformation of the 1923 internees into a political force of unrivalled power twenty years earlier. A bitter school-teachers' strike in 1946 also strengthened the new splinter party sufficiently to deprive Fianna Fáil of a crucial margin of strength. Fine Gael, an apparently dying party, found itself miraculously strengthened by its unexpected accession to power in 1948. Lemass's power base was shaken by the weakening of de Valera and his party in the late 1940s and 1950s. Long before 1952, however, Lemass had turned against protectionism, but he still expressed himself cautiously, not wishing to scare the horses in the forms of the employers and the unions:

> The days of the sellers' market were definitely over [in Ireland], and from every angle that should be regarded as good … The case for a protection policy was that, by assuring the available market to Irish industries, it created the opportunity of expanding output and thereby getting unit costs down. The danger of it was that it might come to be regarded, both by factory owners and their staffs, as an acceptance by the Irish community that costs must necessarily be higher here than elsewhere and an assurance that higher prices would be permanently accepted. That fact was that behind tariff protection, many industries had

now reached the stage of their development at which installed capacity was adequate to meet maximum internal demand, and that any contraction of that demand, due to adverse public reaction to price increases, meant a situation in which total sales would decline, and, in which only those factories could maintain full production which could secure continued public support by reason of better quality or price, and in which those who could not draw support on those grounds might go by the wall ... Where an industry had problems due to rising prices causing sales to contract the remedy would have to be sought first in revised methods of working which would get costs down, and not by trying to bolster up high costs by higher protection.[43]

He was also concerned for the sociological impact of factory work on the sense of local community, arguing in true Griffithian (and de Valeran) fashion for factories in small towns, rather than in Dublin, to help stabilise rural and small-town communities, despite being perfectly well aware that industrialists, by and large, preferred to be in the big towns, where infrastructure, while never marvellous, at least existed and achieved tolerable levels of adequacy. Also, big towns were far more likely to have sufficient supplies of trained labour. In a very localist culture like Ireland's, location was important; capital had to chase labour as much as labour chased capital. In Athlone in 1952, at the opening of a factory, he remarked in a speech that sounds suspiciously like a piece of Lemass trying to sound like de Valera:

With industrial development has come industrial strife and the danger of perpetual class warfare which is one of the gravest problems of our day and a certain destroyer of civilisation as we know it ... [there is a common interest between workers and management so that the workers] recognise that their factory had become for them not merely a place to earn a living, but a stabilising force around which they can develop satisfactory lives ... That sense of common interest ... could be more readily developed in small towns than in the less personal, more materialistic atmosphere of a large city. It is the strongest of practical arguments in favour of industrial decentralisation ...

In this country we should be able—with our deep religious sense and our acceptance of Christian teaching, and because our entry into industrial development has been so long delayed—to produce a better kind of industrial organisation than has developed elsewhere, and maybe show some more powerful nations a way out of their social problems.[44]

By 1955 Lemass had moved further in the direction of free trade, and was making Aesopian references to a possible emendation or partial abolition of the Control of Manufactures Acts introduced in 1932–3 to limit foreign investment in Irish companies. Looking back over the previous quarter-century, he expressed his disappointment at the extent to which economic progress remained pretty much without dynamism and depended on governmental stimuli. The reasons were political and cultural, he felt. There had been a lot of business hostility to Fianna Fáil in the early years, and to the 'national struggle' as well. History had sapped Irish self-confidence and initiative. However, he admitted that the restrictions that had been put on foreign capital by Fianna Fáil governments were part of the reason for Irish economic stagnation. Perhaps, he meditated out loud, these restrictions should be removed. Here, he was clearly flying a kite. On the other hand, he observed, Irish investors and banks were still hostile to Irish development. Full employment would entail the creation of 20,000 jobs per year, apparently envisaged as continuing over at least five years.[45]

Lemass, despite his acceptance of capitalism and state-led private enterprise, saw himself as being left of centre. He felt farmers were politically conservative and economically inefficient, and saw them as a brake on the system; the future lay with the city and with non-agricultural employment. He was keen on welfare programmes for the workforce: he helped to introduce workers' insurance, wet-time pay and unemployment and retraining programmes, and he supported the massive social-housing drive introduced by the Fianna Fáil government of the 1930s. While sympathetic to trade unions, he wished to see them amalgamated and debalkanised, and also disliked seeing so many unions being based in London rather than within Ireland. Lemass's authoritarian and top-down Industry and Commerce protectionist empire, although much weakened after 1957, did hang on well into the 1970s in attenuated form. J.C. Holloway remembered:

Until [Irish entry into] the European Community in the early seventies, Industry and Commerce was ruling by ukase. Every problem big or small could be met by a direction: lower a quota, raise a duty, stop the exporting of scrap metal etc. (for Irish Steel). Every balance sheet should be pre-determined: Ceimicí Teoranta, for example, to a lesser extent Bórd na Móna.[46]

His near obsession with economic transformation was lifelong. Ben Kiely, the well-known writer, reminisced:

> On the one occasion on which I had had a long talk with the great Taoiseach, Seán Lemass, and when I had had the temerity to reproach him (Reproach? Me? Him?) with his cavalier attitude, or so I thought, to what I called the Arts, he said, with kindly forebearance [sic], that if he couldn't make the country pay its way there would be nothing in it for writers, artists, or anybody else. Thanks to the work and inspiration of that great man a change came about.[47]

While being strict-living, he was not without appetite and humour. No drinker, he would occasionally have a glass of wine or a shot of whiskey. He loved pipe smoking, and was addicted to an evil-sounding black tobacco called *Bulwark*. Apparently, he actually *inhaled* the stuff. He bought his regular supply from Flanagan's tobacconists in Merrion Row, around the corner from his office in Kildare Street. Flanagan's also supplied both de Valera and Lemass with the services of a barber. Needless to say, it was a Fianna Fáil shop. At one stage in the post-war period, Wills, the company that made the tobacco, decided to discontinue the manufacture of *Bulwark* plug; Lemass was apparently one of the last users of it in the world. He got on the phone to the company and (presumably humorously) threatened to close them down if they committed such a crime. A compromise was reached: the company manufactured a year's supply, vacuum-packed it and sent him the enormous amount of two pounds of *Bulwark* a week. It is not recorded whether it was free of charge; given his character, he probably insisted on paying for it.[48]

When not running the nascent Irish industrial economy, Lemass had what amounted to an alternative career in journalism while out of office. During his period in opposition between 1948 and 1951, Lemass threw himself into running the Fianna Fáil paper, the *Irish Press*. Unlike its rival Dublin daily papers, the *Irish Independent* and the *Irish Times*, the *Press* ignored the subsistence rural economy and its small farmers from which so many of its readers were descended, other than for purposes of nostalgic recollection and sentimentality. Between October 1949 and March 1950, the paper published 116 articles in a series entitled 'Any jobs going?', which outlined possible careers for its cross-class readership.[49] These jobs covered an astonishing range: from tiler, welder, carpenter, private soldier, cinema usherette and air hostess through to locksmith, bookbinder, silversmith and electrician, up to ship's captain, architect, actuary and secondary-school teacher. Farming, except in the sense of 'scientific farmer', was ignored studiously as were careers as university lecturers or professors as they were well-known Fine Gael, clerical or Trinity jobs.[50] Lemass insisted, admittedly in a context of electioneering in January 1948, that Fianna Fáil was not a 'class party' but a 'Workers' Party.'[51] Actually, it was a party that was creating an entire new range of non-agricultural classes, from a skilled working class through to senior administrators, union organisers and businessmen. Fianna Fáil, after a generation in power, had created its own electorate. Lemass was well aware of this. In particular, he was not keen on lawyers, and latterly prided himself on having participated in a government that contained no lawyers, even though before the Rising he had been probably destined to go for legal training. He remarked that 'legal training was the worst kind of training for a political career', as it taught one to use words to prove a predetermined state of affairs rather than to investigate with an open mind.[52]

John Leydon, secretary, Department of Industry and Commerce; Lemass; John Dulanty, Irish High Commissioner in London; and James Ryan, minister for agriculture, pictured in London during negotiations for the Anglo-Irish Trade Agreement, *c.* 25 April 1938. (© Irish Press Plc)

Fianna Fáil Cabinet, 9 March 1932. Standing, left to right: Seán MacEntee (minister for finance); Seán T. O'Kelly (vice president of the Executive Council and minister for local government and public health); Joseph Connolly (minister for posts and telegraphs); Lemass (minister for industry and commerce); Gerald Boland (not in Cabinet); seated, left to right: Frank Aiken (minister for defence); P.J. Ruttledge (minister for lands and fisheries); Eamon de Valera (president of the Executive Council and minister for external affairs); James Ryan (minister for agriculture); Tomás Ó Deirg (minister for education), unknown. (Courtesy of the National Library of Ireland)

Eamon de Valera and members of his Cabinet (including Lemass (minister for supplies, 1939–43), Seán MacEntee (minister for industry and commerce, 1939–41), James Ryan (minister for agriculture, 1938–43) and Oscar Traynor (minister for defence, 1938–9)) saluting the colours outside the GPO, O'Connell St, *c.* March 1940. (© Hans Wild//Time Life Pictures/Getty Images)

Piles of shells being produced at the Ministry of Supply factory in Northern Ireland, 6 April 1940. While the South remained neutral, Northern Ireland played an active part in the war and the manufacture of munitions. (© Fox Photos/Getty Images)

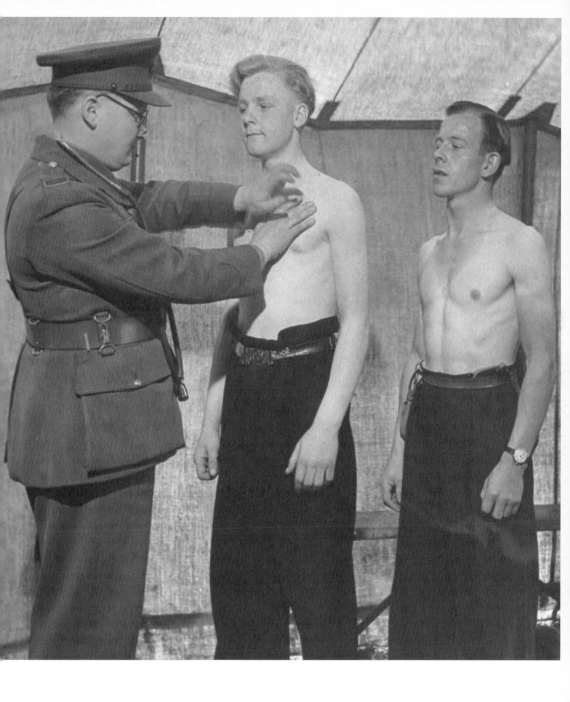

New recruits being examined in an emergency tent at Collins' Barracks, 1941.
Following the invasion of France, Belgium and the Netherlands in May 1940 a
recruitment drive began to bolster Ireland's defences. Just over a month later
25,000 men had volunteered. By March 1941 the army numbered over 41,000.
(© William Vandivert//Time Life Pictures/Getty Images)

Devastation following the Dublin bombings, 1941. (NLI, IND43.965)

ARE YOU A CASUALTY?

"We are in a fight. There must be casualties."

(Mr. LEMASS).

1931	1932
THE BEST IN THE WORLD	**THE WORST IN THE WORLD**
"On the whole it is true to say that the depression has so far affected the Irish Free State probably less than any other Country in the World."	"Of the more important industrial and agricultural countries, the Irish Free State was hardest hit by unemployment during 1932, its unemployed increasing by 241 per cent."
League of Nations, Economic Committee, 1931	International Labour Office Survey, 1932

YET Mr. DE VALERA HAS SAID:—

"There has been no increase of unemployment as has been suggested by our opponents."

(At Strokestown, January, 11th.)

Is the International Labour Office "our opponent"?

Official Statistics issued by Mr. Lemass show an increase of over 73,000 unemployed.

Is Mr. Lemass an opponent of Mr. De Valera?

BRING BACK COSGRAVE
AND BRING BACK PROSPERITY

By Voting in the order of your choice— 1, 2, 3, 4, 5

BECKETT, J. Walter
DOYLE, P. S.
HENNESSY, T., Doctor
KEOGH, Myles, Dr.
McGUIRE, James, B.L.

THE CUMANN NA nGAEDHEAL CANDIDATES

'Devvy's circus', 1932. Cumann na nGaedheal election poster styled as a Victorian circus playbill. Lemass referred to this poster in the Dáil on 20 April 1932. He reported that an acquaintance had commented on the poster and had asked the Cumann na nGaedheal agent if he thought the opposition would do well in the election. The agent responded in no uncertain terms that blood would run in the streets if Fianna Fáil were elected. (NLI, Ephemera Collection, POL/1930-40/1)

Left: 'Are you a casualty?', 1933. Cumann na nGaedheal election poster. (NLI, Ephemera Collection, POL/1930-40/28)

DEVVY'S CIRCUS

ABSOLUTELY THE GREATEST ROAD SHOW IN IRELAND TO-DAY!

57—Star Performers—57

Will Visit this Town any time between now and the GENERAL ELECTION!

SENOR
DE VALERA

World-famous Illusionist, Oath Swallower and Escapologist. See his renowned Act: "Escaping from the Straight Jacket of the Republic." Everyone Mystified!!

JIFFY
GEOGHEGAN

Champion Quick-change Artist! Watch him transforming himself from Toff to Hard-boiled Egg!

FRANK
F-AIKEN

THE FEARSOME FIRE-EATER. See him Make Faces at the British Lion!

JOHNNY MAGINTEE

Fresh from the Gold Rush. In "On Again! Off Again! Gone Again! 'DONE' AGAIN!"

THE GREAT
HUGO

The Mystery Man. Who is he? MISFORTUNES TOLD.

SHAUNTY
O'KELLY

(Who has appeared in every Capital in Europe). "The Man in Dress Clothes!!"

STUPENDOUS ATTRACTION!
MONSIEUR
LEMASS

FAMOUS TIGHT-ROPE PERFORMER. See him cross from the Treaty to the Republic on the tight-rope every night: MARVELLOUS PERFORMANCE!

PERFORMING FROGS
CHAMPION CROAKERS!
MARVELLOUS TRAINED SHEEP!

By Special Request the Senor will try his fifth chance at the Greasered Poll.
LUCKY DIP
(IF IT COMES OFF).

Published by Cumann Na nGaedheal, 5 Parnell Square, Dublin. Printed by the Temple Press, Temple Bar, Dublin.

WILLS'S BULWARK
CUT PLUG TOBACCO

Wills's *Bulwark* Magazine Advert, 1920s. *Bulwark* was Lemass's favourite brand of tobacco. (© Advertising Archives)

Opposite page: 'Bomb havoc in Rialto' news ad, 3 January 1941. German bombs had hit Dublin, Wicklow, Carlow and Wexford the previous day. On 3 January the bombs that hit Dublin injured twenty people. (NLI, Ephemera Collection, NEWS/1940-50/1)

Irish Independent

DUBLIN, FRIDAY, JANUARY 3, 1941.

BOMB HAVOC IN RIALTO

HITLER

HEAR THE TRUTH ABOUT HITLER GERMANY !

ERNST TOLLER

The World Famous Author Who Was Exiled
By The Hitler Government

WILL SPEAK AT A

GREAT PUBLIC MEETING

IN THE

RATHMINES TOWN HALL

On Sunday, January 13, at 7.45 p.m.

MR. F. R. HIGGINS
Member, Irish Academy of Letters, Will Preside

MISS DOROTHY WOODMAN, London, Dr.
A. J. Leventhal, M.A., Mr. R. J. Connolly,
Mr. Peadar O' Donnell, Mr. Sean Murray,
and others will also speak

ADMISSION 6d. and 1s.   (Payable at door)   GALLERY FREE

Support the world demand for release of

ERNST THAELMANN

(The Famous Leader of the German Workers)
and all anti-Fascist prisoners

ISSUED BY THE IRISH LABOUR LEAGUE AGAINST FASCI

'Hear the truth about Hitler Germany!'
handbill, January 1935. Ernst Toller,
playwright was outlawed in Germany on
28 August 1933, the same day as,
amongst others, writer Heinrich Mann.
Artists and critics of the National Socialist
and German Workers' Party had their
citizenship revoked for 'injuring' German
interests and showing a lack of loyalty to
the Reich. (NLI, Ephemera Collection,
POL/1940-50/2)

Opposite page:
'Ireland's position in the war: Dáil debate'
news ad, 23 March 1939. The poster
refers to the debate of the previous night
during which the general consensus was
that neutrality was the ideal but the idea
of achieving it while still retaining close
links with Britain was considered nigh on
impossible. (NLI, Ephemera Collection,
NEWS/1930-40/1)

IRELAND'S POSITION IN WAR : DAIL DEBATE

THE IRISH PRESS

THURSDAY, MARCH 23, 1939

Mr. Lemass opens a New Factory for

'Mr Lemass opens a new factory for making keys for opening new factories', *Dublin Opinion* (n.d.). (Courtesy of the National Library of Ireland)

g keys for opening New Factories.

AIR RAID PRECAUTIONS
ISSUE OF RESPIRATORS

Notice to Members of the Public.

1.   The respirator which has been issued to you is on loan to you from the Minister for Defence.

2.   Only persons resident within the boundaries of the following County Boroughs, Boroughs or Urban Districts will be supplied free with respirators :—Dublin, Cork, Limerick, Waterford, Dundalk, Drogheda, Dun Laoghaire, Bray, Wexford and Cobh.   If you are changing residence to any place outside the areas mentioned, you should notify your Warden and surrender the respirator to him.

3.   You must take proper care of your respirator.   After you have been fitted, the respirator should be left in the box, except you are advised otherwise by the authorities.   The box should be kept in a cool place away from strong light.   If the respirator gets damp from any cause, e.g. from breath, it should be dried gently with a soft cloth before being put away.   It should not be dried by heat.   It should not be carried or hung by the straps, but should be kept properly packed in the cardboard box in which it is supplied.   Care must always be taken to avoid damage to the window which is easily cracked or broken.

4.   From time to time your Warden will ask you to produce your respirator for inspection.   You should facilitate him and any other person whom the Minister may direct to carry out the inspection.

5.   You are responsible for the safe custody of your respirator and it should be retained in your custody.   Should the respirator be lost or damaged, you should report the loss or damage to your Warden immediately.

6.   **The respirator gives no protection whatever against ordinary coal gas.**

7.   Your life and the lives of those dear to you may depend upon the possession of properly fitting respirators in good condition.   The Government, therefore, ask you to co-operate in the preservation of this property.   While the majority of citizens will from common sense motives alone, apart from a sense of civic duty, take proper care of their respirators, unfortunately there may be some who through thoughtlessness or wilfulness may fail to observe the conditions attaching to the issue.   As a deterrent, therefore, it has been necessary to provide for penalties against any person abusing the scheme.   The maximum penalties vary from £5 to £100 and in certain cases also a sentence of imprisonment may be imposed on conviction.

DEPARTMENT OF DEFENCE.

November, 1940.

'Deep litter means better lay for smaller outlay', 1950s. Booklet written by Joseph O'Leary for Bord na Móna encouraging the use of cheap peat as litter in outbuildings to encourage 'peak production' of eggs. (Courtesy of Bord na Móna)

Left: 'Air raid precautions/respirators' handbill, November 1940. Controversy ensued towards the end of November 1940 regarding the manufacture of these gas masks. They were purchased from Britain rather than being manufactured in Ireland. (NLI, Ephemera Collection, POL/1940-50/3)

DEEP LITTER MEANS

BETTER LAY FOR

SMALLER OUTLAY

PUBLISHED BY BORD NA MONA, 28/31 UPPER PEMBROKE STREET, DUBLIN

OIFIG AN AIRE SOLÁTHAIRTÍ,
(OFFICE OF THE MINISTER FOR SUPPLIES),

BAILE ÁTHA CLIATH.
(DUBLIN)

8th January, 1941.

His Grace the Most Reverend John C. McQuaid, D.D.
Archbishop's House,
Dublin.

My Lord Archbishop,

I am anxious to enlist your Grace's active assistance in the promotion of a campaign to safeguard our supplies of essential foodstuffs by securing the maximum measure of agricultural production during the coming season.

The country, as you know, has hitherto been dependent to a very substantial extent on imported wheat to provide bread for the community and on imported maize to feed to livestock and poultry. Because of the scarcity of available shipping the prospects of securing a continuance of such imports are now so poor that unless we are able to grow in this country enough food to support our whole population we are going to find ourselves in a very critical position. The difficulties of the situation can, of course, to a considerable extent be alleviated by the substitution of potatoes and porridge for bread: but the most satisfactory position would undoubtedly be one in which we would grow enough wheat for our requirements.

I would, therefore, ask you, on behalf of the Government, to use your influence with a view to getting farmers in your Archdiocese to produce the maximum possible crop of wheat, as well as of sugar beet, barley, oats and potatoes; and as we cannot reckon on any substantial imports of maize or animal feeding stuffs farmers should produce as much as they can of those crops which can be used for feeding to livestock and poultry.

I should be very glad if, in addition to using your own influence in this direction, you would ask the clergy, teachers, and other influential persons in your Archdiocese to help as much as they can so long as the emergency lasts.

I enclose, for your Grace's information a copy of a recent broadcast address by my colleague the Minister for Agriculture on this subject.

I beg to remain,

Your Grace's obedient servant,

Letter from Lemass to John Charles McQuaid, archbishop of Dublin, asking for assistance in encouraging farmers to maximise the growth of crops, 8 January 1941. (DDA, AB8/b/XVIII/file 51)

[signature]

Minister for Supplies.

2nd March, 1943.

His Grace The Most Rev. John Charles McQuaid, D.D.,
Archbishop of Dublin,
Archbishop's House,
Dublin.

Your Grace,

Encouraged by the good results that have hitherto attended the efforts of the Clergy to stimulate the production of turf during this period of emergency I am taking the liberty of again seeking the favour of your assistance in this matter.

The position with regard to the availability of coal is continually deteriorating, and in this year to a greater extent even than in 1942 we shall be forced to rely on our own resources in the provision of fuel, both for domestic and industrial purposes.

I should be most grateful if you could see your way to use your good offices to ensure that the Clergy in these districts in your Grace's diocese where turf is available may continue to impress on their people the importance of producing the maximum amount of turf during the coming season, so as to meet not only their own requirements but also to provide a large surplus for sale in the neighbouring towns or for removal to the non-turf producing areas. Turf producers may be assured that no turf of good quality offered for sale at a reasonable price will be left on their hands.

I am confident that your valued help will be willingly given in this matter, the importance of which to the welfare of the people you will fully appreciate.

I remain, Your Grace's Obedient Servant,

Minister for Supplies.

Letter from Lemass to McQuaid requesting that the clergy encourage the public to stimulate turf production, 2 March 1943. (DDA, AB8/b/XVIII/file 51)

COPY.

Archbishop's House,

Dublin.
3rd March, 1943.

Dear Minister,

I have just received your note concerning greater turf production.

I shall certainly see to it that the Clergy urge the people of turf-producing areas to obey the Government's instructions.

If, however, you fail to see a pronouncement from me, you will kindly understand that I have my own way of quietly securing that the Priests will assist you.

With kind regards,

I remain, dear Minister,

Yours sincerely,

John C. McQuaid,
Archbishop of Dublin.

Sean F. Lemass, Esq., T.D.,
The Minister for Supplies.

'Travel the easy way', Aer Lingus bookmark, c. 1948. (NLI, Ephemera Collection, TVL/1950-60/4)

IRELAND

CIRCULAR

TRAIN

TOURS

BY  CIE

INFORMATION: YOUR LOCAL TRAVEL AGENT OR COMMERCIAL

AER LINGUS....

Aer Lingus timetable (cover shot), 1950/1. Timetable effective from 22 October 1950 depicting Dublin Airport with the main control tower in the background. (NLI, Ephemera Collection, TVL/1950-60/6)

...flies on **BP**

Aviation Gasoline

A PRODUCT OF ANGLO-IRANIAN OIL CO

FIVE

Leader

Lemass poses at the helm of a ship, 1960s. (© Irish Press Plc)

✸ Propagandist

As the Second World War wound to its grisly end, Lemass had resumed his accustomed role as chief industrialiser, but in very chastened mood. The experience of protectionism had been a disappointment, and it had become obvious that, beyond certain very narrow limits, protectionism was a developmental dead end in a small country, whatever its effectiveness might have been when applied by mighty countries like the nineteenth-century US or Germany. Under protectionism in Ireland, little factories were producing inferior goods at inflated prices for small local markets. British-made goods were smuggled into the country and valued at a premium because of their perceived superiority and fashionability.

However, Lemass resumed his old role as chief booster of the prospects for the country and chief dispeller of traditional pessimism. At a by-election rally in Cork in 1946 he expressed his optimism and hopes for state-led industrialisation:

> Centuries of foreign misgovernment left us with undeveloped resources, defective national organisation, decayed industry and curtailed trade, and a legacy of slums and bad social conditions of which we have not yet got rid.
>
> In the years before the war Fianna Fáil made tremendous efforts to repair our weakness, to develop industries, to build houses, to re-organise our economic life.

The war delayed execution of plans for these purposes, but the road is now clearing again and we can go forward as before if we do not allow ourselves to be distracted by irrelevant issues, or weakened by internal dissentions [*sic*].

We are about to begin a great industrial advance. The number of new industrial projects now being prepared is very large and their effect on employment and the national wealth and security will be very considerable.[1]

He went on to warn that a change of government would constitute a serious national setback; he was well aware of, and afraid of, the electoral challenge being mounted by ex-IRA elements, led by men released from Irish prison camps at the end of the war.[2] Even more galling, it was known in government that Northern Ireland was more prosperous than the South.[3] Taxes were lower in the South, partly due to the relative lack of defence expenditure. However, as Hugh Shearman remarked in Olympian fashion in the *Belfast Telegraph* in late 1947, the reason taxes were lower in Eire was that there were fewer rich people there due to the activities of nationalist revolutionaries over the previous generation.[4] In early 1950, when post-war recovery was more or less complete, the *Irish Times* reported gloomily that industrial employment had indeed risen from 102,000 in 1926 to 200,000 in 1949, but:

Even that figure is, by the standards of other nations, regrettably low; the proportion of industrial workers to the country's population is, possibly, the lowest in Europe … if this process [i.e. the stagnation of the economy] continues, says the Minister [for Industry and Commerce, Mr Daniel Morrissey], there is no hope of checking emigration; for agriculture cannot absorb the surplus of seekers after work. The complaint still rises that Irish 'capitalists' are reluctant to sink their money in Irish manufacturing enterprises. We doubt the truth of that complaint, in view of the evident fact that virtually every issue of shares by a new Irish industrial enterprise is over-subscribed heavily—over-subscribed to such an extent that hosts of investors who want shares cannot get them until they are quoted at a substantial premium. The fault, assuredly, does not lie with the investing public. It lies, rather, with the lack of opportunity for investment. The fact is that we number very few industrialists who are capable of envisaging new industries, which would put the people's idle money to use. What is wanted, in short, is a class of men of vision and courage, who can think of a product that the public need, and can take the necessary steps to see that they get it.[5]

A memorandum from Maurice Moynihan, secretary to the Government, to Taoiseach John A. Costello in late 1948 warned him against getting into a shouting match with Northern spokesmen on the economy:

> There are, I think, two dangers in pursuing the public discussion of the comparative economic and social conditions here and in the six counties. One is that in certain matters, such as prices, wages of agricultural workers, derating and social services, we may not come too well out of the comparisons; and the second, arising from this, is that an encouragement may be given to demands for improvements here which, from the Exchequer point of view, we could not afford.[6]

As early as December 1944 Lemass spoke specifically about co-operation with other countries in pursuing Ireland's economic development. Furthermore, export trade in non-agricultural goods was a practical policy and necessary for the country's prosperity. He argued that countries which Ireland imported goods from could be counted on to reciprocate if the Irish could produce the goods they wanted. This was already a long way from de Valera's old and hopeless dream of total isolation and self-sufficiency, although such a policy had fitted, almost accidentally, with the abnormal conditions of war-time. The real choice was not between dependence on Britain and self-reliance, but between dependence on Britain and becoming a truly international trading nation; Lemass had already realised this before the war ended. Long before the leap forward of 1957–9, he was talking of exports and of the country becoming a trading nation that could and would eventually break its almost abject economic dependence on the UK. This new export trade would have to be mainly non-agrarian, thereby flying in the face of the country's only traditional comparative advantage: agriculture, but an agriculture that was hamstrung by inefficiency and profound underlying structural problems:

During the war we learned, or should have learned, some valuable lessons in applied economics—the extent to which our standard of living depends on international trade; that export of a limited range of perishable products to one market [Britain] did not necessarily give us the free selection of goods we wished to import; and the weakness of total reliance on foreign suppliers for industrial products we could make quite well for ourselves. If we do not apply these lessons in our domestic policy when we get the chance we may have good reason yet to regret it. If we can now judge rightly the conditions of the post-war world they justify a conclusion that our pre-war industrialisation policy was very inadequate.[7]

He went on to suggest, in somewhat contorted prose, that the maintenance of commercial practices which assumed that the separation of Ireland from Britain was a political matter that did not interfere with trade should be terminated. The economic union with Britain, which had in so many ways survived independence in 1922, was to be ended: 'There are many essential commodities which we need and which Britain cannot supply.' The clear implication was that Ireland would have to look determinedly to new export *and import* markets, and end the country's almost total economic dependence on Britain.[8] However, his department sometimes spoke differently, and a certain schizophrenia involving the departmental line and Lemass's growing conviction that export trade was the key to Irish economic take-off was visible. As minister for industry and commerce, he had another voice at times. In October 1945 he wrote, in his official persona, a memorandum to the Taoiseach:

When the Government took up office in 1932, they initiated an industrial policy which had for its object the establishment and development of industries in this country for which it was clear there was adequate scope and an adequate market—a policy designed to establish a better balance between agriculture and manufacturing industry. To this end protection was afforded by the Government for the purpose of developing existing industries and with a view to enabling new industries, particularly in their early stages, to meet competition from outside the country so as to assist them to surmount those initial difficulties which are inherent in most, if not all, newly-established ventures of the kind.[9]

However, this was apparently not just reminiscence but still policy, and the memo had a distinct smell of a departmental official line about it. In July 1946 the *Office* of the Minister for Industry and Commerce (rather than the minister himself) wrote to the Taoiseach: 'The Minister's general objective will be to do everything possible to have trade and commerce restored to normal conditions on the general basis of his policy in the pre-Emergency period of giving protection to native industry, so as to secure maximum employment.'[10] Export-directed economic policy would have to wait, apparently. Lemass seems to have believed deep down that protection versus free trade was only one side of the problem and that psychology as much as the set of incentive systems was at the core of the difficulty; the Irish did not yet have an entrepreneurial culture. A continual problem in Ireland was a kind of defeatism that was deeply planted in people's minds, he felt. As reported in the *Irish Press* in 1949, while he was in opposition, Lemass said

> his experience as Minister for Industry and Commerce had convinced him that industrial progress was largely a matter of morale, which was the product of confidence. If the whole spirit of the nation was vigorous and enterprising, we would make progress against any difficulties.
>
> In relation to industry, confidence could be created by the clear enunciation of a practical policy—a policy which public opinion accepted as practical and desirable—carried out vigorously and decisively.
>
> Those who undertook industrial development must have confidence that the Government was on their side. That did not mean merely assurance of support against external attack, or against difficulties inherent in our economic position. It meant also support against ill-informed or malicious hostility at home.[11]

A priority of Lemass's was the reorganisation or rationalisation of the trade union movement in the 26 counties. In 1946 the Labour Court was set up at his instigation, and with union cooperation, as a pioneering attempt to regulate worker–employer disputes. This certainly preceded German experiments of the 1950s. Tadhg Ó Cearbhaill remembered:

Lemass wanted to hit the ground running after the war. In 1946 he had a big programme of legislation. His relations with the trade union movement were better than with the Labour Party; he would consult widely. He kept in touch with both sides after the split, he gave me the impression that he worked to prevent it. He leaned towards the Congress of Irish Unions; he had a very high regard for young Jim Larkin. When reunification of the trade union movement came in 1959 he was the godmother to that, and facilitated it … Lemass rather resented the [British-based] craft unions recruiting members for work in the United Kingdom on the basis of high wages, but without telling them how much higher the cost of living was too … He didn't want to draft labour legislation if he could avoid it; at meetings with trade union officials he'd invite them to write their own laws.[12]

He never abandoned the proposition that workers and employers were on the same side, despite appearances, and he was very much open to worker participation in management, to shareholding schemes and to any device that did not damage the powerful incentive systems generated by the free market. This consorted oddly with his evident enthusiastic espousal of state enterprise—even to the actual exclusion or crowding out of private enterprise.

Lemass was still quite obsessive about industrial development. This seems to be belied by his engagement in violent anti-partitionist rhetoric in 1948 during the general election, but that can be easily explained by the equally violent anti-partitionism of Séan MacBride's Clann na Poblachta; Lemass's attitude to Northern Ireland was nearly always nuanced, and his 1948 behaviour was out of character. Kevin Boland opined later, 'Of course, one of the reasons for that was because Clann na Poblachta had been eating into our vote.'[13] Lemass's subsequent studied moderation on the North confirms this opinion.

Many years later, in 1962, Lemass reminisced proudly to journalists about the 1932–54 period in which he dominated Industry and Commerce:

The original purpose of the protectionist policy was to encourage the development of industries here which would be able to supply on an economic basis home market requirements in respect of manufactured products previously imported. We have long since passed the point at which that aim has been realised and at which it became clear that any further extension of industrial activities in this country would have to be in the export market. It is for that reason that the policy of protection was changed to one of encouragement of export development and all the new enterprises set up in recent years have been primarily concerned with the export market and have not sought or been given protection in the home market in any form.

I think our economic development had followed classical lines. Of course, when the state came into existence with a very weak industrial structure indeed and exceptional measures of some kind were needed in order to remedy that situation. The new states now coming into existence around the world appear to be following the road we have already pursued.[14]

Another theme he expanded on back in the mid-1940s, was the development of a culture of work, in particular skilled and highly productive forms of work: 'The minimising of production costs does not mean low wages. High wages go with high output per man per hour. But there must be a willing abandonment of all rules and practices which have the effect of reducing output ... our distributive methods will require overhaul.' The best of all post-war plans would be to get everyone to understand that the new world that was coming was one in which the Irish would have to fight hard for prosperity. He inveighed against the zero-sum mentality that saw post-war planning as simply a way of devising new methods of carving up the national income. This amounted to 'putting the cart before the horse'. Productive efficiency was essential, and any concern that failed to meet high standards of efficiency would face the prospect of being scrapped.[15]

Trade unionists were less than totally impressed by Lemass. Gilbert Lynch, president of the Irish Trade Unions Conference, remarked in mid-1945 that 'war on the workers has begun, though in accord with recent international usage, it has not been declared'. Lemass's recent overtures to the unions were 'a threat':

> Mr. Lemass is probably the ablest member of the Ministry ... He is trammelled, however, by adhesion to capitalist ideas about private profit as an incentive to production, and the reward rightly due to ownership as such ... the

position of the workers in the economic scale is to remain permanently subordinate to capital.[16]

There was some truth in this remark; Lemass had a great respect for capitalist entrepreneurship, possibly an exaggerated respect. He found himself in the mainly titular position of Tánaiste, or vice-premier, following the departure of Seán T. O'Kelly from government to the presidency in 1945. This seems to have meant that the 'Old Man' (Dev) had tapped him as favoured successor, and was certainly interpreted that way at the time. It was, however, to be fourteen years before Lemass became Taoiseach, with Dev finally relinquishing the levers of power in June 1959. Following electoral defeat in 1948, Lemass found himself in opposition along with the rest of Fianna Fáil for the first time in sixteen years, and he went quite happily to work in the *Irish Press* as managing director. During these years the Irish Press group of newspapers echoed his opinions as much as anyone else's. From 1948 on, as his sight worsened, de Valera's energy weakened, and, as he approached old age, the Chief quietly ceded more and more authority to his subordinate. James Ryan, minister for finance, remarked in interview, 'Dev finished as an initiator in about 1948; after that he was more an arbitrator'.[17] Fianna Fáil came back into office in mid-1951, and Lemass resumed his seat in Industry and Commerce and his status as Tánaiste. In late 1952, while he was theoretically and legally Taoiseach, de Valera spent the last one-third of the year in Holland having treatment for his eyes. Although Fianna Fáil lost office in 1948, regained it in 1951 and lost it in 1954 only to regain it in 1957, Lemass was to dominate the politics of the Republic throughout this time in a way that is not always visible to historians, but that was certainly evident to Irish journalists of the period. Whether he was back in office or in noisy opposition, the 1950s was to be Lemass's decade, and a long rehearsal for being Taoiseach during the crucial years of 1959–66. This rehearsal was aimed as much at the general public as it was at his own party comrades and Cabinet colleagues. Lemass had bouts of ill-health too; he was laid up after the 1951 election and again in 1956. Some hint of the relationship between Lemass and de Valera is suggested by an anecdote of Whitaker's previously mentioned in Chapter 2:

> In 1956–57 Seán Francis Lemass was laid up and inactive for some months; [I] went to see him in hospital. 'Dev wants me to use this time to brush up on my Irish. But I'd prefer it if you sent me some books on economics. [he said]'—he got Sayers on banking, stuff on development

> economics, and by Lewis, the Jamaican. He had been
> reading about the US division of powers [at that time].[18]

He was still something of a solitary: 'Lemass wasn't a great mixer; you'd see him with his head down, packed briefcase, walking off to Kildare Street from the Dáil.'[19] He read continuously; harangued meetings, conferences, dinners; ghosted newspaper articles; and goaded people to greater efforts in an extraordinary display of energy, initiative and usually creative but occasionally ill-thought-out departures. However, his characteristic watchword was always to the effect that if he was shown a man who never made mistakes, he was looking at a man who had never done anything. He flew around Europe, making contact, both formally and informally, with the new generation of European leaders that had emerged since 1945. Interestingly, he was particularly taken by Konrad Adenauer, first prime minister of the Federal Republic of Germany; he saw analogies, perhaps naively, between partitioned Germany and partitioned Ireland. Many saw the relationship between Adenauer and Ludwig Erhard, architect of the 1950s German *Wirtschaftswunder*, as similar to the de Valera–Lemass partnership; perhaps Lemass did too. He certainly admired Erhard.[20] Even in opposition, Lemass became seen as the leader-in-waiting, but he dominated the increasingly gloomy political debates of the decade, getting considerable attention in all of the Dublin papers, and not just in the *Irish Press*. He inveighed eloquently and repeatedly against what he saw as the nearly pathological pessimism and apathy of the Irish public, almost trying to be a one-man cultural revolutionary, assuring Irish people again and again that all they had to fear was fear itself, to paraphrase Franklin Delano Roosevelt's well-known quote. He was obsessed with political life, but never spoke of it at home, dividing public and private severely. He rarely brought work back with him, preferring to sit in his armchair, living in his private world or reading a book. When his children were young, they scarcely knew their father, as Kathleen did most of the parenting. Sheila, as a child at Muckross School, was once asked to write an essay about her daddy, and she gave her teacher a blank copybook. She told the teacher, 'I don't know anything about my father.' 'He wasn't there.'[21] Similar stories have been told of the children of other Irish political leaders of that generation.

His shyness could be unintentionally intimidating, and his underlying humanity and kindness sometimes showed itself in odd ways. When his son, Noel, and Eileen Delaney got married in 1950, they set up house in Kilmacud in south Dublin; the young couple were strapped for cash, and the house was sparsely furnished. They decided to invite Séan and Kathleen around for dinner one night, and to have a game of poker afterwards. During the game, Eileen drew a full house and raised the stakes. Lemass raised her again, and she folded, only to discover she had lost £5 to a weak hand of two pairs; Lemass had pulled a classic poker bluff. Her housekeeping money for the week or more was gone; £5 was a worker's wages for a week. Some time later in the week, a worker arrived out of the blue from Arnotts department store to measure the house rooms for carpets, as a gift from her father-in-law. [22]

In late 1951, just back in power after more than three years of inter-party government, Lemass celebrated the twenty-fifth anniversary of the La Scala Theatre's hosting of the first meeting of Fianna Fáil by a rousing piece of characteristic boosterism for, of all things, the Irish-language revival campaign:

> If we are to do it, it will be through the enthusiasm of individuals, and where would it be possible to find in this country any body of individuals more capable of generating that enthusiasm ... than in the ranks of Fianna Fáil? ... [The Fianna Fáil policy of industrialisation] had produced an industrial revival without parallel in modern times.[23]

During the early 1950s he repeatedly warned that the country was living on inherited assets—accumulated during the two world wars—that would run out some time in the mid-1950s, while simultaneously assuring everyone that the government was well prepared for the occasion. The *Irish Times* ran a biographical sketch and interview report of him in February 1951, in which he observed that his best asset was a very good memory and the loyal assistance of senior civil servants such as John Leydon, D.F. Shanahan and J.W. Williams.[24] The latter two had won their spurs in Supplies as assistant secretaries, and were transferred to Industry and Commerce on the winding up of Supplies in 1945, being promoted on the way to the nonce rank of deputy secretary.[25] Lemass believed in taking decisions quickly, the reporter commented; sometimes one had to 'take a chance':

> Paramount is the impression of quiet strength in that squarely-built, strong-featured head between the broad line of his furrowed brow (from which the hair is resolutely combed back) and the decisive chin. Yet, for all this controlled power, there is an infectious buoyancy in voice, style and temperament. Friends of the family hold that his activity is the heritage of his mother, still hale and hearty

at 80 … 'Our people have an inferiority complex still, that is historically understandable; and we must aim at building up confidence in ourselves by being fair and not partisan—and alive!'

He did not really believe that a re-Gaelicised Ireland was possible; the old language would never come back. He came across to the journalist as a first-class administrator.[26] He was already being seen as the future leader; day-to-day leadership of Fianna Fáil and of the government had slipped into his hands, although he was careful to emphasise that he was not the declared heir to de Valera's throne. Nevertheless, the article called him the ablest member of the Cabinet after de Valera himself.[27]

It could be argued that his greatest and most dangerous mistake was the condemnation of the IDA, set up under inter-party auspices in 1949–50. The IDA was to be one of the greatest success stories of Irish state-led economic development, and was denounced from the beginning by Lemass in opposition as a Fine Gael attempt to neuter the drive towards industrial-isation and as an asset-strip of his old empire in Industry and Commerce. The idea was to have an independent, if state-financed, body that would research the markets for products that Irish firms were capable of producing, put different firms in the country in touch with one another and develop a grant system to overcome the kinds of market failure endemic in a tiny, Balkanised and underdeveloped economy like Ireland's. It would commence with a survey of Irish industrial resources and possibilities so as to get as clear a picture as possible of past achievements, present omissions and future possibilities; this survey would thereafter be updated regularly. Along with information from the Central Statistics Office and other state agencies, the information would be available to industrialists. Dr T.F. O'Higgins, intro-ducing the IDA Bill in the Senate, painted a scary picture of the utter absence of trade research in the Republic and the utter amateurism and unintellectualism of so much Irish entrepreneurship and management:[28]

> We do not know how industry is financed, for example the extent to which the capital is provided by shareholders, debenture holders, bankers, creditors and reserves. We do not know how many shareholders have provided the capital nor have we any information as to the dividends they receive, which is in itself an indication of whether times are good or bad. Much more information can be obtained than is now available in respect of each industrial

product, as to the extent and type of employment given, as to wages and earnings, labour turnover, welfare schemes, unemployment experience, etc. So also can information be obtained bearing on the manner in which the distribution of industrial products is organised. Generally, the survey will show how and where the country is industrialised, the yearly progress in the case of each important activity, and the extent and location of the human and natural resources which allow of further development.[29]

One model for the IDA was an account of a Czech development board given to Morrissey and company by a Czech industrialist settled in Ireland. Another apparent prototype was a similar agency in Puerto Rico. Lemass saw the IDA as a typical Fine Gael, academic and impractical exercise, designed to avoid real action. His attitude seems to have been partly a 'we knew all that already' reaction; by modern standards, Lemass's scattershot and semi-intuitive approach to development seems primitive, but in primitive conditions, perhaps primitive methods can work surprisingly well; a certain anti-intellectualism, generating an impatience with 'academic' research, seems to have surfaced here. Interestingly, the first chairman of the IDA was Lemass's old schoolmate, the economist J.P. Beddy. A veteran of the Revenue and the Industrial Credit Company, he had lectured part-time for years in UCD on economic geography, a predecessor of development economics. Lemass was later talked around to favouring the agency, apparently mainly by Patrick Lynch and Alexis FitzGerald, and he slowly realised the potential of the IDA. In fact, under Lemass, it morphed into a flotilla of trade organisations dedicated to internationalising Irish trade by investigating foreign markets and making Irish firms aware of foreign opportunities and obstacles. Chief among these, perhaps, was Córas Tráchtála (Trade Board), which investigated foreign markets.[30] Lemass later admitted, with a characteristic refusal to be apologetic, that he had changed his mind and had not recognised a good idea; he had made a mistake. He had been partly blinded by partisanship and his ideological and personal dislike of the Fine Gael tradition, which he saw as smug, privileged and irresponsible, but he was big enough to realise that. It is possibly relevant to note that Morrissey was not classic Fine Gael but an import from the Labour Party.

Another controversial project that Lemass backed during the 1945–60 period was the building up of a production capability for Irish phosphate fertiliser, at the instigation of an enthusiastic civil servant in Industry and Commerce, J.B. Hynes. Lemass was sympathetic to the idea of Irish self-sufficiency in fertiliser because of the disastrous lack of imported phosphates during the war years; subsequently, it took years for Irish land to recover heart after being drained of its fertility—tillage had been preferred over pasturage by government fiat during war-time conditions. Finance, led by Whitaker, adamantly opposed the idea, but a factory was eventually built outside the depressed eastern seaboard town of Arklow. In a chronically marginal constituency, the town was selected partly out of electoral considerations. The factory gave considerable local employment, but the pollution it generated wrecked the hitherto unspoilt sylvan valley that it was plonked down in with no regard for planning or environmental issues. A second monstrous plant was built on the estuary of the River Lee, near Cork, at great financial and environmental cost. The world glut of fertilisers knocked the bottom out of the international market, prices plummeted and the concern operated at a huge and unnecessary loss. The whole venture was predicated on a fear that war-time conditions might easily recur.[31]

'Industrial development' remained Lemass's mantra; by industrialisation he meant mainly the production of physically visible and saleable goods. Services and information, in many ways the real future success stories of the country, he only partially grasped, being a man of his time. In October 1955 he made the famous Clery's Ballroom speech, apparently mostly written by Todd Andrews, in which he proposed a developmental plan that would create 20,000 jobs, primarily in industry, every year for five years until 'full employment' was reached. 'Full employment' was to be a holy grail that would be rhetorically pursued by all Irish governments for the next 30 years. After the first five years of this proposed programme, job creation at the rate of 15,000 a year was envisaged. He completely omitted, or forgot, to mention farming. He also said that it was 'not practicable' to consider the total repeal of protection.[32]

Many years later he was able to deliver a critique of his own economic thinking as it had been in the mid-1950s:

> During the mid-1950s, when we were the party in opposition, I published, I think, the first serious attempt at a plan for economic development. This, reading back on it now [in 1969], was immature in many ways. I left out of the account many of the things that a more sophisticated planner would have regarded as important but the basic fallacy I made was to assume that an increase in total industrial production would represent a corresponding increase in total industrial employment. This hasn't proved

to be so. First of all there was clearly a great deal of slack in the industrial organisation when development became possible and increased production took place for a time, without any increased employment at all.

When we got beyond that stage, with new factories and expansion of existing factories requiring the taking on of additional workers, the pressure of rising wages compelled employers to think of ways and means of getting output per individual up rather than increasing the total labour force.[33]

He felt that wage restraint would be the best way of getting jobs for the unemployed, but he saw that this was impossible to sell to trade union leaders and understood in his hard-headed way that a wish to raise one's members' wages was, in effect, a structural imperative for any true union leader.

In 1957, after Fianna Fáil returned to power, Lemass felt finally able to growl, 'Those who are still pulling long faces and making gloomy forecasts about the future, will look just as foolish, when the future arrives, as the Jeremiahs of the past.'[34] He still felt, as he had done since the 1920s, that one of his major enemies was this culture of settled pessimism. At the end of the decade Séan Lemass became leader of the country. His experience of the Department of Supplies during the war years had decisively disillusioned him about the efficacy of development behind tariff barriers.[35] The decision that the time was coming to stop protectionism was taken by him between 1944 and 1952, and the decision to actually dismantle the system came in 1957–8. On this crucial issue, as on education, he seems to have put trust in his own political instinct and to have been willing to wait until elite and public opinion had come around; the change of heart in the country took fifteen years. A conservative and cautious country looked at change with unease, and only embraced it when self-interest and fear reinforced each other in the collective mind. A shrewd assessment of the public mind without recourse to scientific surveys was more feasible in a small and homogeneous country like Ireland than in a large country.

One of the by-products of the protectionist system was that it reinforced certain rent-seeking tendencies in Irish society that had always existed, in the form of restrictive practices in restraint of trade on the part of employers; craft unions that behaved more like guilds than modern unions; and inheritance customs that, in essence, bequeathed jobs to sons on the deaths of fathers, while preventing anyone else invading their patch and taking up the work. The most obvious example, of course, was the family farm, much extolled by the Catholic Church and the ruralist versions of nationalist ideology; in effect, there was no market in land, as a form of customary entail, enforced by public opinion, frowned on sale to strangers. This custom seems to have derived from the pre-1835 'feudal' entail laws, which enforced inheritance by a son of the property and forbade its sale. The son had the first claim on the farm and had to wait until the father was dead or very old before he received his inheritance. Commonly, marriage was postponed or given up during this long waiting period. After the son, other members of the family and, after them again, interested neighbours were in the queue with a customary, non-legal but socially enforceable claim on the land. This also meant that farmers could not borrow to improve their property, as the banks were reluctant to loan money against property that could not be sold. Thus, the collectivity, by exercising a strong solidarity, denied itself any creditworthiness. The same kinds of quasi-feudal restrictions applied to many trades, among them the trades of carpenter, electrician, marine engineer, printer, hairdresser, auctioneer, tailor, upholsterer, tiler, butcher and instrument maker.[36] More obvious restrictions of great expense and opportunity cost, of course, confined the higher professions to the small moneyed middle and upper classes, unless one were very clever and very determined. In November 1949 the chairman of Cork Chamber of Commerce claimed not only that high taxes inhibited Irish economic progress but also that many walks of life were closed to the young people of the country by what amounted to illegal conspiracies between tradesmen, unions and public sector employees:

> Ministers had deplored the lack of skilled tradesmen in the building industry, but it should be realised that most of those trades were closed and the ministers were making no effort to remedy that state of affairs. No boy who was not an immediate relative of a tradesman would be accepted as an apprentice in most trades and this was seriously affecting the general position. This situation was repugnant to the Constitution.[37]

The new minister of industry and commerce, Daniel Morrissey, chimed in with a denunciation of what was later to be termed 'retail price maintenance' (RPM), involving a conspiracy between shopkeepers that was organised through their trade associations. This involved retailers putting organised pressure on wholesalers to boycott shops that engaged in price-cutting or cash-and-carry trading. These shops were the ancestors of the later supermarket chains, and the traditional firms were echoing the contemporary Poujade-led reaction against supermarkets in France. Morrissey backed the cash-and-carry shops rhetorically. He denounced 'unscrupulous attempts … to exploit the consumer', 'purely arbitrary advances … made in the prices of commodities without any justification', 'artificial scarcities' and 'activities of numerous organisations whose avowed aims are to frustrate deliberately any movement to restore normal competitive trading'.[38]

Back in 1948 being manager of the *Irish Press* suited Lemass, and he seems to have really enjoyed it. Under his stewardship, the daily paper, in particular, became almost a personal megaphone. He made some odd editorial decisions; for instance, he hated the *Sunday Press* Superman comic strip and got rid of it as soon as he could. There was, however, a semi-hysterical campaign against foreign comic strips at the time, and this strange decision should be put into that historical context.[39] After government, journalism was a breeze. Patrick Hillery remembered, '[Lemass] once told me—[he] found himself racing into Mount Street [in 1951?] and saying to himself in the car as he drove down Harcourt Street "Amn't I a fool, rushing into this again—the bad pay, all the hassle!"'[40] He was able to compensate quite easily for the loss of ministerial salary and expenses by taking up directorships, taboo for someone in the Cabinet.[41]

Lemass was later to declare war on the 'rings', as trade conspiracies were termed, but back in 1949 an editorial in the *Irish Press*, while disapproving of these tendencies in Irish labour and trade, was rather defensive; Fianna Fáil was, after all, a party supported by a very large chunk of Irish labour and small traders:

> In reality, these practices are common in every country in the world where free trade unions exist. The United States is no exception. Indeed, in certain respects the Americans have carried the technique of restriction furthest.
>
> The fact is that restriction of output is as old as the trade union movement itself. In the early years of the nineteenth century, the Luddites, who were the forerunners of the modern trade unions, threatened by breaking up machines and destroying factories to call a halt to the industrial revolution while it was still in its infancy. By their own lights they were possibly justified.[42]

This editorial has a strong whiff of Lemass about it: the characteristic mixture of acceptance of capitalism and market forces combined with a sneaking sympathy for the workers who were being pushed around more than anyone else by profit margins, technological change and financial considerations. Electoral opportunism and a cold grasp of political realities also had a fair amount to do with it.[43] Right through the 1950s, a sort of low-level *Poujadisme* pervaded much of Irish industrial and trade relations and, by and large, resisted or evaded governmental attempts to discourage it. Eventually, freer trade and relative prosperity were to make the issue less controversial. The Irish, once they discovered how to trade internationally, became slightly less interested in gouging each other financially.

Another constant theme in Lemass's rhetoric and private conversations right throughout his public career was a blank refusal to get into recriminations over the Civil War. Like many of his entire generation, he was part of a conspiracy of silence to smother the hatred generated by the events of 1913–23 and ensure that they were not transmitted to the next generation. He had moral and emotional reasons for this stance, but there were also prudential considerations; he had a consistent distaste for, and impatience with, pointless political infighting and controversy because they were inefficient. He had polite and even friendly relationships with both W.T. Cosgrave and his son, Liam Cosgrave. As we have seen, he corresponded at length with Ernest Blythe, mainly on things northern. He tended to stay out of political conflicts that he felt he could not gain from, not seeing the point of standing on principle to achieve nothing but a feeling of self-righteousness. Another feature of his style was a restless energy; he was always seeking out a way forward—if one route was blocked, he would try another. Patrick Hillery remarked perceptively, 'Dev put his cloak around Lemass [as his successor], although their styles were quite different. Lemass was always looking for openings'.[44] His almost obsessional foci were the long-term modernisation of the Irish economy, the psychological renewal of the Irish political mentality and the eventual bending of the Irish educational and training systems to these purposes. His means were to be government action, propaganda and a general opening up of the country to Britain, America and the new Europe that was emerging in the 1950s.

The change

A key event among many American-led interventions was the IBEC (Irish Business and Employers Confederation) Technical Services Corporation's study of the Irish economy, compiled between mid-1951 and mid-1952 and published as *An appraisal of Ireland's industrial potentials* in New York in late 1952.[45] This report was commissioned by the inter-party government with some prompting from the IDA and the Americans. It was to give Lemass some unsolicited and possibly unexpected support. It became known in Irish civil service folklore as the 'Stacy May report', after the American economist who was the driving force behind it. It preceded T.K. Whitaker's *Economic development*, also known as the 'grey book', as an Old Testament to his New Testament in the minds of cohorts of junior civil servants and would-be business people in the 1950s and 1960s. 'Stacy May' pointed out that in 1946 nearly half of gainfully employed Irish worked in agriculture, in contrast to the figures of 5% for Britain and of about 33% for Western Europe as a whole. However, agriculture was only dominant demographic-ally; industry was nearly as productive, and was far more dynamic. Essentially, Lemass had won, and his implicit diagnosis that Irish agriculture, with the exception of a small commercialised export sector tied into the British market, was a drag on Irish economic development was correct.[46] According to the report, 'the tempo of overall accomplishment toward dynamic improvement will be severely handicapped so long as the agricul-tural segment remains static in real production terms.'[47] Perceptively, the basic contradiction inside the Irish economic developmental profile was noted in the report and the assumption of so much of Irish opinion was attacked implicitly, particularly as expressed by the *Irish Times* and the *Irish Independent*, that the country's economic future lay in agriculture and that industrialisation was a fantasy. 'Among the many paradoxes that may be found in Ireland is the circumstance that it is progressing best in the field [i.e. industry] where it carries the greatest handicaps, and least in one [i.e. agriculture] in which it has, seemingly, the greatest natural advantages.'[48] However, it argued for a more nuanced and scientific approach towards industrial development. Here an implicit and gentle rebuke to the Lemassian 'try anything' approach was made:

> It is of doubtful national advantage to establish high-cost industries whose output can find domestic buyers only through rigid protective restrictions or high subsidies … For Ireland, then, there is a strong presumption that the trend toward further industrialization should be planned with rifle selectivity rather than with shotgun diffusiveness … hand in hand with … an at least comparable effort to improve agricultural efficiency and output.[49]

The country would have to learn how to produce for export, and investigate foreign trade; 'The only satisfactory remedy [for the chronic balance of payments problem] seems to lie in the arduous but necessary course of committing Irish goods to the high seas in the form of foreign trade exports.'[50] 'Stacy May' echoed Lemass's economic psychologism with a curious accuracy:

> Paradoxically, along with this actively voiced ambition for economic betterment, there runs an undercurrent of pessimism or lack of confidence in the prospects for achieving the pronounced aim. The talk is of economic expansion, but the action of Government, business, and labour alike is too often along the lines of consolidating present positions rather than of accepting the hazards inherent in changed practices upon which expansion depends. There are few evidences of boldness or assurance in economic behaviour to give substance to expressed economic aims. In fact, the declarations of expansive purpose are frequently qualified by expressions of a conflicting, anti-materialist philosophy, of an asceticism that opposes material aspirations to spiritual goals, and hence writes down the former as unworthy.[51]

By 1954 Lemass was both defending his record of industrialisation behind tariff barriers and trying to soften up opinion for an opening up of the economy. In January 1954 he remarked in Kilkenny:

> The Minister for Industry and Commerce has no technical industrial experts in his service, and on the whole that is probably just as well … If all the industries now functioning in the country which were, at one time or another, proclaimed to be impracticable, had never been started, our industrial development in recent years would have been far less substantial …
>
> There are some legislative powers available to the Government by which assistance can be given in the financing of industrial projects. My advice is to have nothing to do with them, if it can be avoided. The less the Government is brought into the operations of a private business enterprise the more successful that business is likely to be. The policy of the Government is based on the

view that a far more extensive development of Irish industry can be secured by means of private business enterprise than by any system of socialised industry.[52]

However, a few days later, he stuck his neck out a little further and said that the time had come to review the whole industrial policy:

In a small country such as ours reasonable home-market security could be guaranteed only by operating restrictions on imports. But it must be made certain that protection was not covering, in any industrial sphere, unduly high production costs … It seemed probable that an expansion of exports would be needed to pay for the increasing imports of materials which the expansion of trade here might necessitate.[53]

His control of the Irish Press group was crucial in affecting public opinion. In the 1950s the *Irish Times* and the *Irish Independent*—the former an ex-Unionist and the latter a middle-class nationalist in political complexion, and both of them rather leaning to Fine Gael in different ways and for different reasons—shared ruling assumptions: that the future of Ireland was agrarian and that industrialisation was a pipe dream, or, alternatively, that Ireland would soon be reunited and suddenly find herself in an imagined weird condition referred to by the epithet 'over-industrialised'. For one example out of many of this attitude, in late 1955 the *Irish Times* editorialised in reaction to one of Lemass's pro-industry speeches that it indicated an undesirable reversal of Fianna Fáil economic policy:

The proper course is surely to work for the rehabilitation of agriculture and at least a doubling of its productivity, rather than to concentrate on manufacturing industries which have no root in our own resources. Has Mr. Lemass—and has his party, if he speaks for it—abandoned all hope of a unified Ireland, which might find itself disastrously overstocked with manufacturing industry?[54]

The *Irish Independent* pushed a somewhat more ambivalent version of the same line, and only came out finally in favour of industrialisation in 1958–9. At times in the early 1950s the paper actually argued that industrialisation had gone as far as it could and that now was the time to turn to agriculture. Only the *Irish Press* pushed relentlessly throughout the decade for a post-agrarian Ireland, in a single-minded fashion that reflected not only Lemass's convictions but also the Fianna Fáil party's growing social-support bases in the new working and middle classes of urbanising Ireland.

Everyone knew that protection had its limits, but no one knew when those limits were being attained or surpassed. If anything, protection intensified during most of the 1950s, despite the increasingly widespread disillusion about its efficacy and the increasingly obvious approach of European free trade in one form or another. Agriculture made some progress in the decade, but still continued to shed labour in the form of emigrants to England in occasionally alarming numbers. The 1956 economic crisis finally convinced everyone—employers, trade unionists, politicians in all parties, journalists and the electorate—that things could not go on this way, but in the first half of the decade opinion remained sharply divided between field and factory, that split replacing the older plough-versus-cow divide. Occasionally, Lemass nodded to agriculture, but his old belief that Irish agriculture was unproductive and inefficient persisted.[55] The scepticism about agriculture and industries derived from agriculture was widely shared, not least by Whitaker, long before he became secretary of the Department of Finance in 1955. Some surviving notes prefigure his historic memorandum on Irish economic development of 1958:

> In some respects it must be recognised that the change since 1929 has been for the worse. If we are not competitive in butter, eggs and only doubtfully in pigs, how can we expect secondary industries based on these to be competitive? ... I would rather see public funds going into industrial development than into less productive channels; it would help towards a better balance between economic and welfare schemes in the State capital programme ... prolonged protection, sheltering high domestic costs or inferior quality, blocks both the incentive and the capacity to expand production for export markets ... personal pref: once for all capital grants such as Undeveloped Areas Act ... profits ... capital; public need £42 million per annum, private savings only £35 million. Only £7–£8 million per annum going into industry. Failure to keep pace with our neighbours in the rate of increase of real output ... savings applied to increased employment rather than to increased production the problem ... Economic development more difficult by stability of population which makes new investments more

risky and less profitable than in a community which is growing quickly.[56]

As early as 1952, as minister for industry and commerce, Lemass turned on his own civil servants—in effect, his political children—in the course of a public lecture. Evidently, he was well aware of 'Stacy May', and possibly informed many of its conclusions. He reminded his audience and the wider public of the original purposes of protectionism: to give the Irish industrial economy a respite from international competition so that it could build itself up and then take on the outside world. It had succeeded, he claimed. He feared, however, that too many people in the protected sector had come to count on the tariff and quota system lasting indefinitely. He warned:

> The results realised to date showed that belief to be well founded, but there was always a danger that in some instances the purposes of Protection might be forgotten, and that it might come to be regarded as a condition which industrial concerns might reckon as permanent, and because of which they might relax their efforts to acquire efficiency.[57]

The system built up by Lemass in the 1930s had, of course, generated its own vested interests. Some trade unionists were naturally fearful for loss of jobs in the protected sector, and, as Lemass remarked acidly in mid-decade, there was 'a danger that the Federation of Irish Manufacturers will become nothing more than a pressure group for the preservation of protection'.[58] He did not add that the same could be said for some of the unions. Whitaker saw the Department of Industry and Commerce itself, in particular its secretary, J.C.B. MacCarthy, as the main bulwark defending an increasingly unworkable status quo; it had been involved in protection for so long it could not imagine doing anything else.[59] Garret FitzGerald remembered:

> [I] used to go into meetings with ... [Lemass] as part of FII [Federation of Irish Industry] delegation. Lemass would push civil servants aside—he knew the details of everything. ... one of his legacies was that he left behind a Department of Industry and Commerce which had been so totally committed to protection that it didn't know how to change gear. [I] went to Beddy [of the IDA] in 1958 to suggest industrial cooperation with the North—was treated almost as a traitor to the State.[60]

Finance versus Industry and Commerce echoed the division within the elites in the aftermath of the gloom that followed the economic crisis of 1956 and the accompanying flood of emigration from the country to Great Britain. In March 1957 Professor Charles Carter of the Department of Economics at Queen's University Belfast gave a public lecture to the Irish Association in Dublin. It was immediately circulated on April Fool's Day 1957 by the minister for finance, James Ryan, to members of the government.[61] It was soon reprinted in *Studies*, a well-known local academic journal.[62] The Republic of Ireland was falling behind the rest of Europe:

> It is falling behind, not only in income, but in the technical progress which creates the promise of further income. Though endowed with the great natural advantages of closeness to wealthy markets, of the absence of substantial defence expenditure, and of large external assets, the Republic achieves her slow progress only by a prodigal dissipation of her external assets, occasionally restrained by emergency measures.[63]

The essentially inefficient and irrational organisation of the Irish economy was a nonsense that could be easily remedied, Carter argued. The hostility to foreign investment was simply silly, and would have to be changed; foreign firms had technical and market information that was denied to local small industries:

> Unfortunately the execution of such a policy runs against a whole lot of favourite illusions. One is that a locally owned business is better than a foreign one; the opposite is the truth, for advanced technical knowledge flows readily from a great firm to its subsidiaries, and a plant which is paid for by foreign capital is a great deal better than one which has to be paid for from the scanty savings of the Republic.[64]

Another illusion was that small was good and big was bad. Partly as a consequence of this kind of thinking, management was poor, investment was weak and technical services were underdeveloped. This argument made headlines in the national papers.

Whitaker himself was famously moved to action by a front-cover cartoon in *Dublin Opinion*, the national humorous magazine, in September 1957, depicting Ireland as a young woman telling a fortune teller to get to work—

'they're saying I have no future!'[65] Whitaker, as secretary of the Department of Finance from mid-1956 onwards, was effectively head of the Irish civil service and a trusted public figure. He felt that he and his fellow officers in the department were sticking their necks out a bit, but he felt he had to comment on settled government policy in a way that would perhaps be seen by some as impertinent, or even worse; there was an undercurrent of despair and a sense that most of the politicians did not really know what to do either. Irish civil servants of that period had a culture that resembled that of an army: you obeyed orders, gave opinions, but were never to go against an established policy line openly; and this is what Whitaker and company were doing. However, Whitaker was actually articulating the sentiments of a growing majority consensus, and his rebellion, if that is what it could be termed, was actually an expression of a broad establishment consensus. His chief opponent was actually the secretary of industry and commerce, J.C.B. MacCarthy, who had genuine fears about an abandonment of a series of policies that, in his view, had served the country well. When the draft of Whitaker's *Economic development* was circulated to government, Lemass contacted him and said it was exactly what was needed. He also told him to publish it *under his own name*, and said that he and the government would back him to the hilt; much to Whitaker's recollected relief, even 50 years later.[66] A memorandum for government recommended publication of the legendary 'grey book' (the book is actually light green) on 4 July 1958.[67] Lemass, like Churchill's Americans, could be relied upon to do the right thing, eventually.

Lemass at an Irish goods trade fair in New York, 1953. He was in the US to launch a campaign, which would allow Irish goods to penetrate the US market. (Courtesy of Seán O'Connor)

Lemass disembarking an aircraft on his US tour, 1953. (Courtesy of Seán O'Connor)

Comharthaí Sóirt
Signalement

Gairm _Reamh_ ~~An~~ Taoiseach
Profession

Ancien _Premier_ Ministre

An áit agus an _Baile Átha Cliath_ : 15·7·1899
dáta a rugadh

Lieu et date _Dublin_ : 15·7·1899
de naissance

Dómas _Éire_ : Irlande
Domicile

Airde _5·9"_ : 1·75 m.
Taille

Dath na súl _Uaithne_ : vert
Couleur des yeux

Dath na gruaige _Donn_ : brun
Couleur des cheveux

Aghaidh _Rialta_ : régulier
Visage

Síniú an t-Sealbhóra.
Signature du Porteur.

Lemass's passport, undated. (Courtesy of Seán O'Connor)

Lemass walking to a meeting in the Mansion House, c. 1961. (© Irish Press Plc)

An Tóċar,
Co. Ċille Manntáin.

Nollaig 1962

A Ṡeáin, a čara díls:

As the big festival of the year
comes close to us once more we send a few
words to say you and Kathleen and the
family are in our thoughts and in our
hearts very much these days.

Phyllis and I send you
our warmest greetings and our very best
wishes for a happy Christmas and a bright
and prosperous New Year.

May 1963 bring you many
graces and benefactions among which
we trust may be good health, peace and
contentment without which it is difficult
to be truly happy. Reading the speeches made
in the Dáil the last day one thought struck me.
If certain spokesmen of the Opposition object
so much to ministers addressing gatherings
outside the Dáil and making important statements there, one good answer to them would be
"at any rate the ministers statements we are
made in their own country. Not like a certain
leader of Fine Gael who went all the way to Canada
to make the most important political pronouncement of his career as P. minister, when
he there told Ireland & the world his government
had decided to cut Ireland's ties with the Commonwealth."

Affectionate regards to you both

Phyllis and Seán T.

BACK
LEMASS

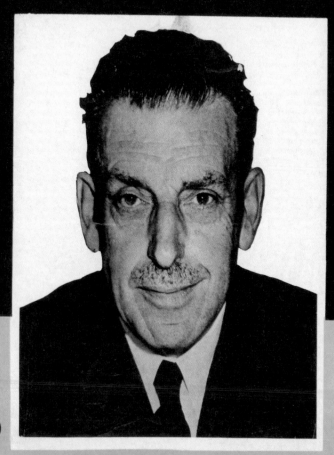

Vote
FIANNA FÁIL

PUBLISHED BY FIANNA FÁIL AND PRINTED BY CRITERION PRESS

SIX

Taoiseach and after

'Back Lemass. Vote Fianna Fáil', *c.* 1961. (UCDA, P176/1242)

✸ Reluctant boss

On 15 January 1959 de Valera announced his intention to retire as Taoiseach and as leader of the Fianna Fáil party. Dev took his time and presided as lame duck for six months, awaiting Seán T. O'Kelly's retirement from the presidency before moving over and letting Lemass into the top job. Not that this annoyed Lemass particularly; he was virtually the boss already. Six months later Lemass was elected leader of the party by acclamation, followed by his election as Taoiseach by the Dáil on June 23. I was nearly sixteen in that beautiful summer month, and I remember walking down the Rathmines Road in Dublin with a friend, who remarked, 'You know, Tom, we mightn't have to emigrate'. The upturn in the economy, which had started hesitantly in 1957, could be sensed, even at our very low level; something had changed. The departure of the Old Man to the president's residence in Phoenix Park symbolised that change. By the end of 1959 Lemass was able to remark in the Dáil that 'the most encouraging feature in the national situation at the present time is the disappearance of the clouds of despondency which hung so heavily over the country only a couple of short years ago'.[1]

His sixtieth birthday occurred in July 1959, as he was adjusting to his promotion. De Valera wrote to him as president from Áras an Uachtaráin in affectionate terms, expressing the hope that his successor would live to be 100:

A Sheáin, a chara,

Just a line to congratulate you on completing your third score [of years]. I hope you will make at least another two [score], and that each one will be as fully packed with purpose and achievement as the last two have been for you, I might have said three.[2]

Lemass gave him a same-day answer, thanking his old friend and mentor and expressing a less than totally triumphalist appreciation of his new role:

Every milestone passed marks so much of life's journey completed and reduces the number still ahead—but two score more, notwithstanding your wish, is an intimidating prospect if I have to try to 'fill each unforgiving minute with sixty seconds worth of distance run'. Since I took over as Taoiseach I have not ceased to wonder how you carried the burden for so long without showing the strain. You are a wonderful man and surely as tough as teak.[3]

James Dillon once remarked rather observantly that Lemass did not really like being Taoiseach all that much, having been the king of Kildare Street at Industry and Commerce for most of the previous 30 years:

I once heard Lemass say, at a public meeting in the King's Inns, that he had never known a day's happiness since he became Taoiseach, that his mission in public life was Industry and Commerce. While he was there he was happy, because he was doing useful work; from the time he became Taoiseach, he felt himself a supernumerary.[4]

Not only did Lemass miss Industry and Commerce but he was missed by the party and by senior executives when he ascended beyond the everyday fray. Brendan O'Regan recalled:

When he became Taoiseach I can remember the feeling of loss that he was gone from the hub of progress—you could feel it in Industry and Commerce as well, he had a vision of Shannon, as a development which would prevent us from being cut off from the rest of the world … We learned during the Lemass period that we had to plug into the rest of the world. We are now doing it not with multinationals as such but by networking with professionals.[5]

A revealing anecdote is supplied by Neil Blaney, who was party director of elections in succession to Lemass. Blaney contacted the Taoiseach about two by-elections that were going badly in 1961. Lemass asked Blaney, 'What are you going to do about it?', handing the problem over to his subordinate and tacitly declining to intervene in his inimitable and direct way. As Taoiseach, Lemass became relatively remote from the detail and the rough and tumble of party politics. Blaney recalled, 'Once he asked me what was wrong. I replied "There's been no Seán Lemass since you became Taoiseach."'[6] Todd Andrews, who knew him well, felt that Lemass had become old and tired by the time he became Taoiseach; 'spun out' was the expression he used. Lemass, Andrews and Robert Briscoe were old political comrades who knew each other well and who made visits to each other's families routinely. Andrews's assessment of Lemass is perceptive and oddly melancholic:

> In my opinion Seán Lemass came too late to power. He was a tired man. Furthermore he had not behind him the sort of disinterested advice which the leader of any large scale organisation requires and which he had enjoyed through all his ministerial life in the person of John Leydon. Collective responsibility was not one of the principles of government to which Seán Lemass subscribed. He came to office a poor man and was a poor man when he left it but in his later years he accepted the ability to make money as a criterion of success in others. It is a standard which enables successful businessmen and speculators to buy their way into politics. I do not think that any politician of any party ever received a personal bribe but I do believe that heavy subscriptions to party funds have redounded to the benefit of the subscribers.[7]

Surviving photographs from this period tend to support one aspect of Andrews's assessment: Lemass did look overworked and old beyond his years at times in the 1960s. Lemass's last achievement as minister for industry and commerce—or, according to one's perspective, as embryonic minister for labour—was actually to help in the successful reunification of the Irish trade union movement in 1959. He had always had fairly good relations with the unions, having kept in touch with both sides after the war-time split into mildly 'green' and mildly 'red' unions. He was friendly with the younger James Larkin, but also with transport union leaders like Fintan Kennedy, John Conroy and Billy MacMullan. As we have seen, in the 1950s 'he didn't want to draft labour legislation if he could avoid it; at meetings with trade union officials he'd invite them to write their own laws'.[8]

However, for a man who was allegedly old and tired, he did quite a job as Taoiseach. He had the good fortune to come to power at a time coincident with a general wave of opinion that looked for sweeping changes in Irish government policy and Irish society. This is quite evident from the newspapers and journals of the period and from the memories of people in positions of influence at that time; there was a ferment of argument in the Ireland of the 1950s, and a generational change was occurring, as people who did not remember the revolution or its passions took over from the older people. Furthermore, the agrarian Ireland that Lemass both needed and resented as a source of political power was dying; de Valera's farmers' republic of small-holders dependent on government handouts, grants and preferences was being replaced by a democracy of businessmen, workers, professionals and, increasingly, big farmers, big business and big unions. Foreign capital, both American and European, began to pour in to the Republic in the late 1950s, ten years or more after it flowed into Great Britain and Northern Ireland. The 1950s begat the 1960s, and there is more continuity between the two decades than is sometimes admitted. What I have termed the 'politics of fear' in an earlier work had something to do with it; simple fear of failure, of political instability, even of some kind of North—South civil war, combined with economic decay and the coming of a sort of 'Peronist' populism.[9] During the debate on Lemass's nomination as Taoiseach in June 1959, Noel Browne, in a generally friendly, if socialist, assessment of Lemass's record as architect of the economy, put it quite vividly:

> His dependence on private enterprise exclusively on the productive side of capital investment in Ireland has obviously proved to be an outstanding failure. In addition to the great weaknesses of the rings and cartels and price monopolies of one kind and another to which, unfortunately, he appears to give a certain tacit acceptance, which have all led to great weakness in Irish industry and which have led thereafter to failure in our national economy, and in the social structure of our society, Irish industry under Deputy Lemass has left us with a constant and near constant 10 per cent unemployed and has led to the best part of three quarters of a million of our choice young people getting out of the country …

In trying to decide what Deputy Lemass may do in the future, one has very little to go on. There is a relatively recent statement by him, when in Opposition, of his ambition to create a new social order and a state of prosperity by the provision of 100,000 new jobs in the country. I do not mention that to sneer at him in any way. I mention it to remind him of it and to hope that the reason we did not see that plan brought to fruition was probably the conservatism of his leader, to the jealousies of his colleagues, or one reason or another. At any rate, those reasons will no longer exist when he becomes Taoiseach, in which case, the validity of that plan can be tested when the problem of unemployment is in the hands of Deputy Lemass.[10]

Browne pointed to the low turnout in the recent presidential election and referendum on proportional representation (PR), which, he claimed, reflected a popular despair of politicians and was 'one of the most frightening, shocking and damning condemnations of our activities here over the past several months'. He went on to express his belief that Lemass was possibly the system's last hope of restoring public confidence in the representative democratic system of government.[11] Browne, with Jack McQuillan, formed a tiny radical party, the National Progressive Democrats, and had a qualified respect for Lemass's equally qualified radicalism; Lemass was fond of claiming that he *was* Fianna Fáil's left wing. During the debate, James Dillon, leader of Fine Gael, denounced Lemass as the author of various follies and as an untrustworthy political figure; he argued that Lemass made public promises he had no intention of delivering on. On the other hand, Dillon dismissed Browne's unease about the survival of parliamentary institutions in the country.[12] Dillon's aspersions on Lemass's personal honesty were, by and large, rejected by most speakers, but they were echoed by Fine Gael's notorious Oliver Flanagan, long-time master of the smear, who accused Lemass of corruption, patronage and general dishonesty.[13] Many opposition deputies accused Lemass of being uninterested in rural affairs, farming, the partition issue or the Irish language. Most of the contributions were admiring or at least sympathetic; a few others were fantastically abusive and occasionally libellous. At the end of the debate, Lemass was elected Taoiseach, and he thanked the house and remarked with some dignity:

I do not think it is possible for any man to face the prospect of becoming Head of the Irish Government without having doubts as to his personal ability to discharge properly the responsibilities of the office and anxiety as to how the country may fare during his term. I have these doubts and that anxiety.

I have been honoured by the confidence shown in me by my Party. Their unanimity and the support given to me by my colleagues in the former Government may, to some extent, reduce my doubts and ease my anxiety, but they cannot remove them entirely. With their assured support, I hope that the country will have reason, when the time comes for me to stand down again, to say that we did our duty well.

During the course of the debate, many things were said to which I would ordinarily like to reply, but I do not think this is the occasion on which to do so. All I will say now is that I shall endeavour to fulfil my duties as Taoiseach to the best of my ability.[14]

Lemass seemed almost impervious to other people's perceptions, and unimpressed by celebrity. Becoming Taoiseach did not change his behaviour or his personality, other than to exhibit respect for the dignity of high office; he stopped going to his beloved race meetings. He came to the job calmly, got on with it, had no celebration, went home in the evening as usual, sat down in an armchair and smoked his pipe. He made no fuss.[15]

The underlying unease about the country's future made a normally cautious people more accepting of change than they had been. After the fiscal and economic crisis of 1956, no one could be smug. Certainly, another ten years of protectionism and redistributive fiscal policies combined with a visible hostility to foreign investment and expertise would have made the Republic truly moribund. Significantly, people in general sensed this at the time.[16] Despite the sometimes slanderous abuse from Fine Gael, echoing old hatreds of Civil War times, as well as an archaic snobbery about new money and new manners, Lemass actually had the wind at his back, in the form of a friendly press; many able senior civil servants in favour of change, particularly the group of senior officials in Finance led by Whitaker; a friendly minister for finance in the person of James Ryan; and a party that was overwhelmingly behind him. Much of the opposition, including much of Fine Gael, were also in support of him. The Catholic Church, because of the Vatican Council, was undermining its own right wing both internationally and in Ireland. The coalition of vested interests intent on preserving the status quo had not quite broken up, but was a great deal weaker than it had been in 1946. Not least, Lemass had the benediction and behind-the-scenes support of Eamon de Valera, who, though departed for the non-executive presidency of the country, acted as a kind of arbiter or referee in the internal affairs of Fianna Fáil much as he had done since 1948. Interestingly, de Valera's valedictory comment about Lemass after he had become president was to the effect that Lemass would be innovative, and would have things going for him. Hillery remembered:

> I went to see Dev in the [Phoenix] Park; I used to go from time to time, he had been from the same constituency [in Co. Clare] and all that. Once he said about Lemass: 'There'll be a breath of fresh air through the country' which was, in a sense, a criticism of himself.[17]

In the 1960s Lemass accelerated the dismantling of the protectionist system and moved the country towards free trade with Britain as a preparatory stage towards free trade with Continental Europe and the world. He tended to be attacked for reneging on his earlier loyalty to de Valera's self-sufficiency policies, but he took the view that, by 1959, Ireland had become ready for free trade and needed to step out of the protectionist cradle. He commented himself in the late 1960s that '[under the First Programme for Economic Expansion] the value of Irish exports increased by 140% and the whole economic atmosphere became lively and exhilarating'.[18]

When Lemass's political career ended in 1969, many of his associates looked upon his record as minister and Taoiseach with some scepticism, a scepticism that tends to run against the verdict of the vast majority of later journalists, historians and political scientists, who have hailed him as a cusp figure, the man who dismantled de Valera's 'dreary paradise' and ushered in the modern world by galvanising the economy, transforming a sclerotic educational system, paving the way for Europe, initiating an era of good feelings with Northern Ireland and normalising relations with the UK.[19] In his spare time he dealt with the representation system, the linguistic revival campaign and the welfare system. Todd Andrews thought he was the greatest Irish administrative leader since Thomas Wentworth Strafford in the early seventeenth century, emphasising his twenty-year marathon in Industry and Commerce rather than his time as Taoiseach. Strafford, who served as an energetic and reforming governor of Ireland, was known as 'Thorough'; he was executed in 1641 by parliament on suspicion of royalism.

Edward MacAonraoi, a veteran Sinn Féiner, *Gaeilgeoir* and civil servant, supported the Treaty in 1922, but changed to Fianna Fáil like many an other later on because he liked the party's ideas on protectionism, separatism and development. He wrote to Todd Andrews in 1980:

> I am amused at your mention of Wentworth because of your naive assumption of your readers' knowledge of history and also because the resemblance is so far-fetched. I assume you think of him (Lemass) as a perfect ruthless administrator. I agree entirely; he would have made [a] perfect [British] Indian civil servant. But as a statesman? As a pragmatist he was an outstanding politician. Immensely clever but not intellectual. As I go on I am more and more baffled. I remember how he used to fill pages of a file on Rank Limerick flour-mill and whether their quota should be 10,000 or 15,000 barrels of flour. Waste of his time, when history was being made, by him and a few others. But I am sure he never thought of himself as a history-maker. But when I call him an enigma I mean it because he must have had charisma to be the leader he was but it was of a strange type. To get a historical parallel I can only think of another, equally far-fetched: Parnell, the same inscrutability, without close friends and few acquaintances. I don't think he knew a civil servant in his Department except [John] Leydon. The story went that he refused to know about any appointment lest he be accused of jobbery. Very like Parnell I imagine there were TDs, even in Fianna Fáil, that he never heard of and very few he would even know in the street.
>
> As for his achievements, I wonder. The industrial development policy was really forced on him by the economic war, but he certainly engineered it well, like the Rank case from day to day. But when it came to high economic and financial policy he left it all to Brennan and McElligott with a complacent [*recte* complaisant?] Finance Minister [James Ryan] so that we had the egregious

('monetarist') Gregory Commission. And then lastly the visit to O'Neill featured by John Healy. Was it perhaps the act of a daring administrator like say the visit of the (British C S India) governor of the Punjab to the governor of Kashmir with Whitaker as go-between? Pace Healy it doesn't seem of much importance now.

But I am writing as I said to suggest that you should set yourself to solve this enigma of Séan Lemass. You said in your last letter that Lynch was trying to emulate him but that Lemass would never kowtow to the Brits. Of course not, no more than Parnell. Unlike Ramsey MacD [Ramsay MacDonald] the DUCHESSES would leave him cold and ditto the Thatcher woman.[20]

He was struck by Lemass's ability to focus on one problem while excluding temporarily all concern with other issues. He applied a version of a rather vivid old Irish proverb to this unusually focused style of working. Noting that Lemass generally left the Irish-language issue to others and got on with the economy, he remarked, '*Ní thig leis an nGobadán an dá traghadh do fhreastal*' ('the pipit cannot attend to two ebb tides at the same time', i.e. do one thing at a time). Like many an old Republican veteran, he distrusted the ability of the younger leaders to stand up to the British as their elders had done in their own day.

Lemass had the huge advantage of revolutionary legitimacy, but he also had another ace in his poker hand. The young men were hungry and increasingly impatient with the clinging to power of the revolutionary veterans. This generational card was one that Lemass had played in the mid-1920s when he pitted the young IRA veterans of Tintown against the ageing romantics of civilian Sinn Féin and created Fianna Fáil. This second time around, the trick worked again, but this time it did not get quite the same harmonious result. His encouragement of competition among the young tigers of the party was to lead to more than a decade of fairly destructive rivalry between Charles Haughey and George Colley after his own resignation in 1966 and his subsequent retirement and death. A divided Fianna Fáil was less than totally equipped to deal with the northern crisis that erupted at the same time. However, Lemass's infusion of new blood into Irish government certainly shook the political system up, and he could scarcely have anticipated violence in the North going on for 30 years after his own death, as indeed happened. He was perhaps too sane to predict such an absurd and tragic scenario. The fairest assessment of the Whitaker–Lemass initiative of the late 1950s is that it had a huge psychologically reassuring effect after years of pessimism and near despair. Ronan Fanning's description suffices:

> Consensus was critical because the larger historical significance of the publication and reception of Economic Development was ultimately psychological. Indeed one of its most often quoted passages opens with the assertion that there was 'a sound psychological reason for having an integrated development … after thirty-five years of native government people are asking whether we can achieve an acceptable degree of economic progress.' At this level the extraordinary success of Economic Development occurred because so many badly wanted it to succeed. People craved the beat of a different drum and if the tunes to which they now began marching were still patriotic—albeit from a new hymnal of economic patriotism—then so much the better.[21]

Old man in a hurry

Lemass, entering his seventh decade, presided over the first generational change in Irish government since independence. The Cabinet that de Valera bequeathed to him had been essentially unaltered since 1932, earning the older man the less than totally complimentary sobriquet of 'Ireland's democratic Salazar'. Lemass commenced to get rid of the old, powerful satraps of de Valera's increasingly gerontocratic power group, all of them appointed because of their roles in the revolution 40 years previously, or because of their relationship to a revolutionary hero. Thus, Kevin Boland, although a younger man, owed his position in government in 1957 to his father, Gerry, who retired under pressure and cajoling from de Valera. Boland became minister for defence on his first day in the Dáil. Erskine Childers owed his governmental position to de Valera's regard for his eponymous father, shot by the Free State in 1922.[22] Jack Lynch, a hurling hero with no old Republican connections, was an exception, being made minister for education in 1957 at the age of 40. Education was not yet seen as an important post. However, Lynch made the first pioneering moves to recognise teachers' unions that were disliked by the bishops and showed an independence of mind and willingness to contemplate wide-ranging reform. Other than these three, there was no middle generation of cadet leaders in Fianna Fáil; an entire middle-aged cohort had been squeezed out. Lemass had to reach over to men who were over 30 years younger than the de Valera generation and half a generation younger than himself. Lynch became minister for industry and commerce in Lemass's first government and a trusted right-hand man; some used a ruder term: 'Lemass's gramophone'.[23] Lynch was 42 years of age by then. Paddy Hillery, the quiet man of the party and a very significant political innovator, was minister for education in the new government at the age of 36. Thirty-eight-year-old Donogh O'Malley was in many ways Lemass's protégé, and was to commence his ministerial career as parliamentary secretary to James Ryan, minister for finance, in 1961. O'Malley served as minister for health from 1965 to 1956 and as minister for education from 1966 to 1968, when he died suddenly. George Colley, aged 34 in 1959, presided over the Department of Education in 1965–6. Charles Haughey, Lemass's son-in-law, was the same age as Colley and evidently very able and energetic. Haughey was to be a chronically controversial figure, and Lemass reportedly opposed his appointment as parliamentary secretary to the minister for justice, but gave in to pressure from Oscar Traynor, old Dublin IRA veteran and fellow northsider. Haughey was to be a brilliant and innovative minister for justice between 1961 and 1964, and a rather more controversial minister for agriculture afterwards. His subsequent heroically corrupt career has become proverbial. Famously, Lemass remarked to him on offering him ministerial office for the first time that as his Taoiseach he advised him to accept and as his father-in-law he advised him to decline.

Haughey's career in Justice really struck a new note: he virtually abolished the death penalty, altered the rights of bequeathal of property so as to protect the immediate family of the deceased, and initiated enlightened measures of penal reform. His shift to Agriculture was sparked off by the surprise resignation in October 1964 of old Cavan veteran IRA leader Patrick Smith from office in protest at Lemass's favouring of industry and the trade unions at the expense of agriculture. Haughey was moved in to office so rapidly and deftly that Smith's dramatic resignation barely caused a ripple. Smith deeply resented the new men; he used to remark grimly, in reference to the mohair-suited young bloods, 'there are worse ways of entering politics than with a rope around your neck'.[24] Another new arrival at that time was Brian Lenihan, who became a parliamentary secretary at the

Department of Lands in 1961 at age 31, followed by a transfer to Justice in 1964. Soon afterwards he was appointed as minister for justice.[25]

The generational shift caused a lot of anger among the older men in the Fianna Fáil elite, but Lemass was quite relentless, playing the same game that he had played with the old Sinn Féiners back in the 1920s. He sided with the young men against the 'boys of the old brigade' much as he had pitted youth against age a generation previously. As a young man, he had also been unusually open to the participation of women in politics and government, but he confronted a very conservative and male-oriented culture in the early 1960s and did not push the issue; as usual with Lemass, one thing at a time. The veterans' anger was well expressed by Gerry Boland's contempt for Haughey and company. In March 1965 he wrote, 'some of the young set make me actually sick and disgusted. And I feel inclined to kick myself for having helped to build up an organisation to be taken over by those chancers'. Seán T. O'Kelly made a similar remark in writing to Seán MacEntee at the same time: 'I hope the bold as brass young fellows will do as well for the country as the old brigade'.[26]

Lemass was quick to abandon the term 'six-county area' as a pejorative title for Northern Ireland, although he tried to avoid the entire sterile quarrel over recognition and nomenclature by a pragmatic acceptance of the facts of Ireland's constitutional condition of division—a division willed by the majority in the North. The British Embassy described him approvingly in July 1959 as being:

> without doubt the ablest of the Fianna Fáil Ministers. He is generally regarded as a realist who is anxious to get away from the barren political controversies of the past. He is no orator but his public speeches are usually very much to the point, and he is certainly less inclined than his colleagues to wander at large over the field of Ireland's ancient wrongs. He has a special standing in the country as the chief architect of Irish economic development, and it may be hoped that once he is firmly in the saddle as leader of the Fianna Fáil party, we may see a gradual shift of policy towards a more practical approach to current problems including particularly the cultivation of friendlier relations with the North.[27]

Two months later, the British ambassador, Peter Clutterbuck, expanded on this theme:

Mr. Lemass, when I have seen him recently, has not only shown himself full of energy and ideas but has seemed positively excited at the opportunities now given him to lead the country forward on more realistic lines. That he wishes to get away from the sterile slogans of the past, there can be no doubt. But in certain respects he will have to move cautiously. It is well known, for instance, that he has no sympathy with the campaign for the restoration of the Irish language; but with Mr. De Valera watching him from the Phoenix Park, and with so many of the 'old guard' still holding high office, he cannot afford too precipitate a change of policy. Meanwhile the emphasis in his public speeches is on the need for a united drive for increased economic development; he is making this his main theme in speeches throughout the country, while he takes stock in other directions …

His references in the Dáil to partition have been couched in notably moderate terms and he urged a quieter approach … Perhaps the most encouraging of his pronouncements … was the absence of any suggestion that it was in some way the fault of, and maintained by, Britain. He seems to recognise that it is a matter for agreement between Irishmen themselves. That, indeed, is an advance …

Indeed, Mr. Lemass said quite frankly to me that he fully realised on looking back that a great number of mistakes had been made by the government here in relation to the North; these he would work to rectify. It was a totally wrong conception, for instance, that this country should seek to bring pressure on the North, whether direct or through Britain or the United Nations. Any such pressure would be self-defeating, as it would only serve to harden opinion in the North, instead of bringing the day of reunion nearer. Reunion, to be genuine and lasting, could only be effectively achieved through goodwill and he was determined to do all in his power to promote goodwill and get the country to turn its back finally on past antagonisms …

In his conversations with United Kingdom ministers and myself, he has made known his anxiety about the economic future of his country … I cannot help thinking that Mr. Lemass, like other Irishmen, is becoming increasingly conscious of the growing political, as well as economic, isolation of his country in a world that his predecessor [Eamon de Valera] had probably not realised was growing ever smaller.[28]

However, something had indeed happened to the economy. The effective repeal of the Control of Manufactures Acts in 1957 had an immediate impact, even before the Whitaker initiative, the Carter lecture or the First Programme for Economic Expansion was promulgated. According to Cormac Ó Gráda, motor vehicle registrations—a useful trace variable for consumer confidence—sank in 1956–7 but climbed from mid-1957 onwards, and were 40% higher in 1960 than in 1959. Irish investors became visibly more confident from 1960 on. Net emigration was lower between 1961 and 1966 than during any intercensal period since independence.[29] Under the First Economic Programme, economic growth was deliberately projected pessimistically at 2% per annum; actual rates of 4% were achieved. Industry was again the star, and in 1961 a historically unprecedented overall growth rate of 8% was recorded. Even without government action, people were keeping their children in school for longer and were waking up gradually to the value of education in the post-agrarian world that Ireland was belatedly entering. Politically, education remained a sleeping giant, but plans for great changes were beginning to be made under Lynch and Hillery. Furthermore, one of Lemass's first announcements as Taoiseach had been the immediate raising of the school-leaving age to fifteen from fourteen, with mention of the prospect of a further rise to sixteen; this was a deliberate and partly symbolic flying in the face of the agrarian and episcopal lobbies. In 1961 Fianna Fáil was returned to office as only a minority government by the electorate, despite this upturn in the country's fortunes. Lemass then went on to form a government with the support of independents. Many have claimed that the minority government of 1961–5 was the best the country had ever seen. Certainly, this government presided over a period of unprecedented prosperity, a prosperity that generated a consumer society of sorts for the first time in history.

Lemass continued to exhibit his fascination with the modern, as symbolised for his generation by the aeroplane. In early 1961 Industry and Commerce suggested giving the French aeronautics firm Potez about £2 million to set up a factory for building light aircraft near Baldonnel airbase in Dublin. There was an obvious attempt to bypass the Department of

Finance, and it is equally obvious that Lemass was behind the idea. Finance hit the roof, and eventually the project collapsed as a palace revolution occurred inside Potez headquarters in France.[30]

Ireland had been a member of the United Nations since 1955, having overcome a Soviet veto. In 1960 the Lemass government assented to Irish troops serving in the newly independent Republic of the Congo, starting a tradition of military involvement in peacekeeping that transformed the Irish Army and broadened public horizons considerably. Under Frank Aiken, the Department of External Affairs experienced an awakening in the form of an array of brilliant, even flamboyant, diplomats such as Frederick Boland, Conor Cruise O'Brien and many others. Talk of Europe had never died, although it was not until the late 1940s that the old Briand project of a European Union began to be talked about seriously, partly at the urging of the Americans. Irish interest in Europe contrasted strongly with British disdain for, or outright hostility to, the idea. Lemass was consistent in his eagerness to see a European market and perhaps some form of European federation. He publicly announced that he would be willing to renounce military neutrality if such an eventuality occurred.

His sensitivity to public opinion and mentality never left him, and he was almost paranoid about the possible impact of the new electronic mass media on the public's thinking and morale. Irish radio and television were seen by him as an arm of government, and he was preoccupied with alleged tendencies of television commentators to hawk left-wing and anti-government points of view in ways that were damaging to national morale and, possibly, to Fianna Fáil electoral prospects.

The term 'Northern Ireland' gradually became official parlance. It is difficult, a generation on, to communicate how great a step this apparently symbolic gesture was in the early 1960s. Long before the famous visit of January 1965, Lemass was making conciliatory noises towards the North in both public and private. This grated on the nerves of some of the older men, and it annoyed some of the younger people on the hard-line Republican wing of the Fianna Fáil party as well. However, he remained an advocate of a federal solution to the problem: the Westminster powers over Northern Ireland being transferred to the Dublin parliament while Stormont continued to rule in the six counties. He was open to other suggestions, but he did to some extent, and like most southerners, retain a certain innocence about northern realities, in particular the implacable collective resistance of the Unionist population to anything that looked even vaguely like a Dublin takeover bid or anything that seemed to threaten the union with Britain.

Even the pronounced views of Blythe, of which he took cognisance, did not really change his mind. Eventually, the North was to defeat him, and he ended up engaged with the problem but openly baffled by it, as Paddy Doherty noted later on.[31] This, however, was in the future. In 1965 Lemass won his second election; he was always conscious of the fact that he had not got the almost magical ability to attract the Irish voter that de Valera had cultivated over the decades, and winning his elections was something of a test and even an ordeal, despite his own genuine popularity. He was always a city man: he regarded rural Ireland as somewhat alien, and he did not possess the cultural reflexes that attracted country people to the party. Despite being regarded by many country people as somewhat alien in return, he did quite well electorally.

His youthful enthusiasm for the European idea never faded away. In June 1961 he said at Shannon that European unity would fundamentally change the relationships between the two Irish political entities:

> It would be a great mistake to underestimate the extent to
> which the full execution of the formal obligations of the
> [EEC] Treaty, even though they bear on economic matters,
> can affect the powers exercised by individual governments in
> a political sense, as this expression is generally understood.
> It is not believed that political unity will grow, automatically,
> from economic unity; rather is it believed that it is only on
> the basis of political agreement that a permanent solution
> of the economic problems can be founded[32]

Of course, the Irish application to join the European Economic Community (EEC) lapsed along with that of the British when de Gaulle put down a veto in 1963. The country did not enter the EEC until 1973, two years after Lemass's death and seven years after the end of his period as Taoiseach. However, due in large part to Lemass's almost prophetic insight of a generation previously, the Irish were far more accepting of the idea of Europe as the future than the British were, and this helped Irish leaders and senior officials to do well in the emergent, larger united Europe of the 1970s.

Education was one of the last areas that Lemass felt should be tackled. He encouraged radical reform, and the long-term drift towards expanding technical education accelerated from a rather low base during his time as Taoiseach. Most spectacularly, he encouraged Donogh O'Malley's drive towards expanded and free education up to age eighteen, a development that came to pass after his own resignation.[33] He also approved of a scheme to amalgamate the two Dublin universities (TCD and UCD).[34] However, the expansion of education actually began earlier. Hillery reminisced:

> I thought we needed a plan to fill the gaps that were there when I came into office. A lot of people think it started with OECD [Organisation for Economic Co-operation and Development] but really it started with the committee of inspectors under Duggan. Finance kept turning it down. I was depressed—I remember expressing my feelings about it to Maeve on a walk along the pier at Dun Laoghaire and at that stage I thought I would bring it directly to government. When I told Lemass about it he said 'You'll never get that through the government.' There were a number of reasons. The obvious one was money—it was like signing a blank cheque in a way, and indeed it turned out very expensive in the end. And at cabinet if any fellow was getting more money someone else was getting less. So he took it to that meeting of himself, myself and [James] Ryan [minister for finance]. Ryan was very helpful. In retrospect I think Ken Whitaker probably was too ... I think educational reform fitted in with his own thinking, especially in relation to Europe.[35]

Hillery described there being resistance by the bishops to the state's plans to expand second-level education and augment the clerically run schools with state-funded comprehensive education. Eventually, the church authorities came round, but not before the secondary teachers had been provoked into staging an examination strike and various other shenanigans. 'Donogh O'Malley—he was always making trouble for somebody—probably put it to Backbencher [John Healy of the *Irish Times*] that I had backed down to the bishops. In fact the opposite was true.'[36]

Lemass used to joke about his allegedly deteriorating health as Taoiseach, and he privately announced his determination to retire to his senior colleagues in September 1966. He had been having blackouts, and he felt the job needed a younger man. This pattern was less dramatic than it sounds: he was commonly required to stand around in stuffy rooms for extended periods at ceremonies of various types, leading to dizzy spells, from which he recovered rapidly.[37] He had always been somewhat unenthusiastic about having the top job, and he possibly thought retirement would be a relief. Characteristically, he encouraged leading younger colleagues to compete against each other for his job. He favoured Hillery, but he was reluctant to run, so he then approached Lynch, who was worried what his wife might think. Colley and Haughey were thought to be too young, and Aiken hated Haughey, for reasons connected in part with his father, Séan Haughey: both older men were northerners, and had been on opposite sides in the Treaty split.[38] Colley's wife was very eager for her husband to run, and Lemass famously remarked about Lynch and Colley that the former had to ask his wife for permission to run, while the latter had to ask his for permission not to run. Lynch was preferred by Lemass, and was also quietly supported by de Valera, but he was to be a reluctant Taoiseach. Not being of a Republican family, Lynch was despised by Blaney and other hardliners, and he had problems controlling the party. Lemass himself tended to lose control towards the end of his tenure, in part because of his rather freewheeling approach to leadership.

The leave-taking

Lemass took his first steps towards retiring in October 1966. A month later, he was nominated as a member of a committee that was one of his own brain-children: the informal Committee on the Constitution, which was set up in August of that year. Lemass had corresponded with W.T. Cosgrave in the early 1960s, asking for his advice on constitutional change among other matters, and back in the mid-1930s he had been quite active in suggesting the phrasing of the draft articles on social policy, in particular advising de Valera against making the Constitution sound too much like a Fianna Fáil social-policy manifesto. By the mid-1950s he was convinced that the PR-STV system was causing a dumbing-down of the Irish political system, because anyone with high qualifications or proven levels of achievement would not be attracted to the over-competitive, particularistic and populist pressures that had to be endured to survive in Irish democratic politics; PR-STV produced a parliament of backbenchers. It made chaos of local elections, he felt. As early as mid-1955, in response to a suggestion that he was 'peeved' by local election results, Lemass had written to the *Irish Independent*, urging PR-STV with a single-seat system, under what was years later nicknamed the 'Norton Amendment', after Patrick Norton, son of William:

> I believe that smaller single-member electoral areas would
> bring the electors into more intimate contact with the
> candidates and produce far greater interest in these

elections, and that a genuine Independent, who had the respect and support of his neighbours, would have a much better chance of securing election under this system.[39]

Neither Lemass nor Patrick Norton was to be heeded by the head honchos of Fianna Fáil, probably to their own and the nation's cost. In 1959 and 1968 the party blundered into ill-thought-out referendum campaigns to change the Constitution and bring in British-style first-past-the-post (FPP) voting rules. In both years a suspicious electorate threw the proposals out, with Dublin displaying a marked suspicion of proposals apparently designed to shore up the Fianna Fáil and culchie vote. Lemass started talking about radical reform of the Constitution in, at least, late 1965 or early 1966, and, characteristically, he tried to hand the whole project over to young people; he favoured women in politics but, significantly, no women were appointed to this inter-party committee. He evidently enjoyed the meetings, chatting and reminiscing about old times in a way quite different from his normal somewhat forbidding mien as minister or Taoiseach. His particular concern was with PR. One of the odder proposals raised at the committee was to permit divorce to people whose religion permitted divorce—a kind of version of the Ottoman *millet* system, by which the state enforced the rules of whatever religion you happened to belong to.[40] Presumably, it dawned on someone that temporary conversions to a more permissive religion would become very popular.

In a general sense, Lemass drove the deliberations of the committee. One of his key concerns was electoral reform; he felt that with the kind of system Ireland had there would always be a problem in persuading people of the right calibre to stand so that they would be available for the Cabinet. At that time, of course, the general body of TDs would not have had, for example, the educational level of TDs of today. It was obviously a concern for him. Michael O'Kennedy, a junior member on the committee, reminisced:

> Although the committee never actually made recommendations there was actually a sort of 'hidden agenda' in the order in which we listed the options, which was in effect an order of preference, with the alternative vote in single-seat constituencies at the top. There wasn't much disagreement about that around the table.
>
> The recommendation on divorce was dreadful—I opposed it. But probably Lemass went for it on the grounds that any change was better than no change, even

though the one actually proposed was full of difficulties and problems.[41]

The committee's proposals were stillborn, but, as with so many of Lemass's initiatives, they served to open debate in a country where such debate was difficult to promote. Divorce did not become a reality for another 30 years, but the committee gave official imprimatur to the proposition that an unconditional ban on civil divorce was simply a non-runner in the modern world that Ireland was, however reluctantly, finally joining. PR in its unreformed version survived Fianna Fáil's rather ineffectual attempts to replace it either with FPP or with a single-seat-constituency PR system.

In retirement Lemass became director of many firms and filled much of his time with private work of that general type. He fished a lot, and considered all his life that to get to know a man you had to spend a day in a boat on a lake with him. His sense of political order and mordant sense of humour seem never to have deserted him. During the Arms Crisis of 1970, Lynch fired Haughey and Blaney; he checked with Lemass first over the firing of son-in-law Haughey, and was told sharply 'You're Taoiseach, it's your decision'.[42] Lynch, not knowing who to trust, skipped a generation in almost Lemassian style and appointed a very young Desmond O'Malley as minister for justice. Naturally, Lemass understood exactly what Lynch was up to, having done generational skipping on a massive scale himself twice over. O'Malley recounted:

> I was at a function in the Gresham Hotel [in 1970] and Seán Lemass was sitting at a table nearby. He called me over, congratulated me on my new job and asked me carefully what age I was—the years, the months, the weeks and the days … Then Lemass looked at me straight in the eye and said: 'Blast you. I was the youngest ever minister before you came along. And now you beat my record by three months.'[43]

His health, never excellent in his later years, continued to deteriorate. His daughter-in-law remembered that he started to have difficulties playing golf due to his hands. His lifelong smoking habit had damaged his lungs, and he underwent several operations to repair them.[44] During his last illness, he received visitors in hospital and continued with one of his lifelong hobbies: betting small amounts on horses. Folklore records that from his sick bed he ordered Haughey to get a haircut. He died on 11 May 1971. Haughey believed that his beloved pipe had killed him.[45]

Frank Aiken and Lemass leaving Admiralty House following talks with Harold Macmillan regarding the Common Market, 18 July 1961. (© United Press)

Kathleen, Lemass and de Valera at the official ceremony to mark the arrival of the *Asgard* at Howth, 30 July 1961. Noel Lemass and Maureen Haughey sit behind their father. (© Irish Press Plc)

Kathleen and Lemass converse with Edward (Ted) Kennedy, US senator from Massachusetts, *c.* 15 October 1963. (Courtesy of Seán O'Connor)

Kathleen, Lemass, Jean Kennedy Smith (future ambassador to Ireland) and her brother President John F. Kennedy at the White House during a state visit, 15 October 1963. (© Irish Press Plc)

President John F. Kennedy welcoming Lemass to the
White House, 15 October 1963. (© Irish Press Plc)

Cardinal William Conway, archbishop of Armagh, welcoming Lemass to Rome, December 1965. (© Irish Press Plc)

Lemass announcing his resignation as Fianna Fáil leader and Taoiseach at a press conference in Leinster House, 8 November 1966. (© Irish Press Plc)

'Why PR means people's rights' news ad, 1965. (NLI, Ephemera Collection, POL/1960-70/1)

"GIVE US THE STRAIGHT VOTE...

... AN

WHY P.R. MEANS

READ THE UNITED

'LL ... ... FINISH THE JOB !"

PEOPLES' RIGHTS

RISHMAN

Personal

Teach Chuilinn,
Cross Avenue,
Blackrock,
Co. Dubl

9th July, 1959

Seán F. Lemass, Esq., T.D.,
Taoiseach,
Government Buildings,
Dublin.

A Sheáin, a chara,

I understand that the following are the up-to-date figures with regard to the Fianna Fáil Trustees' Accounts:

Trustees' Deposit Account ...	£7,338.	15.	2.
" Current " ...	21,705.	17.	6.
F.F. Treasurers' Current a/c.	2,133.	8.	2.

The above figures relate to this day's date. In addition, there are the investments whose total market value at the 15th June, 1959 was estimated at £22,259.

The Trustees' Current Account was allowed to reach the above high figure because of the likelihood of heavy demands for Constituency refunds and for election expenses. The time should now have come, however, when a fair estimate of these can be made, and the greater portion of the balance transferred from the Current to the Deposit Account.

This is the information which, I think, you should know, and which I wished to give you when you were here on Thursday last, but had not the exact figures.

As I think I told you, the important documents, such as the Deed of Trust and the Deeds of No.13 Upper Mount Street, are lodged for safe-keeping with the Munster and Leinster Bank, O'Connell Street Branch. Miss O'Kelly who has been acting as Secretary for the Trustees has the receipt as well as the account records.

Do chara,

Éamonn de Valera

ROINN AN TAOISIGH

Uimhir........................

Secretary.

1.　　I should like the first two sentences of the second
paragraph on Page 3 deleted, and something like the
following substituted:-

　　　　"Because the image of themselves which is
　　　offered by a national television service can
　　　influence the people of any nation to aspire to a
　　　better life, the pretext of objectivity should not
　　　be allowed to excuse the undue representation of
　　　our faults. What you should aim to present is a
　　　picture of Ireland and the Irish as we would like
　　　to have it, although our hopes and aims may well be
　　　helped by the objective presentation of facts in
　　　association with constructive comment".

　　　I am sure this idea could be much better expressed
and I should like you to try your hand at it.

2.　　I think it might be well in the third paragraph on
Page 3, relating to the language, to insert some
qualifying words after "Radio Éireann" at the beginning
of the paragraph such as

　　　　"Within the limits permitted by the primary
　　　purpose of providing the public with entertainment,
　　　information and News"

and later in the paragraph to insert some phrase to the
effect that the aim must be to revive the language
by promoting the love of it rather than pushing it
down the public's neck.

3.　　In the first paragraph on Page 4 I should like to
add at the end some words like "and the inauguration of
a television service affords us a very welcome
new means by which this knowledge and appreciation can
be spread amongst the people".

4.　　In the second paragraph on Page 4, the reference to
national games would, perhaps, be better in a positive
form, i.e. "are a significant manifestation": At the
end of this paragraph also it might be well to give a
more positive direction, i.e. "The Broadcasting service
should cover all forms of sport in which our people are
interested".

5.　　On page 5, first paragraph, the words "educational
medium" might be replaced by some such phrase as

　　　"medium of public information about scientific
　　　developments - particularly perhaps those which
　　　concern agriculture and other rural occupations -."

6.　　I think the final paragraph dealing with Partition
will require changes also. I doubt the wisdom of
referring specifically to the force issue. I suggest
something like this, although it can be considerably
improved:-

　　　Continue from the end of first sentence: "and
　　　our broadcasting services, reaching across the present

Letter from Lemass to the
secretary to the Department
of the Taoiseach setting out
the scope of RTÉ, 8 April
1960. (NAI, Department of
the Taoiseach (DT), S14966)

border, can help to promote that sense of common
nationality and understanding of common interests
which will in time bring about the reunification of
our people.   The natural and traditional unity
of Ireland should be accepted as a matter of course and as
a fact on which special emphasis is not required.   The
programmes which are suited to the needs and tastes
of one part of the nation will appeal equally to the
other.   Care must be exercised, at all times, to
avoid presentations which could cause offence to
any section.   The national aim is to bring about
the solution of the Partition problem by promoting
a general desire amongst the people to remove
the obstacles of misunderstanding and outworn
prejudices, and to seek, by general agreement, the
road to reunification, and this aim must inspire
the conduct of the national broadcasting services."

8. 4. 60.

ROINN AN TAOISIGH

Uimhir..............................

Mr. McCourt will ring

11. 7

Secretary.

    Telefís Éireann had a discussion on the Second Programme last evening. During it some criticisms were expressed some of which, particularly those by Professor Ruane, were misleading, apart from being shallow and unconstructive. In the absence of the Director, Government Information Bureau, I wish to have the Radio Éireann Authority approached to enquire what arrangements they have in mind to enable these criticisms and misrepresentations to be corrected. Their function in this matter should be primarily to support the Programme rather than to facilitate criticism, and certainly criticism must not be allowed to go unanswered. If there is any resistance on the part of the Authority, please let me know and I will deal with it.

SM

10. 7. 64.

Mr. Ó Súilleabháin,

Please speak to the Director General of Radio Éireann about this.

10.7.64.

(6068)E18398E. 25,000. 10-61. F.P.—G28.

Letter from Lemass to the secretary of the Department of the Taoiseach regarding criticisms levelled at RTÉ, 10 July 1964. (NAI, DT, S3532D35)

· ROINN AN TAOISIGH

Uimhir.............................

693/11

Taoiseach,

Please see
in connexion with
your minute of the
10th inst.

Re A/ below,
shall we arrange
for Mr. Andrews &
Mr. McCourt to
come & see you?

J. Slow.
13.7.64.

Rúnaí,

I rang Mr. McCourt on 10th instant as directed.
He said that he had not seen the programme in question
and that he would speak to me as soon as he had had an
opportunity of having it re-run.

Late on the evening of the 10th instant Mr. McCourt
telephoned me at home to say he had now had seen the
programme. He said that 64 was intended to be informative
and in line with his general policy of being constructive
and forward-looking. The method chosen to put the
Second Programme elaboration across was not to have a
pro-and-con discussion but to get four well-known
independent commentators to comment on different aspects
of the White Paper. They had received no instructions
except as regards timing. The compere had two minutes
at the end to wind-up and could have, in a chairman-like
fashion, referred to any of the comments made and said that
it was one man's opinion and that a contrary view could
be held.

From his critical viewing of the programme he felt
that it had served its purpose and that it was at
least 90% favourable to the Second Programme. The major
fault he had found in it was that the compere had not
used his winding-up speech to remark on some of the
comments.

Mr. McCourt said that Telefís Éireann had no other
feature on the Second Programme in contemplation and that
he could see no way of mounting a feature designed to
answer the criticisms or reservations of the commentators
or the questions left unanswered by them. He could well
see that the Taoiseach might feel very dissatisfied at
some of the comments but he felt that it would be
injudicious to attempt such a feature. If he were to call
for it, it would be all over Radio Éireann and outside
that Government pressure had been put on him.

He emphasised many times during the conversation
that he intended no disrespect but that he had in fact
the greatest respect for the Taoiseach's views. He would
discuss the matter with the Chairman and both of them
A would be only too glad to see the Taoiseach if the
Taoiseach wished.

13, Iúil, 1964.

Following enquiry of
Miss Hallin, his private
secretary, he however
phoned today to confirm
appointment, for Mr.
McCourt + himself for
4.30 P.M. on Wednesday
15 id

NX 13/7/64

Letter from an unknown civil servant to the secretary, Department
of the Taoiseach, 13 July 1964. (NAI, DT, S3532D95)

ROINN AN TAOISIGH
DEPARTMENT OF THE TAOISEACH

BAILE ÁTHA CLIATH 2
DUBLIN 2

7th November, 1964.

Dear Seán,

I have received your letter of November 4th accompanying copy of your communication to the Minister for Justice about MacAonghusa's libel on you.

I agree that the existing law gives inadequate protection to public men in respect of libel, and that there are some unscrupulous journalists who will always take advantage of this. Whether your proposals offer a satisfactory solution of this difficulty is a matter which I should like time to consider.

I would, however, strongly advise you not to take libel proceedings in the Courts. Previous experience reinforces me in this view. The newspapers involved will gladly spend money for the resultant publicity and the opportunity of further smearing you.

Juries have shown a strong reluctance to support public men in libel proceedings irrespective of the evidence. I think the dice would be loaded against you from the very start.

Yours sincerely,

Seán MacEntee, Esq., T.D.,
Tánaiste,
Custom House,
DUBLIN 1.

Letter from Lemass to Seán MacEntee advising against litigation, 7 November 1964. MacEntee sued the *Kilkenny Standard* and the *Northern Standard* for libel resulting from a piece written by Proinsias MacAonghusa on 20 December 1963. Lemass publicly supported him. The newspapers settled with MacEntee who received his costs and a payment to charity. (UCDA, P67/821)

2952

25th September, 1965.

Dear Brian,

The question whether the Vatican Council Decree on Religious Liberty calls for any action by the Government needs to be examined. I have in mind, particularly, our divorce law. Do the provisions of the Council Decree oblige or permit us to change this law so as to allow divorce and remarriage for those of our citizens whose religion tolerates it?

I do not consider that we should take any decisions in a hurry, but I suggest that at an appropriate time you might institute informal consultations with some members of the Hierarchy for the purpose of getting their views as to the implications of the Vatican Council Decree in respect of our legislation in this matter and generally.

Yours sincerely,

SEÁN F. LEMASS

B. Lenihan, Esq., T.D.,
Minister for Justice.

248

OIFIG AN AIRE DLÍ AGUS CIRT
(Office of the Minister for Justice)
BAILE ÁTHA CLIATH
(Dublin)

OIFIG AN TAOISIGH
13 FEA 1966
RÚNAÍ PRÍOBHÁIDEACH

17 February, 1966.

Dear Taoiseach,

    In my letter of 16th November last in answer to yours of 25th
September on the implications of the Vatican Council Decree on
Religious Liberty I mentioned that, as the Hierarchy were then in
Rome, Most Rev. Dr. Sheehy, Chancellor of the Dublin Diocese, had
been "sounded" by my Department and had agreed to have an informal talk
on the implications of the Decree after he had had time to consider
the matter.

    Dr. Sheehy called on 14th February and again saw the Secretary
and Assistant Secretary (Law Reform) of my Department.   He said that
what he was about to say was not from himself alone, that he had
consulted "others" (by implication he meant the Archbishop of Dublin).
He said that there would be "violent opposition" from the Hierarcy
to any proposal to allow divorce in the State.   Whether or not there
was divorce did not, he pointed out, affect the question of religious
liberty.   In reply to a question from the Secretary as to whether the
time were opportune for an informal discussion between the Minister
for Justice and His Grace or Representatives of the Hierarchy,
Dr. Sheehy said: "such an approach would not achieve anything."

                        Yours sincerely,

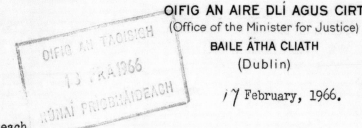

Letter from Brian Lenihan to Lemass, indicating that there
would be 'violent opposition' by the Catholic Church to
divorce, 17 February 1966. (NAI, DT, 966364)

                                            Brian Lenihan

                        Brian Lenihan

Seán F. Lemass Esq., T.D.,
An Taoiseach.

                    P. S.

                        In view of above there would not
                        appear to be much point in
                        pushing the matter any further.   (124)

nusight

IRELAND'S NEWSMAGAZINE

DECEMBER 1969

2/-

(incl. Tax)

(Gt. Britain 2/6)

PROFILE OF
THE SIXTIES

SEVEN

The measure of Lemass

Lemass on the cover of *Nusight,* December 1969. (Courtesy of Vincent Browne)

✹ Incomplete achievement

There is a melancholy proverb to the effect that all political careers end in failure. Seán Lemass would not be included by Irish historians in that sad generalisation. On the contrary, he is generally regarded as one of the most successful Irish political leaders of his generation, or even of his century. As we have seen, some of his friends and colleagues demurred from this view, at least partially. Some saw him as coming to power too late; de Valera, in this view, sat on him and delayed his rise for so long that he did not make the mark that he should have. J.C. Holloway, who worked with him on the Committee on the Constitution that reported in December 1967, remembered that he did not get heavily involved in or lead the discussions on the Constitution, which, even then, was beginning to be seen as outdated and patriarchal. Holloway saw the recently retired Taoiseach as tired and defeated. So much had gone wrong or had not worked out.[1] A photograph on the cover of *Nusight* magazine in late 1969 shows a tired and aging man.[2] Others, however, remembered him in the years after 1966 as being rejuvenated and happily involved in work of a less pressing kind than he had been accustomed to.

Vincent Browne, in a perceptive essay published on Lemass's retirement from politics in 1969, commented, echoing the views of James Dillon:

it may be surprising to state that he really wasn't very happy in that office. Basically, a Taoiseach is Chairman of the Cabinet and has few specific executive or administrative functions of his own. Lemass would very much have liked, and was very tempted, to interfere in the work of some of his Ministers, but he assiduously avoided doing so. Having been in the Department of Industry and Commerce for so long, which afforded him full scope for his considerable administrative abilities, he often felt at a loss presiding over other ministers while he was Taoiseach.[3]

Another way of looking at it would be that he saw the job of Taoiseach as one of conductor of an orchestra, getting the different ministers to do their job and backing them up if he thought they were doing good work. He seems indeed to have preferred running Industry and Commerce with Leydon at his side to having to deal with his peers and even his successors, much as he wanted potential successors around him and encouraged them to compete with each other and to even challenge himself. He often said that dealing with other powerful people was the most frustrating and important task of any political leader, insisting that he preferred being on his own, solving problems in his head. Certainly, his political testament, in so far as he left one, is the classic set of interviews that he gave exclusively, at his own insistence, to Michael Mills, political correspondent of the *Irish Press*, in early 1969. Mills was suggested to Lemass by Tim Pat Coogan, editor of the *Irish Press*, in a letter sent in late 1968.[4] These interviews have been used extensively as basic data by nearly all of his biographers. Lemass was not in the best of health at that time, but he certainly did not speak like a man who had been defeated, but rather as one who had succeeded against many odds and after a lifetime of hard work in starting a process that would be self-perpetuating and even self-accelerating. Progress of an economic nature, once started, would eventually take off on its own, he insisted. Echoing his love of aviation, he used the image of an aeroplane accelerating down a flight path until it started to leave the earth behind, having reached a point of no return at V2. Ireland had reached such a take-off point in the early 1960s and, despite inevitable future setbacks, would now continue to make progress in a self-reinforcing way. Lemass said to Mills in what amounted to a valedictory message to the Irish:

> Progress once it is properly started must accelerate all the time you see; this is the law of life. Just as invention,

scientific invention, is always accelerating because it is working from a basis of established knowledge and that basis is always widening, so the scope for invention is always increasing. The same is true of national progress. As the national economic base widens the scope for progress widens also. You remember there was this fellow who wrote about the various phases of economic development, and talked about the 'take-off' stage. Well, we passed that take-off stage somewhere in the early sixties and now it is certain that our progress will continue. We ceased running down the taxi-way and got into the take-off during that period. And that's why I would say now that progress must continue. Unless there is another international slump of a major kind or some disastrous situation affecting the economy here progress will continue at probably a steadily accelerating pace during the next decade.[5]

His prophecy was to be fulfilled, although rather more slowly and fitfully than he might have wished and hoped for. But he believed that he had instigated an irreversible process, and it is apparent that the Ireland he had railed against so much for its poverty, defeatism and simple archaism was gone forever. Quite uniquely among Irish political leaders of his century, this extraordinary politician achieved almost precisely what he set out to do in his life's work. His own backward look, summarised by him in 1969, was one of overall satisfaction:

When one looks back on the enormous economic and social developments in the country in the past fifty years it has to be admitted that there have been great improvements in that time. I suppose young people today do not appreciate this. They do not understand what it was like fifty years ago when the British were still in occupation of the country, there was little or no industry, social conditions were appalling, and unemployment at the end of the first world war was acute.

We were the first small nation to achieve independence in this century and we had to do everything for ourselves without any help from the experience of other countries … but I think we achieved a great deal also. If we had available to us in the 1920s and 1930s the type of assistance that is available to new states today we would have been able to do a great deal more. Even without it, we might have achieved more. Looking back now, it is possible to see that opportunities were missed, but nevertheless we did a great deal.[6]

Cultural revolutionary

Lemass had always tried to get the population to drop any habits of apathy or self-pity, emotional or cultural conditions that he regarded as self-defeating and self-reinforcing. He thought in terms of cultural vicious circles that could be replaced by cultural benign circles, and spent much of his political career trying to engineer a cultural revolution that would replace the former with the latter. He was fond of saying, 'There is almost nothing on earth that the people of this country cannot do better, or as well, as other people, once they apply their minds to it'.[7] Normally treated as a revolutionary turned political economist, Lemass was as much a social psychologist and cultural revolutionary as anything else. In this sense at least, he was a Sinn Féiner, although not in a way recognisable by some Sinn Féiners.

In his last years he thought he had more or less succeeded in achieving the psychological change in Irish people that he so ardently wanted. He wanted this sea change in Irish collective psychology despite his own occasional misgivings. He was a Victorian man in many ways, which occasionally made him deeply uneasy about the new, commercialised civilisation he was leading Ireland into, in which much that was good and attractive about Irish people might be jeopardised or even destroyed. Horgan points out that he knew little about radio and less about television, other than having an unease about both and a wish to control the possible evil effects that television in particular might have on the mentality of the population.[8] He saw that the permissive society which was already in the ascendant next door in Britain was coming to Ireland and that by the end of the century divorce and contraception would be legalised in Ireland. Strange as it may sound to modern ears, this worried him and made him ask himself whether he was really doing the right thing. After all, in the minds of some of his comrades, he was selling out the communal egalitarian and rural ideas that had fired their own youthful Republican passions a generation previously; he was, to some, the ultimate betrayer. As early as 1946, in a letter to Frank Gallagher (director of the Government Information Bureau), a very thoughtful and perceptive Fianna Fáil backbencher had expressed his unease with the modernisation programme envisaged by Lemass and those around him. Like de Valera himself, this backbencher wondered where Lemass was leading the Irish people, long before he became Taoiseach. Lemass was seen as a threat to the neo-Gaelic programme of moral rearmament, which combined with an agrarian egalitarianism dreamed of by priests and patriots since the time of Canon Patrick Sheehan:

> The Land Commission has ceased to function except to collect Annuities and two Ministers (Lands and Agriculture) are proclaiming in best [Patrick] Hogan style that there are too many people on the land … the [Fianna Fáil] Cabinet through long office have lost their moorings.
> We'll have English Holiday Camps in Gormanstown etc. and beautiful international airports and as sure as your name is Frank Gallagher the Irish-Ireland programme in schools will be watered down before Fianna Fáil quits office.[9]

Even back then, Lemass felt deep down that capitalist modernisation had to happen and that it had to be made irreversible; as a city man, he saw the countryside as representing the past, and the town the future. The Irish countryman would have to be replaced by the Irish citizen, the *Gemeinschaft* by the *Gesellschaft*. Interestingly, despite all the received stereotypes of his leader and mentor, de Valera agreed with him, though his agreement was more tinged with sentimental regret; Lemass's revolution had to happen or the country would die, and Dev understood that perfectly.

Lemass's central political thesis, endlessly reiterated by him over his long political career, was that the spirit of the public was all-important in a democratic polity, and that if public opinion was not with you, you would get nowhere; he did not say it, but certainly this is something that the top leadership of what became Fianna Fáil had learned the hard way in 1922–3, when they lost connection with the public mood, marched into a political fantasyland and did not regain rapport with the Irish people until the end of the 1920s. De Valera's five years in the political wilderness, to use the phrase of the time, was a sour but lasting lesson. The public mood could be changed, but only by a long process of private argument, public lectures, good political journalism and local group meetings. The founding of the

Irish Press symbolised de Valera's grasp of this salient fact of political life. This was the real stuff of democratic life. A good public leader could distinguish readily between a genuine expression of a general public mood and the clamour of a noisy but unrepresentative minority. Good government decisions came when elected leaders informed the public and reached mature conclusions in a public way. Lemass said to Mills, in terms that should be considered carefully by modern Irish governments, that governments which made decisions regardless of public feeling could find themselves in Queer Street very quickly:

> To say that decisions are always made at the top is not correct. In my experience as head of the Government for a number of years and as an active Minister for a very long number of years, most of the important decisions develop by a process of growth. Ideas emerge from a variety of sources. Most of the important decisions are built up by a slow process. Ideas are expressed in newspapers, in speeches in the Dáil, at party meetings, or in discussions between deputies and amongst ministers. It is only after protracted debate and discussion on new ideas that the possibility of a policy decision occurs. John F. Kennedy said something about the function of an expert being to examine a question to a conclusion, while the function of a politician is to examine it to a decision.
>
> This process of examining to a conclusion new possibilities for development policy is going on all the time, but the speed at which political decisions followed by action become feasible is something that you have to determine from time to time. This is where I suppose the question of Government leadership arises. You realise that people are talking about certain possibilities. You may have initially rejected these as impractical or premature and then they come to you in a new form, or your own ideas develop in such a way as to make you realise that a decision is now possible. Then you get down to talking about ways and means, costs and administration, and you are now reaching a policy decision; but this is never born complete with arms and eyes and legs overnight. It's something that grows over a long time. In the type of democracy that we are

developing here, where action very largely follows upon the development of public opinion, the building of a consensus, the influence of the grass roots is enormous. Many of the ideas which ultimately emerge as Government policy decisions in the form of legislation began with the discussions with some local group in some area where something is suggested that would be acceptable to public opinion and something which on examination proves to be practical also, because, of course, practicability is always of great importance ... The most effective means of consultation I found was at personal level, with individual deputies who reported back on the discussions that had been taking place in their areas.[10]

Full of promise

Lemass regarded the way of reacting to a recession by ceasing to spend money through government as old-fashioned and wrong, and he felt that it had had been exploded by John Maynard Keynes and by the experience of the 1930s. He argued that during hard times, government spending should actually be maintained and even increased in some directions; to cut back would be to exacerbate the economic slowdown. From direct and indirect evidence, it seems he was particularly thinking of education and social welfare here.[11]

Lemass in retirement, with not too long to live in the nature of things, evidently thought that his work was incomplete but that was itself the nature of political work in general, there being to his mind no apparent end to the making of nations. He had spent his political life trying to get people to try new methods, new ideas and new projects. He cajoled, bribed, bullied, helped, begged and pushed people into overcoming objections, both real and unreal, so as to grow industrial activity and to bypass the extraordinary thicket of institutional and cultural obstructiveness that characterised Ireland's little emergent democratic polity. He often bewildered people around him by his single-mindedness and his unconcern with what he saw as peripheral and inconsequential issues. He felt that he had made mistakes but that he had, by and large, done more right than wrong, and had woken his country up to the great task of economic achievement and social reform. He was a classic national radical; no socialist, he was a believer in a managed welfare capitalism of a type that was being devised in interestingly different ways during his lifetime by all of the western democracies in the aftermath of the Great Depression and the Second World War. He was one of the originators of a quasi-corporate style of economic management that attempted to harness employers, organised labour and government together to promote collective solidarity and cross-class alliances. He comes across finally as a very modern western European political leader rather than as an Americanised political thinker. However, the image of Roosevelt's leadership bulked large in his imagination, as it did in the western democracies in general during the crisis of the 1930s and afterwards.

Nevertheless, he always insisted that he *was* in person the left wing of the Fianna Fáil party, and certainly, compared with Séan MacEntee or Frank Aiken, he was supportive of a developed welfare state, unemployment benefit, public-housing initiatives and wet-time insurance. He was a workaholic who worked hard and played hard, who was intensely private in his personal life outside politics and who was loyal to his childhood friends in a very Dublin way. Only Northern Ireland baffled him, and like many an other he never quite managed a radical change of mind about it, despite real and conscientious efforts to shake off inherited passionate convictions; about everything else he was willing to say he was wrong and to embrace the views of his opponent if he felt the opponent had had the better of him in argument. He was a man of immense ability, with not least of his powers being an unusual willingness to examine where he had gone wrong and attempt to rectify it. In a generation that was less than totally self-assured and that partook of an oracular political style which occasionally pretended to near-infallibility, this characteristic was doubly unusual.

Perhaps the best assessment was the fulsome tribute paid to his memory by his old colleague, rival and sparring partner Seán MacEntee—like Lemass, a city boy among countrymen. Lemass used to refer to MacEntee genially and with typical acerbic humour as 'my colleague, the minor poet'. MacEntee noted his restless energy and focused mind, contrasting it with a private geniality and ability to relax with friends and old comrades:

> The authentic personality of Seán Lemass centred upon one fixed, one constant nucleus: an abiding, restless, ever active urge to make his country and her people, not only prosperous and peaceful, but of some account in the world as well. Those who did not recognise that this was the

source of his abounding, venturous ambition and energy could never understand Seán Lemass. His love of his country and her people was innate and ineradicable, like that of Patrick Pearse and James Connolly, though Seán himself would have scoffed at the comparison.[12]

His favoured role was that of the calculating and cold detached man of affairs, and he tried in his mature political years to separate his political passions from the low-level cunning and hard realities of everyday political matters, MacEntee recalled. However, a fierce Republican nationalism would occasionally break through the carapace of the reasonable man during the crucial years of the war, and his fiercely held political opinions would surface in a growling reaction to the remarks of an ambassador or a complaint about Irish neutrality.[13] An appreciation in the *Irish Times* exhibited a common bewilderment about Lemass as a man. A quiet agnostic, he was willing to recruit allies from unexpected sources, and was well aware of the cultural power of international Catholicism on Irish public opinion. At least one pope was among these unwitting allies. He was, underneath a public outgoingness, quite shy. Michael McInerney of the *Irish Times* wrote in an obituary:

> Lemass had a difficult personality. Dark with a sallow complexion, he had a quick winning smile and an easy relaxed charm, but his greatest charm was his interest and his intelligence. He never missed a word, particularly if it had an idea. And yet he was not a good mixer and in this he lacked Dev's love of people. He was quick as lightning to grasp an idea, to develop it and to implement it. He was a great admirer of Pope John XXIII and insisted that every Minister should have a copy of his Encyclicals in his desk. A glutton for work, he would be at his office before any other Minister at 8 a.m., work until 6 p.m. and then take files home.
>
> He had a happy way with political journalists and they had a mutually beneficial arrangement with him. During the war he met the political correspondents weekly and developed a good relationship. He did the same in the years 1957–'59.[14]

When asked what kind of a man Lemass was, Todd Andrews replied, 'Interviewing him was both exciting and informative. He never wasted time on small talk. He went straight into the subject. Many times he was already answering before I was half-way through the question'.[15] Lemass could play the role of the business leader, the moulder of public opinion, the international negotiator, the friend of the union leaders and the blunt-talking killer of sacred cows with cutting comments, while being, in private, a kind and considerate family man and a friend of a rather fastidious but genial and conventional type. He loved card games, mathematical problems, chess, fishing, the races and golf. He was fond of motor cars and fascinated by aeroplanes. His energy and drive; extraordinary memory for detail, which permitted him on occasion to dispense with his civil service aides; ability to work long hours; and rapidity in decision making were legendary. You could argue, although he would have laughed sardonically at the assessment, that he worked himself to death for his country. For Ken Bloomfield, Lemass reminded him of veteran French left-wing politicians rather than of any other Irish nationalist leaders he had met.

As he himself anticipated after his visit to Stormont in January 1965, nothing was to be the same after his seven years as Taoiseach. Ireland underwent a seismic change, from a society that many still saw as unchangeably rural and pastoral to one that accepted the future was post-agrarian. Some accepted the change with foreboding and even anger; others with eagerness and impatience. No one could say he made no difference.

His political legacy is somewhat more ambiguous. He left many uncompleted projects behind him, the most conspicuous being the revision of relationships between Northern Ireland, the Republic and London. Another was the vexed question of education, and yet another was the European project that he had pursued with enthusiasm and characteristic single-minded persistence throughout his political career. He admired the US and saw it as a role model for Europe, but, because of his age and historical era, he never fully engaged with the emergent superpower of the west in the few years left to him after 1959. After all, the US he knew at a distance as a young man was the isolationist America of the 1920s and 1930s, the Smoot–Hawley protectionist tariff of 1932 and, given the communications technology of the time, a country that was very far away. He hugely appreciated American expertise, advice and, of course, investment, and he knew intellectually, if not quite instinctively, that the future was American. He enthusiastically welcomed John F. Kennedy to Ireland in 1963, and was fond of quoting the American president when discussing political leadership and decision-making. He also grasped that the old European empires were dead and that Ireland's future lay with a united Europe which would rival the

US. Quite certainly, he assumed automatically that such a future Europe would be a partner, rather than an opponent, of the US.

He was not quite as indifferent to culture and the arts as he was sometimes accused of being, but he saw such issues as secondary to the big issue, which was the painful and costly process of transition from a moribund peasant-proprietor economy to a post-agrarian economy of industry and off-farm employment generally. As he said to Benedict Kiely, the economy had to be created before anyone could live in Ireland long enough to create anything else.[16]

Robert Savage has pointed out that another major contribution of Lemass to Irish political development was his very *early* awareness of the potential of Europe, an awareness that was, as we have seen, already formed in his mind as a young man in the late 1920s.[17] At that time, when the British Empire was still intact, the US was a mighty but faraway country, and Continental Europe was still recovering from a crippling war and about to descend into an even worse one; to have seen the long-term potential of Europe was certainly percipient and very unusual. However, a strong sense of Ireland as a European country is traditional in Irish culture, dating back at least to the sixteenth century and originally derived in part from hope for an anti-England alliance with a Continental power, be it Spain, France or Germany. The fact that Ireland was a mainly Catholic country also opened a cultural conduit of sorts to the European mainland through clerical networks.[18]

Lemass might be accused of weakness in the face of the Catholic Church's obduracy; several times as Tánaiste he had to bring de Valera on board so as to face down or persuade John Charles McQuaid. His attitude to the Church's power was one of characteristic pragmatism: when he could not win by direct action, he sought ways around the obstacle or shelved the issue for future reference. He saw the Church as only one of many road-blocks on his planned pathway towards the future, and he did preside in the 1960s over determined and eventually successful efforts to push through educational reform against the wishes of some, though not all, clerical opinion. It could be argued that he saw the semi-state bodies as educational institutions as much as economic enterprises; they were intended to show Irish people how to run large modern organisations, coming as they generally did from a culture where the biggest organisation many of them knew how to run was a farm or a country shop. The hope was that these semi-state bodies would eventually produce a pool of native managerial and entrepreneurial talent. This whole enterprise was itself seen tacitly as a way of getting around the general inadequacy of Irish technical and nonacademic school training. A legitimate complaint might be that he left the country with a bewildering maze of parastatal bodies and quangos, which could be accused of crowding out private enterprise and being sometimes of doubtful efficiency while constituting a convenient source of political patronage for ruling parties. Protection took a long time to die, and left a legacy of 'golden circles' that had privileged access to political power and contractual preference. Incorruptible, he left room for the corrupt.

Northern Ireland did indeed stump him, but he can be scored highly for trying to break up the political logjam that bedevilled relationships between the two parts of Ireland since the early 1920s. Also, despite the long-drawn-out and pointless violence of the 1969–96 period, his initiative of the 1960s can be credited with sowing seeds that did eventually flower into the multi-lateral initiatives that put an end to the conflict 30 years after his death.

Envoi

Lemass injected an honesty and intelligence, an emotional control and a fastidiousness into Irish political life. He was impatient with, and angered by, any wallowing in self-pity or blaming of one's failings on others. He does not seem to have been all that interested in money. The Irish could rely on their own abilities; 'Sinn Féin' was his motto, but not his party. As Brian Farrell has emphasised, he was fairly impatient with, and even contemptuous of, other political parties than his own, but was paradoxically able to maintain courteous relationships and even friendships with people of different political allegiances and philosophies; he was no tribal Fianna Fáil partisan.[19] Despite the occasional lapse, he did not suffer overmuch from his party's besetting sin of condemning someone's idea because Fianna Fáil had not thought of it first; his delayed ratification and expansion of Fine Gael's IDA in the 1950s was an important example of this open-mindedness, as was his adoption of Sweetman's policy of export tax relief and his expansion of it as government policy. His pouncing on Whitaker's initiative and backing of it in 1958 is yet another example of the intellectual freedom he exercised and enjoyed.

Perhaps his greatest legacy of all is his preaching and practising of politics as the art of the possible rather than the art of posturing. Politics was about real people leading real lives in one place, and slogans, megaphone diplomacy and obsession with unreal issues such as symbols, oaths of allegiance, flags, religious affiliations and moralising were, by and large, pointless to a man of Lemass's mentality. The promotion of a politics of the practical and a rhetoric of reality may have been the most lasting and important of his many legacies to the peoples of Ireland. Eileen Lemass felt that he had an extraordinarily focused personality and that he was the most severely honest man she had ever met. He was extremely straight, and expected the same straightness of others; his characteristic attitude towards others was quite tough. Generally, he was reluctant to give advice or to help; things were up to you. 'He was his own man, and expected others to be the same.'[20] He never wanted to be a celebrity, and he left no money after him; even the mortgage on the family bungalow was not paid off at the time of his death.[21] He cared little for money to the end.

The *Irish Times* editorial obituary described his legacy in extraordinarily affectionate and moving sentences:

> He was the supreme pragmatist. Doctrinaire attitudes held no appeal for him in any field. He protected Irish industry with tariffs, and he lived to dismantle them; he fought the British, and didn't hesitate to trade profitably with them. He could and did espouse radicalism; yet, in office, while proclaiming himself to be a little Left of Centre, he acted on the reality of the situation by occupying from the safe base of the Centre any political openings to Left or Right as they emerged. …
>
> Séan Lemass left, in the totality of his life, a stamp for good on his country: it cannot be interred with his generous, if essentially lonely, bones. The landscape of modern Ireland, for all its faults, he marked heavily from the jet scream of the sky to the lumbering of Bord na Móna machinery on the Bog of Allen.[22]

Lemass at the Skerries Golf Club Jubilee Day, 15 April 1956. Lemass was a keen golfer and proposed the provision of a municipal golf course in the Phoenix Park in the 1970s. (Courtesy of Seán O'Connor)

SKERRIES GOLF CLUB
JUBILEE DAY 15·4·56

Lemass and Kathleen, c. 1963.
(Courtesy of Seán O'Connor)

Lemass; his son-in-law, Charles Haughey; and Haughey's son, Seán, c. 1963. (Courtesy of Seán O'Connor)

Fianna Fáil election posters at a demolition site, Fitzwilliam Street Lower, *c*. October 1961. Two of Lemass's Fianna Fáil running mates, Philip A. Brady and Patrick J. Cummins were also elected that year in Dublin South Central. (NLI, WIL 14(4))

Lemass outside the GPO, photo by Colman Doyle, c. 1966. (NLI, Colman Doyle Collection)

LEMASS, Mr. Sean

T.D. (Fianna Fail) for Dublin City South.
TAOISEACH (PRIME MINISTER)

Curriculum Vitae.

Born 1899. Married and has four children.

T.D. for Fianna Fail for Dublin City South from 1924.
Tanaiste (Deputy Prime Minister) from June, 1945 to February,
1948, from 1351 to 1954 and 1957 to 1959. Minister for
Industry and Commerce from 1932 (combined with Minister for
Supplies from 1939 to 1945) until 1948, and again from 1951
to 1954 and 1957 to 1959, Taoiseach 1959. Took part in the
1916 (Easter Rising) Rebellion; taken prisoner at the General
Post Office but released on account of his youth; served with
the Irish Republican Army on the renewal of hostilities;
remained with the I.R.A. after the Treaty, and appointed to
Headquarters staff. Nominated a Sinn Fein candidate in 1923
but failed to secure election; first elected to Dail in
1924. In 1925 he suggested that the disintegrating Sinn Fein
should be reorganised as the Fianna Fail. Director of
Elections for Fianna Fail from 1927 to 1932 and Honorary
Secretary of the Party Organisation. Elected President of
the International Labour Conference, Geneva, 1937. Manager
of the "Irish Press" (Fianna Fail paper) 1948.

Personal.

Mr. Lemass, though as a very young man he took an active
part in the Rebellion of 1916 and subsequent troubles, seems
to have little of the typical Irishman in his make-up. He is
said to be of Jewish origin and his appearance does not belie
this theory. He is sensible, courageous and cool-headed, a
man of affairs with his feet on the ground, and it is to be
hoped that in his present office he will bring, so far as is

/politically ...

politically possible, a more realistic approach to relations with the United Kingdom and Northern Ireland. Lord Rugby recorded the view that at the outbreak of war Mr. Lemass did not favour Eire's policy of neutrality, and had always viewed the dissocation from the Allied cause with concern.

Since before the war Mr. Lemass had been the apostle of establishment of and protection for industries in the Republic, regardless of the effects upon the costs of production. He is the architect of (amongst others) the Irish Air Services, the peat industry, mineral exploration, the extension of the electricity, sugar and shipping industries. He set up the Labour Court in 1946. His views on economic self-sufficiency for the Republic seem to have now been considerably modified. He is probably more progressive than the majority of his colleagues and fellow countrymen, but is too shrewd to try to force the pace.

Less rabid on the subject of Partition than most Republican politicians, his negotiation of the Great Northern Railway Agreement (now unfortunately undone by the disappearance of the G.N.R.) with the Government of Northern Ireland was something of a personal triumph.

Mr. Lemass is pleasant and courteous to meet but is not endowed with much charm or personal magnetism. On the other hand he commands the respect of the Irish business men and the devotion of his officials. His speeches are well pondered and well expressed. Since becoming Taoiseach in June, 1959 he has indicated that he is alive to the need for changes in the economic policies which he had himself forsaken.

(Received in 1959)

May 12, 1971

Dear Mr. President:

The death of Sean Lemass has deprived Ireland of a distinguished leader and the world of a much-admired citizen.

Skilled architect of Irish industrial and commercial expansion, courageous and steadfast in his efforts for peace: he will be remembered by men of good-will everywhere for generations to come.

On behalf of my own fellow citizens, I hope that you will extend to the people of your country our deepest sympathy and that you will tell them how much we will continue to value the life's work of this great son of Ireland.

Sincerely,

Richard Nixon

His Excellency
Eamon de Valera
President of Ireland
Aras an Uachtarain
Phoenix Park
Dublin 8
Ireland

Letter of condolence from President Nixon to de Valera on the death of Lemass, 12 May 1971. (UCDA-OFM, P150/3497)

Caricature of Lemass, c. 1969.
(Courtesy of Henry Sheridan)

Lemass photo by Colman Doyle, 1960s. (© Irish Press Plc)

ENDNOTES ✹

Chapter one

[1] Interview with T.K. Whitaker, 4 April 2008; interview with Henry and Evelyn Sheridan, 11 November 2008.

[2] Interview with Henry and Evelyn Sheridan, 11 November 2008.

[3] John Horgan, *Séan Lemass: the enigmatic patriot* (Dublin, 1997), 278.

[4] Horgan, *Séan Lemass*, 278.

[5] Interview with T.K. Whitaker, 4 April 2008.

[6] Terence O'Neill, *The autobiography of Terence O'Neill* (London, 1972), 72.

[7] Interview with T.K. Whitaker, 4 April 2008.

[8] Michael Yeats, *Cast a cold eye* (Dublin, 1998), 88.

[9] Kenneth Bloomfield, *Stormont in crisis* (Belfast, 1994), 80.

[10] Bloomfield, *Stormont in crisis*, 80.

[11] Michael O'Sullivan, *Seán Lemass: a biography* (Dublin, 1994), 178.

[12] O'Sullivan, *Seán Lemass*, 178.

[13] John Horgan Archive (JHA), in my possession, Interview with T.K. Whitaker, 10 October 1994.

[14] Tom Garvin, 'The north and the rest: the politics of the Republic of Ireland', in Charles Townshend (ed.), *Consensus in Ireland: approaches and recessions* (Oxford, 1988), 94–109.

[15] Kevin Myers, 'Lest we forget, they died for our freedom', *Irish Independent*, 7 November 2008.

[16] Richard Rose and Tom Garvin, 'The public policy effects of independence: Ireland as a test case', *European Journal of Political Research* 11 (4) (1983), 377–98.

[17] See, for example, Michael Sheehy, *Divided we stand* (London, 1955); Frank Gallagher, *The indivisible island: the story of the partition of Ireland* (London, 1957); J.V. Kelleher, 'Ireland…and where does she stand?', *Foreign Affairs* 38 (1957), 485–95.

[18] O'Sullivan, *Seán Lemass*, 181.

[19] JHA, Interview with Patrick Hillery, 14 December 1994.

[20] National Archives of Ireland (NAI), S17246 W/63, 4 June 1961, as cited in JHA.

[21] Robert Savage, *Seán Lemass* (Dundalk, 1999), 41–2; for Blythe's line on partition, see the definitive study by Daithí Ó Corráin, '"Ireland in his heart north and south": the contribution of Ernest Blythe to the partition question', *Irish Historical Studies* XXXV (137) (May 2006), 61–80.

[22] Ó Corráin, '"Ireland in his heart north and south"', 73.

[23] Savage, *Seán Lemass*, 30–1.

[24] As quoted by Savage, *Seán Lemass*, 43. For Lemass–Blythe correspondence, see NAI, S16272 D.

[25] As quoted in Ó Corráin, '"Ireland in his heart north and south"', 75.

[26] Sheehy, *Divided we stand*; Donal Barrington, 'Uniting Ireland', *Studies* 46 (Winter 1957), 379–402.

[27] R.F. Foster, *Luck and the Irish* (London, 2007), 104.

[28] Brian Farrell, *Seán Lemass* (Dublin, 1991), 117.

[29] O'Neill, *Autobiography*, 59.

[30] O'Neill, *Autobiography*, 80.

[31] Personal experience of this writer, who travelled extensively throughout Northern Ireland for the first time as an innocent abroad from Dublin in the summer of 1964 and listened uncomprehendingly to conversations in which Protestants and Catholics alike resignedly predicted a resumption of inter-community conflict, possibly with armed escalation.

[32] JHA, Interview with Paddy Doherty, 24 February 1995.

Chapter two

[1] JHA, Interview with Peggy O'Brien, November 1994.

[2] Liam Skinner, in *Politicians by accident* (Dublin, 1946), 86, mentions five boys and four girls in the family. There is some uncertainty as to the exact number, and infant mortality at that time was high by modern standards and regarded as an almost routine fact of life.

[3] O'Sullivan, *Seán Lemass*, 2–3.

[4] Philip P. Ryan, *Jimmy O'Dea: the pride of the Coombe* (Dublin, 1990), 27–8.

[5] Horgan, *Seán Lemass*, 32.

[6] Horgan, *Seán Lemass*, 4–7.

[7] Tom Garvin, *1922: the birth of Irish democracy* (Dublin, 1996), 63–91; Tom Garvin, 'Defenders, ribbonmen and others: underground political networks in pre-Famine Ireland', *Past and Present* 96 (1982), 133–55.

[8] Tom Garvin, *The evolution of Irish nationalist politics* (Dublin, 1981), 69–88.

[9] University College Dublin Archives (UCDA), P91 (Papers of C.S. Andrews)/158, Letter from Edward MacAonraoi to Todd Andrews, 6 March 1980.

[10] UCDA, P91/158, Letter from Edward MacAonraoi to Todd Andrews, 6 March 1980; on Parnell and his MPs, I am indebted to Art Cosgrave for conversations we had in the 1980s.

[11] Horgan, *Seán Lemass*, 105.

[12] JHA, Interview with Kevin Boland, 24 November 1994.

[13] Michael Mills, 'Seán Lemass looks back—1', *Irish Press*, 20 January 1969.

[14] Mills, 'Seán Lemass looks back—1'.

[15] Edward MacLysaght, *The surnames of Ireland* (Dublin, 1973), 193.

[16] See the dust jacket of O'Sullivan, *Seán Lemass*.

[17] Horgan, *Seán Lemass*, 20.

[18] Interview with Henry and Evelyn Sheridan, 11 November 2008. Henry Sheridan.

[19] Horgan, *Seán Lemass*, 9.

[20] Conversations with Alvin Sanford Cohan at UCD in 1967–8 and at University of Georgia in 1969–70.

[21] Mills, 'Seán Lemass looks back—1'.

[22] JHA, Interview with Charles J. Haughey, 24 October 1994.

[23] Michael Mills, 'Seán Lemass looks back—9', *Irish Press*, 29 January 1969.

[24] Mills, 'Seán Lemass looks back—9'.

[25] For the best account, see Horgan, *Seán Lemass*, 17–18. Charles Dalton gives a similar, autobiographical account of his *own* use of the ferry on Bloody Sunday in his *With the Dublin Brigade* (London, 1929), 106–08. This fact makes the entire story look a little folkloric; however, maybe both took the ferry. If so, it seems odd that the police did not think of it.

[26] Mills, 'Seán Lemass looks back—9'.

[27] Interview with Michael Mills, 16 January 2008.

[28] C.S. Andrews, *Dublin made me* (Dublin, 1979), 153.

[29] JHA, Interview with Maureen Haughey, 27 February 1995.

[30] Michael Mills, 'Seán Lemass looks back—2', *Irish Press*, 21 January 1969.

[31] Interview with T.K. Whitaker, 4 April 2008.

[32] JHA, Interview with James Ryan, 6 December 1968.

[33] O'Sullivan, *Seán Lemass*, 191.

[34] NAI, S16663 B/61 *c.* 1960s.

[35] JHA, Interview with Kevin Boland, 24 November 1994.

[36] Horgan, *Seán Lemass*, 26–7; Andrews, *Dublin made me*, 222.

[37] JHA, 31 August 1993.

[38] UCDA, P161 (*Seán Lemass: nation-builder* by Liam Skinner), 1–2.

[39] JHA, Interview with Charles J. Haughey, 24 October 1994.

[40] Conversation with Rory Barnes, 4 November 2008.

[41] Sheila Walsh, 'Wife of a statesman', *Irish Press*, 7 February 1969, 9.

[42] 'The dynamic lifestyle of Seán Lemass', *Irish Independent*, 12 May 1971.

[43] JHA, Interview with Kevin Boland, 24 November 1994.

[44] Interview with Henry and Evelyn Sheridan, 11 November 2008. Henry Sheridan.

[45] Kees van Hoek, 'Lemass: minister who maps Republic's future', *Times Pictorial*, 4 April 1953.

[46] JHA, Interview with T.K. Whitaker, 1994.

[47] UCDA, P53 (Papers of Michael Hayes)/303, 235–507.

[48] UCDA, P53/304, 238.

Chapter three

[1] Andrews, *Dublin made me*, 208.

[2] UCDA, P53/54.

[3] UCDA, P53/54.

[4] Andrews, *Dublin made me*, 218.

[5] Seán O'Faoláin, *De Valera* (London, 1939), 114–19, and throughout.

[6] Seán O'Faoláin, as quoted in Dick Walsh, *The party* (Dublin, 1986), 12–13.

[7] R.M. Fox, *Smoky crusade* (London, 1938), 357–8. The account may be exaggerated, but the emotional atmosphere seems authentic.

[8] P.S. O'Hegarty, *The victory of Sinn Féin* (Dublin, 1924, repr. 1998).

[9] Michael Mills, 'Seán Lemass looks back—4', *Irish Press*, 23 January 1969.

[10] National Library of Ireland (NLI), LO p.117 (122).

[11] UCDA, P80 (Papers of Desmond FitzGerald)/875, *Comhairle na dTeachtaí, Cruinniú 18–19 Mí na Nodlag, 1926*.

[12] UCDA, P80/847, 14 January 1924–July 1926.

[13] Mills, 'Seán Lemass looks back—4'.

[14] Mills, 'Seán Lemass looks back—4'. There were two general elections in 1927: one in June, when Fianna Fáil baulked at taking the oath; and one in August that was precipitated by the assassination of Kevin O'Higgins by three young men from George Gilmore's 'Red IRA'. This, plus new emergency legislation, forced de Valera and his colleagues to take the oath while declaring that they were not taking it. De Valera was twitted for declaring this apparently all-important oath as an 'empty formula', but Lemass remarked frostily that the Cumann na nGaedheal pro-Treaty government had itself declared it to be so and had used exactly the same phrase.

[15] Mills, 'Seán Lemass looks back—4'.

[16] See, for example, Garret O'Connor, 'Canada moving towards freedom', *An Phoblacht*, 2 October 1925, 2.

[17] NAI, 2B/82/117, Sinn Féin Standing Committee minutes, 4 May 1925, see section on Sinn Féin funds case.

[18] NAI, 2B/82/119, Sinn Féin funds case.

[19] NAI, 2B/82/119, Sinn Féin funds case.

[20] UCDA, P80/847, *Monthly summary (no. 11), November, 1925.* 27 November 1925.

[21] Seán Lemass, 'Reorganisation committee', *An Phoblacht*, 11 September 1925, 6.

[22] Seán Lemass, 'Sinn Féin in Dublin: what is wrong with it?—a personal view', *An Phoblacht*, 18 September 1925, 5.

[23] Maighréad Bean Uí Bhuachalla, 'Sinn Féin in Dublin: what is wrong with it?—another personal view', *An Phoblacht*, 25 September 1925, 2.

[24] Fingan, 'The need for education', *An Phoblacht*, 9 October 1925, 2.

[25] Seán Lemass, 'New leaders for Sinn Féin: the coming year', *An Phoblacht*, 9 October 1925, 2.

[26] Patrick O'Shea, 'Sinn Féin in Dublin: what is wrong with it?', *An Phoblacht*, 16 October 1925, 2.

[27] Seán Lemass, 'The turning tide', *An Phoblacht*, 23 October 1925, 2.

[28] UCDA, P80/847, *Report by no. 70*, 30 October 1925.

[29] Seán Lemass, 'The need of Sinn Féin', *An Phoblacht*, 29 January 1926, 3.

[30] On this entire saga, see Farrell, *Seán Lemass*, 10–15. On the suggestion that Boland engineered the suicide vote of Sinn Féin, see [Vincent Browne], 'Lemass: a profile', *Nusight*, December 1969, 84. See also R.K. Carty, *Party and parish pump: electoral politics in Ireland* (Ontario, 1981), 104–8; Peter Pyne's path-breaking study 'The third Sinn Féin Party, 1923–1926', *Economic and Social Review* I (1969–70), 29–50 and 229–57, and his 'The politics of parliamentary abstentionism: Ireland's four Sinn Féin parties, 1905–1926', *Journal of Commonwealth and Comparative Politics* XII (July 1974), 2, 206–27.

[31] [Browne], 'Lemass: a profile', 84.

[32] O'Sullivan, *Seán Lemass*, 33.

[33] *Irish Press*, 21 February 1949.

[34] JHA, Interview with Charles J. Haughey, 24 October 1994.

[35] JHA, Interview with James Ryan, 12 April 1967.

[36] JHA, Interview with James Ryan, 12 April 1967.

[37] Michael McInerney, 'Politics is war by other means', *Irish Times*, 18 February 1974, 6.

[38] Walsh, *The party*, 13.

[39] Richard Dunphy, 'The soldiers set out: reflections on the formation of Fianna Fáil', in Philip Hannon and Jackie Gallagher (eds), *Taking the long view: 70 years of Fianna Fáil* (Dublin, 1996), 7–20.

[40] UCDA, P80/800, Copy of document intercepted on its way into Tralee Gaol, consisting of a directive from de Valera calling on all prison and internment camp inmates to maintain their morale, and to organise and convert their prisons into miniature universities, 18 July 1923.

[41] Irish Military Archives, Cathal Brugha Barracks, Department of Defence, Captured documents, 1923–5 (Collins collection). See also Garvin, *1922*, 143–4.

[42] Michael McInerney, 'The making of a national party', *Irish Times*, 16 February 1974, 9.

[43] McInerney, 'Politics is war by other means', 6.

[44] McInerney, 'The making of a national party', 9.

[45] McInerney, 'The making of a national party', 9.

[46] 'From Sinn Féin to Fianna Fáil', *Irish Times*, 23 July 1974, 12.

[47] McInerney, 'The making of a national party', 9. The future minister was Neil Blaney; see Chapter 1.

[48] O'Sullivan, *Seán Lemass*, 38.

[49] 'From Sinn Féin to Fianna Fáil', *Irish Times*, 23 July 1974, 12; Carty, *Party and parish pump*, 105.

[50] Dunphy, 'The soldiers set out', 7.

[51] Uinseann MacEoin, *Harry* (Dublin, 1985), 106. From the context, it is not clear who 'shot Kevin O'Higgins', but it seems to have been Archie Doyle, with two others, apparently Coughlan and Gannon.

[52] Farrell, *Seán Lemass*, 20–1.

[53] Farrell, *Seán Lemass*, 21–2.

[54] The Davin–Lemass exchange is in *Dáil Debates*, vol. 22, cols 1613–16 (21 March 1928).

[55] *Dáil Debates*, vol. 22, cols 1618–19 (21 March 1928).

[56] UCDA, P150 (Papers of Eamon de Valera)/3497, Letter from Lemass to de Valera, 13 January 1930.

[57] UCDA, P150/3497, Letter from Lemass to de Valera, 10 March 1930.

Chapter four

[1] UCDA, P161.

[2] van Hoek, 'Lemass: minister who maps Republic's future'.

[3] UCDA, P150/2019, Draft address by de Valera rallying supporters, 1926.

[4] NLI, MS. 18,339, Frank Gallagher papers. See also Tom Garvin, *Preventing the future* (Dublin, 2004), 45–54, and Horgan, *Seán Lemass*, 51–3.

[5] NLI, MS. 18,339, 1–2.

[6] NLI, MS. 18,339, 5.

[7] NLI, MS. 18,339, 3–4.

[8] Garvin, *Preventing the future*, 47.

[9] NLI, MS. 18,339, 5.

[10] NLI, MS. 18,339, 11.

[11] NLI, MS. 18,339, 20.

[12] NLI, MS. 18,339, 32–3.

[13] NLI, MS. 18,339, 2–3.

[14] JHA, Interview with James Ryan, 31 May 1967.

[15] Henry Boylan (ed.), *A dictionary of Irish biography* (3rd edn, Dublin, 1999), 223–4.

[16] Donal O'Sullivan, *The Irish Free State and its Senate* (London, 1940), 224, 295, 441, 577.

[17] UCDA, P53/298, Notes for draft book, never published, on 1916–23.

[18] UCDA, P53/298, Notes for draft book, never published, on 1916–23.

[19] Robert Skidelsky, *John Maynard Keynes* (London, 2004), 494–7.

[20] UCDA, P161, 89–91. The tariff phrase '*ad valorem*' was to get into James Joyce's *Finnegans wake* as 'Da Valorem', also a pun on de Valera as the most Valorous Daddy of them all, while meaning, ironically, 'give value'; see James Joyce, *Finnegans wake* (Paris, 1939).

[21] UCDA, P161, 123.

[22] UCDA, P161, 126–7.

[23] UCDA, P161, 48–9 and 63.

[24] Interview with T.K. Whitaker, 4 April 2008.

[25] JHA, Interview with Tadhg Ó Cearbhaill, October 1994.

[26] 'National honours Lemass', *Irish Press*, 9 April 1954, 9, 11.

[27] NAI, S1036A, 7 January 1943, as cited in JHA.

[28] UCDA, P161, 97–8.

[29] UCDA, P161, 98–9.

[30] UCDA, P161, 38.

[31] Garvin, *Preventing the future*, 178; for an argument by Garret FitzGerald in favour of the closures, see 'First service to US by Aer Lingus failed to get off to a flying start', *Irish Times*, 3 May 2008.

[32] JHA, Interview with Kevin Boland, 25 November 1994. CKD (completely knocked down) referred to the assembly in Ireland of cars from components imported unassembled from Britain and elsewhere.

[33] JHA, Interview with Jack McQuillan, 18 November 1994.

[34] JHA, Interview with Jack McQuillan, 18 November 1994.

[35] Eileen Lemass Collection (ELC), Seán Lemass to Gerry Boland, 30 December 1947.

[36] 'Monopolies inquiry', *Irish Independent*, 5 March 1949.

[37] JHA, Interview with Sheila O'Connor, 30 November 1994; Interview with Eileen Lemass, 3 December 2008.

[38] JHA, Interview with Tadhg Ó Cearbhaill, October 1994.

[39] JHA, Fianna Fáil party minute book, FF 440b, 12 November 1958.

[40] JHA, Interview with Tadhg Ó Cearbhaill, October 1994.

[41] JHA, Interview with T.K. Whitaker, 10 October 1994.

[42] ELC, [undated (1960s)].

[43] NAI, GIS 1/212, Speech made by Lemass at the Annual Dinner of the Federation of Irish Manufacturers, 12 February 1952.

[44] NAI, GIS 1/212, June 1951–February 1952, Lemass speeches, 8 February 1952.

[45] 'Fianna Fáil look to future', *Irish Press*, 18 January 1955, 7.

[46] JHA, Interview with J.C. Holloway, 2 July 1995.

[47] Benedict Kiely, *The waves behind us* (London, 1999), 140.

[48] Interview with Henry and Evelyn Sheridan, 11 November 2008. Henry Sheridan.

⁴⁹ *Irish Press*, 17 October 1949 to 3 March 1950.
⁵⁰ See my study of Dublin newspapers in the 1950s: Tom Garvin, *Dublin Opinions* [provisional title] (Dublin, forthcoming).
⁵¹ 'Fianna Fáil the workers party', *Irish Press*, 10 January 1948, 7.
⁵² 'Tánaiste on lawyers in politics', *Irish Press*, 24 November 1951, 2.

Chapter five

¹ 'By-election important, Mr. Lemass on consequences', *Irish Press*, 4 June 1946, as clipped to UCDA, P150/2728.
² 'By-election important, Mr. Lemass on consequences', as clipped to UCDA, P150/2728.
³ NAI, S14186, 'Twenty-six counties versus Northern Ireland, contrast of conditions', 1947.
⁴ Hugh Shearman, 'Ulster's success and Éire's failures', *Belfast Telegraph*, 8 December 1947, 4, as attached to NAI, S14186.
⁵ 'Openings for industry', *Irish Times*, 10 March 1950, 5.
⁶ NAI, S14186, Memorandum from Moynihan to Costello, 11 November 1948.
⁷ 'Can, must expand industrial exports, Mr. Lemass says', *Irish Press*, 4 December 1944, 1.
⁸ 'Can, must expand industrial exports, Mr. Lemass says', 1
⁹ NAI, S11987B, October 1945, as cited in JHA.
¹⁰ NAI, S11987B, 2 July 1946, as cited in JHA.
¹¹ 'Wanted—a bold plan for industry', *Irish Press*, 14 January 1949, 1.
¹² JHA, Interview with Tadhg Ó Cearbhaill, October 1994.
¹³ JHA, Interview with Kevin Boland, 24 November 1994.
¹⁴ NAI, S17246 W/63, 4 June 1961, as cited in JHA.
¹⁵ 'Mr. Lemass points road to prosperity: work, efficiency, low costs', *Irish Press*, 20 November 1944, 1.
¹⁶ 'All Éire unity maintained by Irish trade unionists', *Cork Examiner*, 5 July 1945, 2.
¹⁷ JHA, Interview with James Ryan, February 1968.
¹⁸ JHA, Interview with T.K. Whitaker, [undated, 1995?].
¹⁹ JHA, Interview with Patrick Hillery, 14 December 1994.
²⁰ JHA, Interview with Tadhg Ó Cearbhaill, October 1994. Professor Michael Laffan of the Department of History, UCD, suggested the Adenauer–Erhard analogy to me.
²¹ Interview with Eileen Lemass, 3 December 2008.
²² Interview with Eileen Lemass, 3 December 2008.
²³ *Irish Press*, 7 November 1951.
²⁴ Kees van Hoek, 'Vignette: Seán Lemass', *Irish Times*, 17 February 1951, 5.
²⁵ *Cork Examiner*, 14 July 1945.
²⁶ van Hoek, 'Vignette: Seán Lemass', 5.
²⁷ van Hoek, 'Vignette: Seán Lemass', 5.
²⁸ *Senate Debates*, vol. 39, cols 5–6 (6 December 1950).
²⁹ *Senate Debates*, vol. 39, cols 5–6 (6 December 1950).
³⁰ T.K. Whitaker, *Interests* (Dublin, 1983), 8, 74–5, and throughout. On Lynch and FitzGerald and their influence on Lemass, see Ronan Fanning, 'The life and times of

Alexis FitzGerald', *Magill*, September 1985, 34–49.

31 Horgan, *Seán Lemass*, 237–9.

32 'Fianna Fáil announces full employment plan', *Irish Times*, 12 October 1955, 1, 7.

33 Michael Mills, 'Seán Lemass looks back—10', *Irish Press*, 30 January 1969.

34 'Money for Shannon is an investment', *Irish Press*, 27 May 1957, 1.

35 Interview with T.K. Whitaker, April 2008.

36 *Irish Press*, series entitled 'Any jobs going?', published from 17 October 1949 to 3 March 1950.

37 'Industry hindered by taxation', *Irish Independent*, 23 November 1949, 7.

38 'Prices blame put on public', *Irish Press*, 9 November 1949, 5.

39 JHA, Interview with Patrick Hillery, 14 December 1994.

40 JHA, Interview with Patrick Hillery, 14 December 1994.

41 O'Sullivan, *Seán Lemass*, 122.

42 'Man and machine', *Irish Press*, 21 November 1949, 6.

43 On Lemass and the *Irish Press*, see Mark O'Brien, *De Valera, Fianna Fáil and the Irish Press* (Dublin, 2001), 81–3, and throughout.

44 JHA, Interview with Patrick Hillery, 14 December 1994.

45 Irish Business and Employers Confederation (IBEC) Technical Services Corporation, *An appraisal of Ireland's industrial potentials* (New York, 1952).

46 IBEC Technical Services Corporation, *Appraisal*, 4–5.

47 IBEC Technical Services Corporation, *Appraisal*, 11.

48 IBEC Technical Services Corporation, *Appraisal*, 13.

49 IBEC Technical Services Corporation, *Appraisal*, 15.

50 IBEC Technical Services Corporation, *Appraisal*, 19.

51 IBEC Technical Services Corporation, *Appraisal*, 80.

52 NAI, GIS 1/213, Speech made by Lemass at Annual Dinner of Kilkenny Chamber of Commerce, 20 January 1954.

53 'Economy buoyant, says Lemass but warns of trade problems', *Irish Press*, 26 January 1954, 5.

54 'The wrong accent', *Irish Times*, 12 October 1955, 5.

55 *Irish Press*, 14 January 1952.

56 JHA, Interview with T.K. Whitaker, [1995?].

57 'Industry depends on efficiency: Mr. Lemass on aims of protection', *Irish Press*, 23 January 1952, 5.

58 'Lemass: need is for efficiency—not protection', *Irish Press*, 2 March 1955, 5.

59 Interview with T.K. Whitaker, April 2008.

60 JHA, Interview with Garret FitzGerald, 30 May 1995.

61 NAI, S16211, 'The Irish economy viewed from without', 19 March 1957 and 1 April 1957.

62 C.F. Carter, 'The Irish economy viewed from without', *Studies* XLVI (1957), 137–49.

63 Carter, 'The Irish economy viewed from without', 137.

64 Carter, 'The Irish economy viewed from without', 140.

65 Interview with T.K. Whitaker, April 2008; see also JHA, Interview with T.K. Whitaker, 30 May 1995.

66 Interview with T.K. Whitaker, April 2008; See in particular the important documentation in T.K. Whitaker, *Protection or free trade: the final battle* (Dublin, 2006), throughout.

67 NAI, S15359, 4 July 1958.

Chapter six

[1] *Dáil Debates*, vol. 178, cols 1531–2 (11 December 1959).

[2] UCDA, P150/3497, Letter from de Valera to Lemass, 15 July 1959.

[3] UCDA, P150/3497, Letter from Lemass to de Valera, 15 July 1959.

[4] James Dillon, 'The Memoirs', 72, unpublished in personal possession.

[5] JHA, Interview with Brendan O'Regan, 3 May 1995.

[6] JHA, Interview with Neil Blaney, October 1993.

[7] C.S. Andrews, *Man of no property* (Dublin, 1982), 250–1; conversations with Andrews during the 1960s and 1980s.

[8] JHA, Interview with Tadhg Ó Cearbhaill, October 1994.

[9] Garvin, *Preventing the future*, 195–8.

[10] *Dáil Debates*, vol. 176, cols 15–16 (23 June 1959).

[11] *Dáil Debates*, vol. 176, col. 16 (23 June 1959).

[12] *Dáil Debates*, vol. 176, cols 16–18 (23 June 1959).

[13] *Dáil Debates*, vol. 176, cols 43–9 (23 June 1959).

[14] *Dáil Debates*, vol. 176, cols 87–9 (23 June 1959).

[15] Interview with Eileen Lemass, 3 December 2008.

[16] Garvin, *Preventing the future*, 167–9, 195–8.

[17] JHA, Interview with Patrick Hillery, 14 December 1994.

[18] ELC, [undated, 1969?].

[19] In particular, see Paul Bew and Henry Patterson, *Seán Lemass and the making of modern Ireland, 1945–1966* (Dublin, 1982).

[20] UCDA, P91/156, Letter from Edward MacAonraoi to Todd Andrews, 6 March 1980.

[21] Ronan Fanning, 'The genesis of economic development', in John F. McCarthy (ed.), *Planning Ireland's future: the legacy of T.K. Whitaker* (Dublin, 1990), 74–111, at 104–5.

[22] Conversations with John Garvin during the 1960s.

[23] JHA, Interview with Jack McQuillan, 18 November 1994.

[24] Conversations with John Garvin during the 1960s.

[25] Vincent Browne and Michael Farrell (eds), *The Magill book of Irish politics* (Dublin, 1981).

[26] UCDA, P67 (Papers of Seán MacEntee)/403, Letter from Gerry Boland to Seán MacEntee, 19 March 1965; Letter from Seán T. O'Kelly to Seán MacEntee, 23 March 1965.

[27] Public Record Office, London (PRO), DO 35/5291, Irish Republic fortnightly summary, 2 July 1959.

[28] PRO, DO 35/5379, Peter Clutterbuck to Earl of Home, 1 September 1959.

[29] Cormac Ó Gráda, 'The Irish economy half a century ago', *UCD working paper series* (August 2008), 16.

[30] NAI, S17066 A/61, 'Commercial aircraft: proposed manufacture in Ireland', 11 May 1961; 19, 21, 23 October 1961; personal memory.

[31] JHA, Interview with Paddy Doherty, 24 February 1995.

[32] NAI, S17246 W/63, as cited in JHA.

[33] *Irish Press*, 18 June 1969.

[34] JHA, Interview with Kevin Boland, 24 November 1994.

[35] JHA, Interview with Patrick Hillery, 12 December 1994.

[36] JHA, Interview with Patrick Hillery, 12 December 1994.

[37] Interview with Henry and Evelyn Sheridan, 11 November 2008. Henry Sheridan.

[38] JHA, Interview with Kevin Boland, 24 November 1994.

[39] Seán Lemass, 'Letters to the editor—local elections', *Irish Independent*, 14 July 1955, 4.

[40] Committee on the Constitution, *Report of the Committee on the Constitution* (Dublin, 1967), 21–6, 43–6.

[41] JHA, Interview with Michael O'Kennedy, 22 June 1995.

[42] Interview with Henry and Evelyn Sheridan, 11 November 2008. Henry Sheridan.

[43] Michael Hand, 'Waked in his lifetime', *Sunday Tribune*, 10 October 1993, 10.

[44] Interview with Eileen Lemass, 3 December 2008.

[45] JHA, Interview with Charles J. Haughey, 24 October 1994; Interview with Henry and Evelyn Sheridan, 11 November 2008. Henry Sheridan concurs.

Chapter seven

[1] JHA, Interview with J.C. Holloway, 2 July 1995.

[2] [Browne], 'Lemass: a profile'.

[3] [Browne], 'Lemass: a profile', 92, 96.

[4] ELC, Letter from Coogan to Lemass, 4 September 1968.

[5] Michael Mills, 'Seán Lemass looks back—15', *Irish Press*, 5 February 1969.

[6] Mills, 'Seán Lemass looks back—2'.

[7] 'The dynamic lifestyle of Seán Lemass', 8.

[8] John Horgan, *Seán Lemass*, 315–22.

[9] NLI, MS. 18,336, Frank Gallagher papers, 18 December 1946. Patrick Hogan was Cumann na nGaedheal minister for agriculture in the 1920s, and he gave preference to the commercialised big farmer over the small subsistence farmer during his term of office, 1922–32. He was killed in a car accident in 1936.

[10] Michael Mills, 'Seán Lemass looks back—14', *Irish Press*, 4 February 1969.

[11] Mills, 'Seán Lemass looks back—14'.

[12] 'One abiding, restless, active urge …', *Irish Press*, 12 May 1971, 4.

[13] *Irish Press*, 12 May 1971.

[14] 'A pragmatic man who saw opportunity in everything', *Irish Times*, 12 May 1971, 8.

[15] UCDA, P150/3497, *Éire/Ireland: Bulletin of the Department of Foreign Affairs*, 18 June 1971.

[16] Kiely, *Waves behind us*, 140.

[17] Savage, *Séan Lemass*, 80–1.

[18] Tom Garvin, 'The French are on the sea', in Rory O'Donnell (ed.), *Europe: the Irish experience* (Dublin, 2000), 35–43.

[19] Farrell, *Séan Lemass*, 124.

[20] Farrell, *Séan Lemass*.

[21] Interview with Eileen Lemass, 3 December 2008.

[22] Editorial, 'Séan Lemass', *Irish Times*, 12 May 1971, 13.

INDEX *Page numbers in italic refer to documents, illustrations and photographs.*

PICTURE CREDITS ✸

The Academy would like to thank the archives and individuals which/who opened their collections to our researchers in the creation of this book. The help of such bodies/persons in producing a publication like this cannot be underestimated.

Seán O'Connor, private collection—*see pages vi–vii, 32, 56, 57, 61, 63, 64, 65, 67, 68–9, 195, 196–7, 198, 200, 230–1, 242, 266–7, 268, 269 and 270–1*

Eileen and Seán Lemass, private collection—*see cover image*

Henry Sheridan, private collection—*see page 279*

Irish Press Plc—*see pages x, xx, 143, 168, 199, 225, 226–7, 229, 232–3, 234–5, 236–7, 238–9 and 280*

National Library of Ireland (NLI)—*see pages viii, xii, xviii, xix, 33, 60, 62, 66, 70, 99, 100–01, 108, 109, 110, 111, 112, 118, 119, 120, 144–5, 150–1, 152, 153, 155, 156, 157, 158–9, 160, 165, 166, 167, 201, 240–1, 272–3 and 274–5*

UCD Archives, School of History and Archives (UCDA)—*see pages 102–03, 106, 107, 202 and 247*

UCD–OFM Partnership (UCDA–OFM)—*see pages 23, 114–15, 116–17 and 278*

National Archives of Ireland (NAI)—*see pages 24, 25, 26–9, 243–4, 245, 246, 248 and 249*

Dublin Diocesan Archives (DDA)—*see pages 162, 163 and 164*

Getty Images—*see pages 104–05, 146–7, 148 and 149*

Ken Bloomfield, private collection—*see pages 20–1 and 22*

The *Irish Times*—*see pages 30–1 and 113*

The National Archives, London (TNA)—*see pages 276–7*

TIME—*see page ii*

United Press International—*see page 228*

Advertising Archives—*see page 154*

British Pathé Film—*see page 34*

ILO Historical Photographic Archives—*see endpapers and spine*

Bord na Móna—*see page 161*

Vincent Browne—*see page 250*

Lensmen Photographic Archive—*see pages 58–9*